Conversations with August Wilson

Literary Conversations Series
Peggy Whitman Prenshaw
General Editor

Photo credit: © 2005 Nancy Crampton

Conversations with August Wilson

Edited by
Jackson R. Bryer and Mary C. Hartig

University Press of Mississippi
Jackson

Books by August Wilson

Ma Rainey's Black Bottom. New York: Plume, 1985.
Fences. New York: Plume, 1986.
Joe Turner's Come and Gone. New York: Plume, 1988.
The Piano Lesson. New York: Dutton, 1990.
Three Plays [*Ma Rainey's Black Bottom, Fences, Joe Turner's Come and Gone*].
  Pittsburgh: University of Pittsburgh Press, 1991.
Two Trains Running. New York: Dutton, 1993.
The Piano Lesson and Joe Turner's Come and Gone. London: Penguin, 1997.
Seven Guitars. New York: Dutton, 1996.
Jitney. Woodstock, NY: Overlook Press, 2001.
The Ground on Which I Stand. New York: Theatre Communications Group, 2001.
King Hedley II. New York: Theatre Communications Group, 2005.

www.upress.state.ms.us

The University Press of Mississippi is a member of the Association of American University Presses.

First edition 2006

∞

Library of Congress Cataloging-in-Publication Data

Conversations with August Wilson / edited by Jackson R. Bryer and Mary C.
  Hartig.— 1st ed.
    p. cm.—(Literary conversations series)
  Includes index.
  ISBN 1-57806-830-4 (cloth : alk. paper)—ISBN 1-57806-831-2 (pbk. : alk. paper)
    1. Wilson, August—Interviews. 2. Dramatists, American—20th century—
Interviews. 3. African Americans in literature. 4. Historical drama—Authorship.
I. Bryer, Jackson R. II. Hartig, Mary C. III. Series.

PS3573.I45677Z63 2006
812′.54—dc22
  [B]   2005042432

British Library Cataloging-in-Publication Data available

Contents

Introduction

Because he was so prolific and received so much critical attention and so many accolades, it is often difficult to keep in mind that August Wilson's career as a playwright was little more than twenty years in length. While he wrote his first play, *Recycle*, in 1973 and had his first professional production in 1981, when the Penumbra Theatre in St. Paul staged his musical satire *Black Bart and the Sacred Hills*, his emergence onto the American theatre scene as a significant presence began with the October 11, 1984, opening of *Ma Rainey's Black Bottom* at Broadway's Court Theatre. In the two decades since, eight more Wilson plays have been produced in New York, seven of them on Broadway and one in an Off-Broadway theatre. This statistic is particularly noteworthy because serious new plays by American dramatists have become an endangered species on Broadway in recent years; especially since 1990, it has been a rare season when more than two or three such plays have opened. Since 1984, no American playwright has had nearly the number of new plays receive Broadway productions as Wilson. And as John Lahr pointed out in his April 16, 2001, *New Yorker* profile of Wilson, "His audience appeal almost single-handedly broke down the wall for other black artists, many of whom would not otherwise be working in the mainstream." Lahr quotes director Marion McClinton's observation that, because of Wilson, "American theatre now looks toward African Americans as viable members."

But Wilson's significance extends well beyond the African American community. Two of his plays, *Fences* (1987) and *The Piano Lesson* (1990), won the Pulitzer Prize; *Fences* also won the Tony Award. He received seven New York Drama Critics' Circle Awards for best American play. Since that award was inaugurated in 1936, only Tennessee Williams, who won it four times, has won it more than twice. Wilson received some twenty-five honorary degrees. He was also awarded the National Humanities Medal, Rockefeller and Guggenheim Fellowships, and The Whiting Writers' Award;

and he was elected to both the American Academy of Arts and Sciences and the American Academy of Arts and Letters.

With the April 2005 opening at the Yale Repertory Theatre of *Radio Golf*, Wilson completed his ambitious and unprecedented ten-play cycle depicting African American life during the twentieth century, with each play taking place during a different decade. The cycle includes (the dates in parentheses are those of the first New York production):

1900s   *Gem of the Ocean* (2004)
1910s   *Joe Turner's Come and Gone* (1988)
1920s   *Ma Rainey's Black Bottom* (1984)
1930s   *The Piano Lesson* (1990)
1940s   *Seven Guitars* (1996)
1950s   *Fences* (1987)
1960s   *Two Trains Running* (1992)
1970s   *Jitney* (2000)
1980s   *King Hedley II* (2001)
1990s   *Radio Golf*

The interviews collected in this book cover the full range of Wilson's career. In several of them, Wilson acknowledged that he did not set out to write a ten-play cycle; but, as he explained to Sandra G. Shannon in 1991, "I wrote a play called *Jitney!* set in '71 and a play called *Fullerton Street* that I set in '41. Then I wrote *Ma Rainey's Black Bottom*, which I set in '27, and it was after I did that I said, 'I've written three plays in three different decades, so why don't I just continue to do that?' " Doing so, he told Vera Sheppard in 1990, "gave me an agenda, a focus, something to hone in on, so that I never had to worry about what the next play would be about. I could always pick a decade and work on that."

The cycle also enabled Wilson to pursue others of his goals—to make African Americans aware and proud of their history and heritage and to change what he described to Kim Powers in 1984 as "the glancing manner in which white America looks at blacks and the way blacks look at themselves." This, in turn, came from his belief, expressed to, among others, Bill Moyers in 1988, that African Americans "participate in life" in ways that are "very much different than white America." "There is no way that you can dispute the fact that we are African, and we have a culture that's separate and distinct from the mainstream white American culture," he asserted to Moyers. "We have different philosophical ideas, different ways of responding to the world, different ideas and attitudes, different values, different ideas about style and linguistics, different aesthetics—even the way we bury our dead is different." As he told Vera Sheppard and repeated to other interviewers, "[F]or the white man, nature exists to be conquered," while "Africans, . . . see themselves as part of everything, the trees, all of life on the planet."

Wilson's aim was to make African Americans acknowledge these differences and understand their history. "If we're going to be pointed toward a future, we must know our past," he told David Savran in 1987. "What I want to do," he explained to Vera Sheppard, "is place the culture of black America on stage, to demonstrate that it has the ability to offer sustenance, so that when you leave your parents' house, you are not in the world alone." That past, Wilson often insisted, should not exclude African Americans' roots in African culture nor should it overlook slavery. Speaking with Savran, he called slavery "the most crucial and central thing to our presence here in America," "nothing to be ashamed of," and an important part of "our uniqueness in being African." In fact, he lamented to Bill Moyers, "I find it criminal that after hundreds of years in bondage, we do not celebrate our Emancipation Proclamation, that we do not have a thing like the Passover, where we sit down and remind ourselves that we are African people, that we were slaves."

Because African Americans are constantly striving to assimilate themselves into the majority white culture, Wilson saw as part of his mission to point out what that implies. "The real struggle since an African first set foot on the continent," he told Moyers, has been "the affirmation of the value of oneself. If in order to participate in American society and in order to accomplish some of the things which the black middle class has accomplished, you have had to give up that self, then you are not affirming the value of the African being. You are saying that in order to do that, I must become like someone else." It is this conflict, between assimilation and pride in one's uniqueness and one's heritage, that is the basis of much of Wilson's work. As he put it to Vera Sheppard, "I think the fundamental question that has confronted blacks since [the] Emancipation Proclamation is, Are we going to adopt the values of the dominant culture, or are we going to maintain our cultural separateness and continue to develop the culture that has been developing in the southern United States for some two to three hundred years?"

Clearly, Wilson believed that assimilation has not been productive for African Americans. To several interviewers he asserted that black people in the United States are in a worse situation now than they were a half-century ago, and he blamed this fact on their efforts to mimic the dominant white culture. "[B]lacks must be allowed their cultural differences," he said to Savran, adding, "the process of assimilation to white American society was a big mistake. We didn't want to be like you." This bold stance led Wilson to make some controversial assertions, as when he outlined to Richard Pettengill in 1993 his belief, mentioned in other interviews as well, that black Americans would have been more successful if they had never left the South, recommending that "What we should do is to return to our ancestral homeland. . . . We should move down there and register to vote, elect ourselves as representatives within the framework of the Constitution of the United States of America, and begin to provide do-for-self food, clothing, and shelter. I think if we did that, fifty years later we'd be in a much stronger position in society than we are today."

This view underlies Wilson's much-publicized 1997 debate at New York's Town Hall with critic Robert Brustein, the artistic director of Boston's American Repertory Theatre. On that occasion, Wilson harshly criticized the policy of so-called "color-blind casting," in which black actors and actresses are cast in roles normally played by white performers. As quoted by Elisabeth J. Heard in her 1999 interview, in the debate Wilson asserted, "We do not need color-blind casting; we need some theatres to develop our playwrights. . . . Without theatres we cannot develop our talents, then everyone suffers: our writers; the theatre; the audience." In the debate with Brustein, Wilson pointed to the dearth of African American theatre companies in America and urged black theatre professionals not to play white parts or to participate in all-black productions of plays originally written for white actors but rather to establish theatres of their own and produce African American plays in them. He elaborated on this idea in his 2003 interview with Sandra G. Shannon and Dana A. Williams, where he pointed out that white American theatre was created out of "European conventions" brought by Europeans who "came to America to settle here"; while "[t]he African, who came to America, stripped of his culture and language, didn't have any conventional baggage." As a result, "if you're going to have . . . an *American* theater, then it has to include and probably be led by African Americans." However, in that same 2003 interview, Wilson admitted that his 1997 call for more black theatre companies had gone unanswered: "after the speech there was less money given to black theatres than before"—because "in certain ways there's not a value for black theatre." In a similar way, Wilson's insistence that a film version of *Fences* must be directed by a black director has resulted in the movie, to date, never being made; the saga of this effort is recounted or referred to in several of these interviews.

In many of the interviews reprinted here, August Wilson speaks about his background and how it formed the basis of his beliefs, his aesthetics, and his literary career. He was born Frederick August Kittel in 1945 in Pittsburgh's Hill District (the setting for all of his plays, despite the fact that he left the city in 1978, to live first in St. Paul and then in Seattle) to a white father and a black mother. Because his father was largely absent during Wilson's adolescence, Wilson explained to Bill Moyers, "The cultural environment of my life, the forces that have shaped me, the nurturing, the learning, have all been black ideas about the world that I learned from my mother." Daisy Wilson Kittel, whose maiden name her son eventually took, was a strong, proud woman who believed in the value of education and in the uniqueness and limitless possibilities of her children. Her refusal to settle for the used washing machine that she was offered—because she was found to be black—when she won a contest that promised a new washing machine as its prize is an emblematic story her son told often; and it lies behind those characters in his plays—most obviously Hambone in *Two Trains Running*—who, as the playwright explained to Nathan L. Grant in 1993, confront the questions, "Should you accept partial payment for what you know is due you—or should you get the whole thing? . . . Is something better than nothing? Not always."

Brought up a Catholic—"I was going to be a priest, until I discovered Nancy Ireland in the second grade," he told Michael Feingold in 1984—Wilson attended parochial schools and lived first in a mixed neighborhood of mostly Jews, Syrians, and blacks in the Hill District. When Daisy and her six children moved to another Pittsburgh neighborhood, Hazelwood, he told Dinah Livingston in 1987, "someone threw a brick through the window that said, 'Nigger Stay Out' "; but, he added, "knowing my mother, that just made her more determined." Because reading was very important to his mother—"She stressed the idea that if you can read, you can do anything. . . . you could be anything you wanted to be if you knew how to unlock the information," he explained to Bill Moyers—Wilson got a library card at age five and at fourteen discovered the Negro section in the local public library. "I read *Invisible Man*, Langston Hughes, and all the thirty or forty books in the section," he told Bonnie Lyons in 1997. At Central Catholic High School, he was the only black student and that was, he acknowledged to Feingold, "really the first time I had confronted anything like racism." As he described it to Livingston, "The principal on various occasions would . . . walk me through these forty guys who were waiting to beat me up, and put me in a cab and send me home. What he failed to realize was . . . he didn't send a cab to pick me up in the morning, and I had to come to school by myself the next morning. So I got in a lot of fights."

It was also at Central Catholic High School, however, that Wilson encountered Brother Dominic, an English teacher who, he told Watlington, "would always tell me I could be an author, and I needed to hear that." Despite Brother Dominic's encouragement, Wilson eventually left Central Catholic because of the harassment and, after a brief stay at a trade school, enrolled at Gladstone High School, the public school across the street from where he lived. There his history teacher, a black man Wilson referred to as Mr. B, gave him a failing grade on a term paper on Napoleon for which he had done extensive research. Mr. B accused Wilson of having his older sisters write the paper for him ("I write *their* papers," he recalled to Dinah Livingston that he told Mr. B). Wilson, as he recounted the incident to Livingston, "took the paper, tore it up, threw it in the trash basket, and walked out" of the school, never to return again—except to shoot baskets on the court "right outside the principal's office" for the next two weeks in the hope that someone would wonder why he wasn't in school. No one did and Wilson's formal education ended.

He held a series of jobs, eventually got his own apartment, began writing poetry on a typewriter he bought for $20 his older sister had paid him for writing a college term paper for her, and chose to call himself August Wilson. His friends at the time were other writers and artists, among them Rob Penny, who, in 1968, wrote a play and with Wilson started a theatre called Black Horizons. Wilson, who at the time had never seen a play, volunteered to direct and soon began to write plays himself. At this point, Wilson had almost no knowledge or experience of dramatic history. Because his early poetry had been highly derivative—it took him a long time, he told Vera Sheppard, "before I could find my own voice as a poet, before I could write a poem that was *my* poem, that was not influenced by John Berryman or Amiri Baraka"—when he turned to playwriting, he deliberately avoided reading the classics so that, he explained to Sheppard, he could "do it my way." In 1987, he admitted to David Savran, "I haven't read Ibsen, Shaw,

Shakespeare—except *The Merchant of Venice* in ninth grade . . . I'm not familiar with *Death of a Salesman*. I haven't read Tennessee Williams." He estimated to Savran that, by 1987, he had seen about fourteen plays.

Without any background in the dramatic tradition, Wilson found his major influences elsewhere. The first of them was poetry, the genre in which he began writing and one in which he continued to write. "The foundation of my playwriting is poetry," he told Savran, "not so much in terms of the language but in the concept." Each play is "different," he explained, "each has its own form. But the mental process is poetic; you use metaphor and condense." "I think I write the kind of plays that I do," he declared to Sandra G. Shannon in 1991, "because I have twenty-six years of writing poetry underneath all of that."

His other formative influences were what he often referred to as his "four Bs." The first B was the blues and he dated his acquaintance with the form from the moment he heard Bessie Smith's recording of "Nobody in Town Can Bake a Sweet Jelly Roll Like Mine." He played the record over twenty-two straight times because he realized, he explained to Bill Moyers, that it "was something I could connect with that I instantly emotionally understood . . . . all the rest of the music I was listening to did not concern me, was not a part of me." But this music "spoke to something in myself. It said, this is yours." He began to look at the black people around him "a little differently than I had before. I began to see a value in their lives that I simply hadn't seen before. I discovered a beauty and a nobility in their struggles to survive." The blues became what he described to Vera Sheppard as "without question the wellspring of my art." It is, he asserted to Sheppard, "the cultural response of black America to the world that they found themselves in. I simply transferred these things over to all the ideas and attitudes of my characters."

Wilson's three other "Bs," writers James Baldwin and Amiri Baraka and artist Romare Bearden, similarly gave him encouragement to write about and celebrate his own people. He frequently cited Baldwin's call for "a profound articulation of the things that can offer a man sustenance once he leaves his father's house" as an inspiration for his explorations of African American culture. In a like way, two of Wilson's plays, *Joe Turner's Come and Gone* and *The Piano Lesson*, were specifically inspired by Bearden paintings. The significance of Bearden's work, he told Michael Feingold, was that it was "the first time I encountered anyone who dealt with black life in a large way. He shows through his work a black life that has its own sense of self, its own fullness."

He acknowledged to Sandra G. Shannon that Baraka was "less" of an influence than Baldwin or Bearden and that it was not "the way he writes or his writing style" that affected him as much as "the ideas of the '60s that I came through and improved a lot using that influence." To Carol Rosen in 1996 and to others he described Baraka's anthology *Four Revolutionary Black Plays* with its "ideas of black nationalism in the '60s" as "very beautiful." A later influence Wilson acknowledged was Argentinean writer Jorge Luis Borges. What fascinated him about Borges, he explained to Shannon, was "the way he tells a story." One of his techniques is "that he tells you exactly what is going to happen" at the beginning, but you don't know how or why—and that is the suspense of the tale. Wilson consciously adopted this approach in his play *Seven Guitars*.

As important as these literary and musical influences were on Wilson's plays, they were surely no more crucial than the day in August of 1982 when he first met Lloyd Richards, the head of the Yale Drama School and the director of the O'Neill Playwrights Conference, to which Wilson had unsuccessfully submitted scripts on several occasions. Richards and the O'Neill Conference had accepted *Ma Rainey's Black Bottom* to be given a staged reading and Richards was to direct it. Eventually, the play was produced at Yale in April 1984, before its October 1984 opening on Broadway. Thus began a playwright-director partnership that was to last through *Seven Guitars* in 1996; Richards directed the first six of Wilson's ten cycle plays. *Ma Rainey* also inaugurated Wilson's process of having the luxury of working with Richards on his play through several pre-Broadway productions (his later plays often were produced in several cities—among them Chicago, Los Angeles, Boston, Seattle, and Washington—before opening in New York). "The important thing I learned [at the O'Neill]," he told David Savran, "was to rewrite. Not just patchworking here and fixing there, but exactly what the word means—re-writing." The O'Neill also made him, he explained to Savran, "more conscious of what theatre is about"; for the first time, he encountered "the problems of costume, light, [and] set design."

Richards was twenty-five years older than Wilson and was an experienced theatre professional who had directed the groundbreaking Broadway production of Lorraine Hansberry's *A Raisin in the Sun* in 1959. At the first rehearsal of *Ma Rainey's Black Bottom* at Yale, when the actors started asking questions, Richards answered them and Wilson realized that not only were the answers the same as those he would have given but they often provided the playwright with insights into his own play that he hadn't had previously. "[F]rom that moment," he told Sandra G. Shannon, "I visibly relaxed. I said, 'Everything's going to be all right. Pop knows what he's doing.' It's been that way ever since." Wilson, who grew up without a father, acknowledged to Dennis Watlington that "I always view [Richards] in a fatherly way," adding, "I came [to the O'Neill] to learn about theater, but I learned a lot about life." It was Richards who helped Wilson shape his plays and make them theatrically viable. Over the years, the two men got "to the point where there is not a lot of talk about the plays," he explained to Vera Sheppard. "It is an intuitive almost nonverbal kind of communication." The plays, he told Bonnie Lyons, were "the product of the same two artistic sensibilities" and "became seamless."

In the interviews collected for this book, Wilson speaks a good deal about his writing process. "I generally start with a line of dialogue," he told Elisabeth J. Heard in 1999. "Someone says something and they're talking to someone else. I don't all the time know who's talking or who they're talking to, but you take the line of dialogue and it starts from there. . . . the more the characters talk the more you know about them." "Very often," he acknowledged to Heard, "I don't know what the ending is or what the events of the play are going to be, but I trust that these characters will tell me or that the story will develop naturally out of the dialogue of the characters."

Despite his rather shy and soft-spoken manner—Michael Feingold remarked that "his lines are memorable in inverse proportion to the likelihood of his saying them himself" and Carol Rosen described his "hesitant and thoughtful hum of a voice"—Wilson is remarkably candid and expansive in discussing and analyzing his plays and in giving his views on virtually any subject that is raised by his interviewers—be it race relations, the state of the American theatre, critics, his background, television, or religion. He deals willingly with such provocative questions about his plays as their emphasis on male characters, the violence in them, the prevalence of long speeches, and whether they are directed primarily at black audiences. With respect to the long speeches, he suggested to Vera Sheppard that they are "an unconscious rebellion against the notion that blacks do not have anything important to say." He also assured Sheppard, "I don't write for black people or white people. I write about the black experience in America. And contained within that experience, because it is a human experience, are all the universalities." Wilson frequently quotes Romare Bearden's remark, "I try to explore in terms of the life that I know best those things which are common to all culture."

This book went to press as Wilson completed his cycle, celebrated his sixtieth birthday, and seemed poised to move on to the next phase of his already illustrious career. In late August 2005, we learned that he had been diagnosed with inoperable liver cancer. His death on October 2, as Peter Marks wrote in the *Washington Post* two days later, did not "simply leave a hole in the American theater, but a huge yawning wound, one that will have to wait to be stitched closed by some expansive, poetic dramatist yet to emerge." It now seems especially appropriate to gather in one volume what we judge to be the most useful and informative of the many interviews he gave. In making our selections, since Wilson was so forthcoming in discussing his plays in detail, we have tried to include interviews that deal extensively with as many of those plays as possible. In all but two instances, the interviews are reprinted uncut; Carol Rosen and Elisabeth J. Heard graciously allowed us to omit non-interview portions of their pieces. In addition, we have silently corrected obvious errors, such as misspellings, and we have regularized all titles into italics. For significant assistance in putting together this collection, we wish to thank Sandra G. Shannon, Jeffrey Eric Jenkins, Christopher G. Hale, and Anne Stascavage, as well as the interviewers and editors who gave us permission to reprint the interviews. Seetha Srinivasan and Walter Biggins of the University Press of Mississippi were invariably as supportive as they were patient.

JRB
MCH

Chronology

1945	Frederick August Kittel is born on 27 April in Pittsburgh, Pennsylvania, to Frederick Kittel, a white—and mostly absent—German-American baker, and Daisy Wilson Kittel, who supports her family as a cleaning lady. He is the fourth of six children, three girls followed by three boys.
1945–1957	AW learns to read at age four. The Kittels live in the Hill District of Pittsburgh until AW is twelve.
1957	AW's mother, now divorced from Kittel, moves the family to Hazelwood, a blue-collar, steel workers' neighborhood, where AW lives from his twelfth through his eighteenth year. Around the time of the move, Daisy Kittel marries David Bedford, a black man to whom AW becomes very close.
1959–1960	At fourteen, AW becomes the sole black student at Central Catholic High School, where he is made so uncomfortable by racism that he eventually transfers to Connelly Trade School, a vocational high school which proves far too easy for him academically. At fifteen, he transfers to Gladstone public high school, where his history teacher gives him a failing grade on a term paper on Napoleon, believing it was written by one of AW's older sisters; AW drops out of school, much to his mother's dismay. Always a reader, he begins to spend much more time in the public library and reads widely over the next four years.
1962–1963	AW enlists in the U.S. Army for three years, but leaves after serving only one year.
1965	Frederick Kittel dies. On 1 April, AW buys a typewriter, begins to write poetry, and adopts the name August Wilson. In the fall, AW moves to a rooming house in the Hill District

and lives among writers—including Rob Penny—and painters; he begins to listen seriously to old blues recordings of the 1930s and 1940s, which he buys from secondhand stores. For the next twelve or thirteen years, he supports himself with a variety of jobs—dishwasher, short-order cook, porter, stock boy, gardener, and mail room clerk.

1966–1967   Continuing to write poetry and listen to the blues, AW begins to frequent Pat's Place, a cigar store and pool hall, where he listens to his black male elders tell stories. With friends, AW starts a small magazine, *Signal*; they change the name to *Connection* and AW becomes the poetry editor. *Connection* then becomes the Center Avenue Poets' Theatre Workshop.

1968   AW founds the Black Horizons Theatre with Rob Penny, who becomes the company's house playwright. Although AW directs plays by Amiri Baraka, Ed Bullins, and others, he himself is not yet writing plays (the group folds in 1971).

1969   AW marries Brenda Burton, a member of the Nation of Islam. David Bedford, AW's stepfather, dies.

1970–1972   On 22 January 1970, AW's daughter, Sakina Ansari, is born. In 1972, AW and Brenda Burton divorce. AW publishes poetry in the periodicals *Negro Digest, Black World,* and *Black Lines* and in the anthology *Black Americans: Anthology of the Twentieth Century*, edited by Arnold Adoff.

1973–1976   While AW continues to write poetry and short stories, after seeing Athol Fugard's play *Sizwe Bansi Is Dead*, he begins also to write one-act plays, including *Recycle* (1973), which is produced at a Pittsburgh community theatre; *The Coldest Day of the Year* (1976), not produced until 1989; and *The Homecoming* (1976), which is produced in 1976 by the Kuntu Theater, an amateur group in Pittsburgh. His friend Claude Purdy suggests AW turn his "Black Bart" poems into a piece for the stage and AW does so, calling it *Black Bart and the Sacred Hills.*

1977   AW visits Purdy in St. Paul and rewrites *Black Bart and the Sacred Hills* for Purdy (at the time, Purdy is directing Penumbra Theatre's first show). In the fall of this year, he discovers Romare Bearden's paintings, which will become an important influence.

1978   In January, the Inner City Theatre of Los Angeles does a staged reading of *Black Bart and the Sacred Hills*, "a musical satire." On 5 March, AW moves to St. Paul and takes a job with the Science Museum of Minnesota, writing children's plays which dramatize events and people connected with anthropology and science (these scripts include *How Coyote Got His Special Power* [1978], *An Evening with Margaret Mead* [1979] and *Eskimo Song Duel* [1979]). AW eventually quits the Science Museum to take a job as a cook for a social service organization, The Little Brothers of the Poor, where he works for about two and a half years.

1979   In ten days, writing in a fish and chips restaurant, AW completes an early version of *Jitney!*, which he later submits to the Eugene O'Neill Theater Center's National Playwrights Conference; it is rejected. He resubmits it and it is rejected again. He also submits *Black Bart and the Sacred Hills* to the O'Neill and it is rejected.

1980–1981   AW writes *Fullerton Street*, which is also sent to and rejected by the Eugene O'Neill Theater Center's National Playwrights Conference. However, when he submits *Jitney!* to the Playwrights' Center of Minneapolis, he is awarded one of their $2,500 Jerome Fellowships, allowing him to develop his work at the Center while receiving the stipend; the Playwrights' Center does staged readings of both *Jitney!* and *Fullerton Street*. *Black Bart and the Sacred Hills* is produced at the Penumbra Theatre in St. Paul. In 1981, AW marries Judy Oliver, a St. Paul social worker.

1982   Lloyd Richards, then Dean of the Yale School of Drama and Artistic Director of the Eugene O'Neill Theater Center's National Playwrights Conference, reads *Ma Rainey's Black Bottom*; the play is given a staged reading at the National Playwrights Conference during the summer. In October, *Jitney!* is produced at Pittsburgh's Allegheny Repertory Theatre.

1983   In the summer, *Fences* is given a staged reading at the Eugene
        O'Neill Theater Center's National Playwrights Conference.
        Wilson's mother dies of lung cancer.

1984   On 6 April, *Ma Rainey* opens at the Yale Repertory Theatre, under
        Lloyd Richards's direction. Wilson's play, originally called *Mill
        Hand's Lunch Bucket* after a painting by Romare Bearden and reti-
        tled *Joe Turner's Come and Gone* during the summer, is read at the
        Eugene O'Neill Theater Center's National Playwrights Conference.
        On 11 October, *Ma Rainey's Black Bottom* opens at New York's Cort
        Theatre and runs for 285 performances.

1985   *Ma Rainey's Black Bottom* wins the New York Drama Critics' Circle
        Award. On 30 April, *Fences* opens at the Yale Repertory Theatre.
        Jitney! is produced at the Penumbra Theatre in St. Paul.

1986   On 29 April, *Joe Turner's Come and Gone* opens at the Yale
        Repertory Theatre.

1987   On 26 March, *Fences* opens at New York's 46th Street Theatre and
        runs for 536 performances. It wins the Pulitzer Prize, the Tony
        Award, and the New York Drama Critics' Circle Award. The *Chicago
        Tribune* names AW Artist of the Year. In the summer, *The Piano
        Lesson,* also titled after a Romare Bearden painting, is given a staged
        reading at the Eugene O'Neill Theater Center's National
        Playwrights Conference. On 27 October, *Joe Turner's Come and
        Gone* opens at Arena Stage in Washington, D.C. On 26 November,
        The Piano Lesson opens at the Yale Repertory Theatre. AW meets
        Constanza Romero, who designs the costumes for the Yale produc-
        tion, whom he will later marry.

1988   On 9 January, *The Piano Lesson* opens at Boston's Huntington
        Theatre. On 26 March, *Joe Turner's Come and Gone* opens at New
        York's Ethel Barrymore Theatre, runs for 116 performances, and
        wins the New York Drama Critics' Award.

1989   *The Piano Lesson* is produced at the Center Theatre
        Groups/Ahmanson Theatre in Los Angeles and at the Kennedy
        Center in Washington, D.C.

1990   On 16 April, *The Piano Lesson* opens at New York's Walter Kerr
        Theatre and runs for 336 performances; it wins the Pulitzer Prize
        and the New York Drama Critics' Circle Award. On 27 March, *Two
        Trains Running* opens at the Yale Repertory Theatre and goes from

there to Boston's Huntington Theatre. Late in the year, AW moves
to Seattle after divorcing his second wife. In Seattle, he marries
Constanza Romero.

1991   *Two Trains Running* is produced at the Seattle Rep, San Diego's
Globe Theater, and at the Kennedy Center in Washington, D.C.

1992   *Two Trains Running* opens at Center Theatre Groups/Ahmanson
Theatre in Los Angeles and on 13 April, it opens at New York's
Walter Kerr Theatre, runs for 167 performances, and wins the New
York Drama Critics' Circle Award.

1995   On 21 January, *Seven Guitars* premieres at Chicago's Goodman
Theatre. On 5 February, the television adaptation of *The Piano
Lesson* airs on CBS's Hallmark Hall of Fame; AW writes the
screenplay and serves as a producer. In the spring, AW is
inducted into the American Academy of Arts and Letters.
On 15 September, *Seven Guitars* opens at Boston's Huntington
Theatre; it later moves to the American Conservatory Theater in
San Francisco.

1996   In January, *Seven Guitars* opens at the Ahmanson Theatre in Los
Angeles. On 28 March, it opens at New York's Walter Kerr Theatre,
runs for 201 performances, and wins the New York Drama Critics'
Circle Award. *Seven Guitars* is the last AW play to be directed by
Lloyd Richards. In April, AW receives the William Inge Award for
Achievement in the American Theatre at the William Inge Theatre
Festival in Independence, Kansas. On 26 June, he gives his speech,
"The Ground on Which I Stand," to the 11th Biennial Theatre
Communications Group Conference at Princeton University; it sets
off a controversy about race and American drama that leads to
AW's 1997 Town Hall debate with Robert Brustein. In July, a
revised version of *Jitney* (with the exclamation mark removed from
the title) opens at Pittsburgh's Public Theater; AW chooses Marion
McClinton to direct the production.

1997   On 27 January, Wilson debates Brustein, the artistic director of
Boston's American Repertory Theatre, at New York's Town Hall
about the best way to preserve African American identity in
American theatre. In April, the further revised *Jitney*, directed by
Walter Dallas, opens at Crossroads Theatre in New Brunswick,
New Jersey.

1998   *Jitney*, once again under the direction of Marion McClinton, opens
        at the Huntington Theatre in Boston.

1999   On 29 September, AW is awarded the National Humanities Medal
        by President Clinton in Washington, D.C. On 11 December, *King
        Hedley II* premieres at the Pittsburgh Public Theater under the
        direction of Marion McClinton.

2000   *King Hedley II* opens at the Seattle Rep in March, at the
        Huntington Theatre in Boston on 24 May, at the Mark Taper
        Forum in Los Angeles on 5 September, and at Chicago's Goodman
        Theatre on 11 December. After some fifteen regional productions,
        many with the same core cast, *Jitney* opens off-Broadway on 25
        April at New York's Second Stage Theatre and wins the New York
        Drama Critics' Circle Award.

2001   On 25 February, *King Hedley II* opens at the Kennedy Center in
        Washington, D.C. On 1 May, it opens at New York's Virginia
        Theatre and runs for ninety-six performances.

2002   In the summer, AW is writer-in-residence at the Eugene O'Neill
        Theatre Center's National Playwrights' Conference, where *Gem of
        the Ocean* is given a staged reading.

2003   On 28 April, *Gem of the Ocean* opens at Chicago's Goodman
        Theatre. From 22 May through 1 June, Wilson's one-man-show,
        How I Learned What I Learned, runs at the Seattle Rep. On 20 July,
        Gem of the Ocean opens at Los Angeles's Mark Taper Forum. In
        December, AW receives the Heinz Award in Arts and Humanities.

2004   In March, AW receives the Freedom of Speech Award at the
        Comedy Arts Festival in Aspen, Colorado. In August, AW wins the
        Chicago Tribune Literary Prize for Lifetime Achievement. On 24
        September, *Gem of the Ocean* opens at Boston's Huntington
        Theatre. On 6 December, it opens at New York's Walter Kerr
        Theatre and runs for eighty-seven performances.

2005   On 28 April, the day after AW's sixtieth birthday, the last of his cycle
        plays, *Radio Golf*, opens at the Yale Repertory Theatre. In August,
        Radio Golf opens at the Mark Taper Forum in Los Angeles. In late
        August, it is announced that AW has liver cancer. On 2 October,
        AW dies. On 16 October, Broadway's Virginia Theater is renamed
        the August Wilson Theater.

Conversations with August Wilson

An Interview with August Wilson

Kim Powers / 1984

From *Theater*, 16 (Fall–Winter 1984), 50–55. Reprinted by permission of Duke University Press for Yale School of Drama/Yale Repertory Theatre.

August Wilson's play *Ma Rainey's Black Bottom* garnered rave reviews at the Yale Rep last Spring. It met with even greater success this Fall in New York, where the play opened at the Cort Theatre on October 11, with the same production staff, including director Lloyd Richards, and a majority of the original Rep cast. Wilson leapt from virtual obscurity as a playwright to the leading ranks with only this one play. *Ma Rainey*, originally produced at the Eugene O'Neill National Playwrights Conference in 1982, is, in part, an examination of race relationships in America, set in 1927 against the backdrop of one of the legendary blues singer's recording sessions at a "race division" of Paramount Records. The battling egos of the musicians, and the transitory status of the blues itself, become metaphors for rage and injustice.

At our interview, conducted in New Haven in mid-May 1984, Wilson had just returned from the O'Neill's "Pre-Conference," during which each playwright reads his or her play aloud. August had read his play *Mill Hand's Lunch Bucket* (retitled *Joe Turner's Come and Gone* during the summer), and was both exhilarated by the new creation and alerted to the hard revisions ahead. Our focus on this play in the interview is indicative of his excitement. *Joe Turner* is set in a boardinghouse in Pittsburgh in 1911 and uses a sort of "Grand Hotel" strategy to take in a number of characters who are searching for a racial and spiritual identity. As Wilson explains in the interview, the play has a more mystical and less realistic base than *Ma Rainey*. The Yale Rep has already optioned *Joe Turner* for its 1985–86 season. (Wilson is quickly becoming a sort of resident playwright at the Rep. His play *Fences*, read at the 1983 O'Neill Conference, will be directed by Lloyd Richards at the end of the 1984–85 season.)

August Wilson says he came to playwriting out of arrogance and
frustration, certain he could write just as well as other playwrights about the
Black experience in America. He didn't use other plays as a primer on how to
write but combined his poetry background with fledgling efforts as a director
at a small theater in Pittsburgh, which devoured the plays from the early
seventies anthologies of Black drama. His first play written for that theater
was called *Jitney!* it concerned a group of jitney cab drivers, two of whom
are involved in a pivotal father/son conflict. The play was an SRO success; a
large portion of the black audience going to the theater for the first time
refused to leave when told the show was already sold out. The play came back
the next year to satisfy the demand. In his second play, Wilson deliberately
tried to expand the dramatic world from the rather narrow "slice" of the first
play. Although Wilson considers the play a failure, it did lay the groundwork
for the expanded fictional realm and overlapping scenes of *Ma Rainey*.

August Wilson was born in Pittsburgh, Pennsylvania, and now lives in
St. Paul, Minnesota. He is a member of New Dramatists and an Associate
Playwright at the Playwrights' Center in Minneapolis. Mr. Wilson is the
recipient of Bush, Rockefeller, and McKnight Foundation Fellowships in
playwriting. In addition to his summers at the O'Neill National Playwrights
Conference (1982, '83, and '84), Mr. Wilson's poetry has been published in
various magazines and anthologies.

KP: You've written other plays before *Ma Rainey's Black Bottom*, but is that
the one you wanted to hit the public first? Did you instinctually know it
might be a bigger play?
AW: Oh, no—I wanted to hit the public with all of them. But about *Ma
Rainey* I felt that I was growing as a playwright and moving toward learning
more about the craft and how to articulate my ideas dramatically. I had
submitted a couple of other plays to the O'Neill, but I'm glad they weren't
selected. I'm glad my exposure was with *Ma Rainey* because I think it is a
stronger play than the others I had submitted.

KP: You've mentioned a cycle of history plays you have in the works. What
is that?
AW: As it turns out, I've written plays that take place in 1911, 1927, 1941,
1957, and 1971. Somewhere along the way it dawned on me that I was
writing one play for each decade. Once I became conscious of that, I realized

I was trying to focus on what I felt were the most important issues confronting black Americans for that decade, so ultimately they could stand as a record of black experience over the past hundred years presented in the form of dramatic literature. What you end up with is a kind of review, or re-examination, of history. Collectively they can read, certainly not as a total history, but as some historical moments.

KP: Why did you switch from writing poetry to playwriting? Did you need something as "big" as a play?

AW: I would describe my poetry as intensely personal. I needed something as big as a play because my ideas no longer fit in the poems, or they fit in a different way, for myself only. I needed a larger canvas that would include everyone.

KP: Your concern with history hasn't been evidenced by many other American playwrights. Although there is a contemporary tone to your historical plays, what would you write in a 1984 play, a play without a past framework?

AW: I don't know. But if, as you pointed out, my historical plays are contemporary in tone, I think you can write a play set in 1984 that is historical in tone. A play set in 1984 would still have to contain historical elements—as the lives of the people do not exist in a vacuum. The importance of history to me is simply to find out who you are and where you've been. It becomes doubly important if someone else has been writing your history. I think blacks in America need to re-examine their time spent here to see the choices that were made as a people. I'm not certain the right choices have always been made. That's part of my interest in history—to say "Let's look at this again and see where we've come from and how we've gotten where we are now." I think if you know that, it helps determine how to proceed with the future.

KP: What is your response to some of the *Ma Rainey* reviews that said you were just repeating incidents and attitudes from the past that people already knew existed?

AW: I would hope that the play as a whole provides a different view—which is what art and literature are about—to present the familiar with a freshness and in a manner never quite seen before. What I tried to do in *Ma Rainey*, and in all my work, is to reveal the richness of the lives of the people, who show that the largest ideas are contained by their lives, and that there is a nobility to their lives. Blacks in America have so little to make life with compared to whites, yet they do so with a certain zest, a certain energy that is fascinating because they make life out of nothing—yet it is charged and luminous and has all the qualities of anyone else's life. I think a lot of this is hidden by the glancing manner in which white America looks at blacks, and the way blacks look at themselves. Which is why I work a lot with stereotypes, with the idea of stripping away layer by layer the surface to reveal what is underneath—the real person, the whole person.

KP: What do you think of the angry young black playwrights of the early seventies—Ed Bullins, LeRoi Jones, Papp's people?
AW: I think it was an absolutely great time, much needed, and I'm sorry to see it dissipated. It was a response to the time, the turbulence of the sixties. I think it goes back to a person like Malcolm X, who began to articulate for the first time what the masses of black people were saying on the street corners. It was all a part of the people's lives; they had been given a platform, and there was an explosion of black art and literature comparable to the Harlem Renaissance.

KP: When you write your sixties play, will you write about a real historical figure such as Malcolm X or Martin Luther King, or will you use that as a background for imagined characters?
AW: So much has been written about them that I don't think I would attempt it. Here again, I would try to find the major idea of the decade and examine that. The play I write about the sixties will be about what happened prior to the sixties, its historical antecedents. I think the ideas of the sixties are rooted in the morality of American society of the fifties. I would try to uncover what made the sixties a troubled, turbulent and violent decade not only for black but for white society as well.

KP: Let's start with your historically earliest play, *Joe Turner's Come and Gone*, set in 1911. You pervade the storytelling with alien folklore, or mysticism.
AW: I set the play in 1911 to take advantage of some of the African retentions of the characters. The mysticism is a very large part of their world. My idea is that somewhere, sometime in the course of the play, the audience will

discover these are African people. They're black Americans, they speak English, but their world view is African. The mystical elements—the Binder, the ghosts—are a very real part, particularly in the early twentieth century, of the black American experience. There was an attempt to capture the "African-ness" of the characters.

KP: And yet there are characters, such as Seth and Bertha, who own the boarding house, who seem very "American."

AW: Well, they are of African descent though their experiences in America have been different. Seth is a Northern free man. His father was not a slave. His grandfather was not a slave. He was born in the North. So his experiences are totally different from the rest of the characters who have come up from the South, whose parents have been slaves. The fact that he owns the boarding house and that he is a craftsman, that he has a skill other than farming, sets him apart from the other characters. That was also a part of the black experience.

KP: There is a part of the character of Loomis that is similar to Levee from *Ma Rainey*—an anger or drive, a sense of something not being accomplished.

AW: I don't know if Levee's angry. For some reason I don't like that word. Levee is trying to wrestle with the process of life the same as all of us. His question is, "How can I live this life in a society that refuses to recognize my worth, that refuses to allow me to contribute to its welfare—how can I live this life and remain a whole and complete person?" I think Loomis and Levee are very similar in some elements of their character, as you pointed out, but Levee has a firmer sense of who he is—where Loomis is more clearly on a search for identity, on a search for a world that contains his image.

KP: How did you get the ideas for the characters of the People Finder and the Binder in *Joe Turner*?

AW: Well, the first title of the play was the title of a painting by Romare Bearden, *Mill Hand's Lunch Bucket*. It's of a boarding house in Pittsburgh in the twenties. There is a figure in the painting that my attention was drawn to. The figure of a man sitting at a kitchen table in a posture of defeat or abandonment. And I wondered, "Who is this man and why is he sitting there and what are the circumstances of his life?" That became Herald Loomis. It occurred to me that at the time and particularly after slavery there was a lot of dispersement among blacks. Families were separated. I had been working on a series of poems called "Restoring the House" in which a man set out in search of his wife who had been sold from Mississippi to a family in Georgia maybe five years before the Emancipation. Of course, when he finds her, all kinds of things have happened in the interim. That idea of people leaving each other, of people being separated—there has to be someone who wants to heal them and bind them together. So that's how the idea of the Binder came about. I gave him the name Bynum, which was my grandfather's name, and which seemed appropriate. The People Finder is almost the same concept, but it's a White application of it. Rutherford Selig is a peddler of pots and pans. He travels about knocking on people's doors, and as a result he's the only one who knows where everybody lives. So if the people were looking for someone, it's only logical they would ask Selig. I don't think he called himself the People Finder—this is something the people of the community called him.

KP: Do you see him as more evil than Bynum?

AW: Oh, no, he's not evil at all. In fact, he's performing a very valuable service for the community. The fact that his father was a "People Finder" who worked for the plantation bosses and caught runaway slaves has no bearing on Selig's character. That was his job. That was something he did and got paid for. His grandfather was a "Bringer" working on a slave ship. Selig doesn't make any apologies for any of this. It's not his fault. It was his grandfather's job. It was hard work. His grandfather got married and had some kids. This contact with blacks, of being paid for performing some service that involved blacks, has been going on in his family for a long time. Selig is the guy who opens up a hardware store in a black community. He's got a long history of involvement.

KP: What about the story of Joe Turner, who took slaves and kept them for seven years?

AW: Joe Turner was a real person. He was the brother of Pete Turner who was the Governor of Tennessee. Joe Turner would press blacks into peonage. He would send out decoys who would lure blacks into crap games and then he would swoop down and grab them. He had a chain with forty links to it, and he would take blacks off to his plantation and work them. The song

"Joe Turner" was a song the women sang down around Memphis. "Joe Turner's got my man and gone."

When I became aware of this song somehow it fit into the play. Because the seven years Loomis is with Joe Turner, seven years in which his world is torn asunder and his life is turned upside down, can in fact represent the four hundred years of slavery, of being taken out of Africa and brought to America. At some point someone says, "Okay, you're free." What do you do? Who are you, first of all, and what do you do now that you're free, which is Loomis's question. He says, "I must reconnect and reassemble myself." But when he goes to the place where he lived, his life is no longer there. His wife and daughter aren't there. He is, in effect, a foreigner to the place. So he goes off on a search. He searches for a woman to say goodbye to and to find a world that contains his image, because there's nothing about the world that he finds himself in that speaks to the thing that's beating inside his chest. And in the process of that search, he falls into an ancestral drove and is witness to bones rising up out of the ocean, taking on flesh and walking up on the land. This is his connection with the ancestors, the Africans who were lost during the Middle Passage and were thrown overboard. He is privileged to witness this because he needs most to know who he is. It is telling him, "This is who you are. You are these bones. You are the sons and daughters of these people. They are walking around here now, and they look like you because you are these very same people. This is who you are." This is what Bynum tries to guide him toward. And the scene where Loomis reveals his vision can be read as a baptism, as a naming. Loomis's recognition of that, his "learning to sing his song," and his acceptance of that is what makes him luminous.

KP: When did you find the end of the play, with Loomis slashing his own chest?
AW: When I wrote it. It's something that just happened. I said to myself, "What was that?" and I looked and examined it. At first it read as a liberation, a severing of the bonds, a blood-letting rite. But I think its larger meaning, especially in relation to the Christian context, is that Loomis accepts the responsibility for his own presence in the world, and the responsibility for his own salvation. It says, "I don't need anyone to bleed for me, I can bleed for myself." Because your god should resemble you. When you look in the mirror you should see your god. If you don't, then you have the wrong god.

KP: Were you conscious that *Ma Rainey* also ended with a knife?
AW: There are knives in the two, but that's the only similarity. In *Joe Turner*, it's accepting the responsibility for your own salvation. In *Ma Rainey*, it's a transference of aggression from Sturdyvant to Toledo, who throughout the play has been set up as a substitute for the white man. It happens in a kind of blind rage as opposed to something that comes from an inner life. When Loomis slashes himself, he's conscious of all the meanings. He knows he must do it. The thing he's been looking for those four years he finds in that moment.

KP: Are you consciously writing religious symbols in the plays?
AW: I don't try to. I write whatever's there. Whatever comes out of me.

KP: As we've said, one of the aspects of your plays is a sort of looking back at history, or even a contemporary involvement in that history. (For example, in compiling program notes for *Ma Rainey*, you didn't want primary source documents from the Harlem Renaissance writers of the twenties and thirties, but rather contemporary writing examining that period.) In *Joe Turner*, the integrations of both worlds seems particularly complete, even forging an unknown sort of "otherworld" through an elevation of language and ideas.
AW: I think you just said it—the ideas are universal ideas. When I started I knew it wasn't like my other plays. I knew I wanted to create the sense of a whole other world. It's a blending together, an overlap. You're looking at the familiar in a new way.

KP: Do you have a total stage picture from the audience's perspective as you write, or do you write from the viewpoint of each character, dropping into each voice as you write?
AW: The characters actually do what they want to do. It's their story. I'm like Bynum in *Joe Turner*: walking down a road in this strange landscape. What you confront is part of yourself, your willingness to deal with the small imperial truths you have accumulated over your life. That's your baggage. And it can be very terrifying. You're either wrestling with the devil or Jacob's angel, the whole purpose being that when you walk through that landscape you arrive at something larger than you had when you started. And this larger something should be illuminating and as close to the truth as you can understand. I think if you accomplish that, whether the play works or not,

you've been true to yourself and in that sense you're successful. So I write from the center, the core, of myself. You've got that landscape and you've got to enter it, walk down that road and whatever happens, happens. And that's the best you're capable of coming to. The characters do it, and in them, I confront myself.

KP: The characters in your plays are each trying to find their songs, or they receive a gift from someone who perceives what their songs might be. In your fifties play, *Fences*, the father has a beautiful speech that sums up his life, his song. Would you quote that?

AW: "I come in here every Friday. I carry a sack of potatoes and a bucket of lard. You all line up at the door with your hands out. I give you the lint from my pockets. I give you my sweat and blood. I ain't got no tears. I done spent them. We go upstairs to that room at night and I fall down on you and try to blast a hole into forever. I get up Monday morning . . . find my lunch on the table. I go out. Make my way. Find my strength to carry me through to the next Friday. That's all I got. That's all I got to give. I can't give nothing else."

August Wilson's
Bottomless Blackness
Michael Feingold / 1984

From *The Village Voice*, 39 (27 November 1984), 117, 118. Copyright © 1984 Village Voice Media, Inc. Reprinted with the permission of *The Village Voice*.

The play happens in a recording studio in Chicago, 1927. Toledo, the piano player in Ma Rainey's backup band, has just explained to his colleagues how slavery got blacks from every part of Africa mixed up together, like ingredients in a stew:

"See, we's the leftovers. The colored man is the leftovers. Now what's the colored man gonna do with himself? That's what we waiting to find out. But first we gotta know we the leftovers . . . The white man knows you just a leftover, cause he the one who done the eating, and he know what he done ate. But we don't know that we been took and made history out of. . . ."

The stocky, bearded, caramel-colored man sitting across the desk from me does not look like the author of a Broadway hit. Soft-spoken, pensive, almost meek in manner, August Wilson is an anomaly among playwrights, who are by and large a demonstrative breed. We've been friends for three years, since the summer we met at the O'Neill Center's National Playwrights Conference, where I worked as dramaturg ("the crank on the side," as Edith Oliver defines it) on the staged reading of his play *Ma Rainey's Black Bottom*. Since then, there have been two more August Wilson plays at the O'Neill; *Ma Rainey* has gone on to the Yale Rep and now to Broadway, accompanied by yelps of enthusiasm from the press; two subsequent plays are set for full productions at Yale. The day we meet for this interview, my mail contains a plea for funds from a nonprofit organization dedicated to helping playwrights; the grabber is a xeroxed letter from August Wilson. In a dauntingly short time, he's become a theatrical force.

Yet, superficially at least, August hasn't changed. The warm but reticent, guarded, shyly stammering man across from me is still the writer I met in 1982, when the first surprise was the disparity between his refined, low-toned speech and the flamboyant vernacular of his characters. Black playwrights, many of whom are actors, aren't largely noted for their undemonstrativeness either, and August's plays are treasure houses of street talk, blunt, saucy, and extravagant: "Good times done got more niggers killed than God got ways to count." "Man would sit down and eat two chickens and give you the wing." "You got more shit piled up in your head than the devil got sinners." "He look like he done killed somebody gambling over a quarter." It's high praise to a playwright's imagination, I muse, when his lines are memorable in inverse proportion to the likelihood of his saying them himself.

The tape recorder plunked between us is of course one good reason for August's reserve, but as I start getting his biographical data, he loosens up: born in Pittsburgh, April 27, 1945; one of six children; father a baker. I ask him if he ever watched his father work, and suddenly there's a pause. The answer comes slowly, as if from a painful distance: "He . . . didn't live with us." I wince—trespassing on family secrets isn't my forte—but I press on. He attended public schools in Pittsburgh? No, parochial. The family was Catholic; one sister was a nun for ten years: "I was going to be a priest, until I discovered Nancy Ireland in the seventh grade." Around the same time, he turned from a prize student into a problem, one that was compounded by a change of schools:

"I started at Central Catholic High School. That was a very prestigious school, you had to have very good grades to get in. I was the only black in the school, first of all. They wouldn't let me play on the football team. They said I was too small—and I was, like, 5' 7", 175 pounds. . . . So I had a lot of problems at school. See, the grade school I went to, as well as the neighborhood I grew up in, was very mixed, there were white, black, all sorts of people. So going from there to Central Catholic at fourteen was really the first time I had confronted anything like . . . racism, actually. I would come to school and there would be a note on my desk that said 'Go home, nigger.' And every morning, like clockwork, I just would pick it up and throw it away. You weren't allowed to stand around outside [at recess], you had to walk around the quadrangle, and someone would throw a potato chip bag, you know, kids being kids, and hit you in the back, or run up and step on the back of your shoe, then say 'excuse me.' So it was really . . . it wasn't a very good experience. I got into a lot of fights. One particular day there was, like, forty-some kids waiting outside after school for me, the principal had to send me home in a cab. And I just said, this is not what I want to do, I don't care to go to school here."

Ma Rainey's Black Bottom, *a series of conversations punctuated by increasingly violent events, happens in the interstices of a recording session, during the endless waits while artists' egos are soothed and technical glitches repaired. During one of these lulls, after a colossal tantrum, Ma is talking to Cutler, the elderly trombonist who leads her band:*

"*Wanna take my voice and trap it in them fancy boxes with all them buttons and dials . . . and then too cheap to buy me a Coca-Cola. And it don't cost but a nickel a bottle. . . . They don't care nothing about me. All they want is my voice. . . . As soon as they get my voice down on them recording machines, then it's just like if I'd be some whore and they roll over and put their pants on. Ain't got no use for me then. I know what I'm talking about.*"

From Central Catholic High, August went, at his mother's behest, to a vocational high school, where he spent half the day doing "fifth-grade work" and the other half in a sheet-metal shop. "So that wasn't any fun." In the middle of that year, at fifteen, he transferred to a public high school, where he wrote for a history class a paper on Napoleon; the teacher gave it a failing grade, assuming it was by one of his older sisters. "Which was odd, because I was writing papers for them, actually." He refused to go to that class again. "And instead of going to school I would go right outside the principal's office—they had a basketball court there—and just shoot baskets all day. And . . . I just never went to school."

Instead, "I spent a considerable amount of time in the library. I don't remember too much else I did." He wrote poetry. And he worked on and off, mainly as a cook. ("In pizza places, in barbecue places, all over.") At the same time, the civil rights movement was happening, with a great upsurge of black culture and black consciousness. The poet-cook found himself a public personage, at least in Pittsburgh: "In 1968 I founded this troupe, called Black Horizons Theatre, to politicize the community. I wasn't writing any plays then. I was directing—I mean, I didn't know how to do that either; I'd never even seen a play. We did Baraka, we did Bullins, we did whoever was out there during that brilliant time. I didn't ever think about writing one myself until much later."

Another part of that brilliant time, which he's less willing to talk about, was a marriage, which lasted from 1969–72, produced a daughter (now living in Cleveland with her mother), and ultimately fell apart because of "religious differences." Even this much of the story takes some digging to bring out.

I feel uncomfortable prying, and August is obviously squirming—I notice that he carefully avoids mentioning his ex-wife's name—but I keep at it because it's relevant: *Ma Rainey*, like all of August's produced plays to date, contains among its narrations the story of a man whose marriage crumbles as his wife becomes increasingly devoted to the church.

Interestingly, in the plays the religion that comes between husband and wife is Christian; in August's own life it was Muslim. Not that he objected to the Black Muslim movement itself: "I thought that they were important. I still do." Even after Farrakhan? A truly long pause, during which I feel a gulf between us deeper than I've ever felt with a theater artist of any race or religion. Then, softly, "I think yes. Yes." Then why was his wife's religion a problem? "A house divided against itself cannot stand. Someone said that once." The joke, made gently, gets us off the topic, with a sigh of relief on both sides.

The white exploitation of black artists is one ongoing theme of Ma Rainey, *but reviewers who see this aspect of it as banal—misled partly by the conventional and somewhat stodgy production—have missed the way this theme is mirrored by the second one: the inability of blacks—and of artists—to make common cause in the face of the exploiters. Ma speaks of Levee: "He ain't gonna mess up my song with none of his music shit." At the same time, she gives convincing expression to the vision of music all the black characters share:*

"I never could stand no silence. I always got to have some music going on in my head somewhere. It keeps things balanced. Music will do that. It fills things up. The more music you got in the world the fuller it is. . . . White folks don't understand about the blues. They hear it come out but they don't know how it got there. They don't understand that's life's way of talking. You don't sing to feel better. You sing 'cause that's a way of understanding life."

Ironically, listening to records of the real Ma Rainey underscores the historical truth of the script: The vocal power and obvious authenticity of feeling in her singing don't obscure the fact that her musicianship is stolid and undistinguished compared to, say, Bessie Smith's; Levee's put-downs of it in the play are justified. Which, ironically again, is no justification of his actions.

Black Horizons Theatre and the marriage both faded out of existence around the same time, 1971–72, "and I was just hanging around writing poetry and stories and that." What transformed five years of hanging around and "that" into playwriting was a director, Claude Purdy, who invited August to turn his poems into a stage piece ("I thought it was a ridiculous idea, but I sat down and wrote a script") for Penumbra, a tiny theater in St. Paul, Minnesota. "He called me from there and said, why don't you come out and rewrite this script? And he sent me a ticket, so I went; and I said, this is a nice place, I should move up here. And a couple of months after that I did."

By a stroke of luck, he was able to get something few playwrights have ever had—a job writing plays, for a theater troupe in the anthropology wing of The Science Museum of Minnesota: "I would dramatize tales of the Northwest Indians, you know, 'How Coyote Got His Name.' I did a series called Profiles in Science, one on Margaret Mead, one on William Harvey. So almost without knowing it I'm becoming more involved with theater."

Some of August's involvement, naturally, was conscious: he joined the Playwrights Center of Minneapolis, received a grant from the Jerome Foundation, and began writing a series of plays that dramatized his own myths—tales of black people in Pittsburgh instead of the Northwest Indians. *Jitney!* was about five black drivers sitting around a gypsy cab station swapping stories, *Fullerton Street* about the migration of southern black workers to the industrial north during World War II. These, and other plays, were submitted to the O'Neill Conference, "which promptly sent them back." In all, he submitted five scripts before *Ma Rainey,* none of which got past the preliminary screening.

The climactic violence in Ma Rainey *comes from a dissension between two of the band members that is masked for most of the play by the musical disputes and the white-black tensions: the ambitious young trumpet player Levee— desperate, driven, success-hungry—is balanced against Toledo, the amiable, philosophic drifter. They represent two ways of making music, and of dealing with the white world. Toledo's is rational and acceptive, but Levee's, which is impulsive and veers to extremes, stems from a childhood trauma that, as he describes it, becomes a core image of the black experience in America:*

"I was eight years old when I watched a gang of white mens come into my daddy's house and have to do with my mama any way they wanted. . . . She standing there frying that chicken and them mens come and took hold of her just like you take hold of a mule and make him do what you want. . . . My daddy had a knife that he kept around there for hunting. . . . I tried my damndest to cut one of them's throat. I hit him on the shoulder with it. He reached back and grabbed hold of that knife and whacked me across with it.

(He raises his shirt to show a long ugly scar.)

*"That's what made them stop. They was scared I was gonna bleed to death. . . .
[My daddy] got four of them before they got him. They tracked him down in
the woods. Caught up with him and hung him and set him afire."*

*Toledo is destroyed by the conflict, but in the elegiac epilogue that closed the
play's first version, it was Levee who was mourned, Levee whose torment
and whose gifts sum up the aspects of black life that common sense and common
experience have no way of explaining, the blackness, so to speak, at the bottom
of Wilson's dramatic vision.*

It comes as a surprise to learn that August isn't a musician, that his
interest in the subject matter of *Ma Rainey* is historical and intellectual: "I
knew very little about jazz, and I wanted to find out something about it, so I
started at the very beginning. I got as far as Jelly Roll Morton and I got
bagged down." The classic blues singers of the twenties attracted him for a
variety of reasons: As women making notable careers in a male-dominated
world, as artists giving universal feelings a highly personalized expression ("I
was always interested in songs in which the singer said her name."), and as
representatives of a culture with ties to his own black awareness: "I was struck
by the use of the word black. I mean they didn't say negro fellas or colored
fellas. 'All you brown and black gals.' People weren't afraid of the word
black in the twenties. And yet in the sixties it took them some time to get
used to it."

His interest in blues as black myth and history was echoed by the
inspiration he found in the paintings of Romare Bearden; both *Joe Turner*
(originally called *Mill Hand's Lunch Bucket*) and the play he's currently
working on, *The Piano Lesson*, took their titles from Bearden canvases:
"Bearden for me is very important, because it's the first time I encountered
anyone who dealt with black life in a large way. He shows through his work a
black life that has its own sense of self, its own fullness, and he does this
in terms of myth and ritual." Does August see himself as writing rituals, then?
"Yes, because I try to define the ritual that's attendant on everyday life, to
uncover and expose it. It exists in ordinary life anyway; you just don't always
recognize it."

Tied to the mythic sense is August's love of storytelling, which as a
mode of theatrical performance has stronger roots in the African than in the
Western past. Some of the stories in *Ma Rainey* are background data;

others, like Levee's story about murder in a New Orleans brothel, reveal the character's preoccupations; the last story of all, Cutler's tale of a black minister attacked by a mob, is another mythic instance, summing up the white-black theme. For August they're expressions of the characters' relative positions in the group as well as of their psychology: "In African storytelling, how long you can keep the story going is a mark of a good personality. And I discovered if you sit around, and you hear one guy tell a story five times, he'll tell it five different ways, depending on who he's telling it to. So what I tried to do is isolate them and find out why he told it this way then, and this way another time. It's a conscious thing."

The consciousness, however, is the character's: "I don't have a strong sense of myself being in there at all. It's like, I'm there, I'm writing this down, but the characters are really in control. I have the choice to censor them, to say, no, I don't want you to do that. But basically I just watch them and they do or say whatever they want." Does he hear the white characters the same way? "I do. I have to listen a little differently, but I do." This delights me, since I've always thought of playwriting as essentially a mystical process.

What is *The Piano Lesson* about, I ask him? "A woman who is trying to acquire a sense of self-worth by denying her past." Which is? "Which is something you cannot do." I mean, what is her past? "I don't know yet. I have no idea, but it will have something to do with the piano, how the piano got into the house."

"It's not coincidence," he adds wryly, "that the piano has both black and white keys."

August Wilson
David Savran / 1987

From *In Their Own Words: Contemporary American Playwrights* by David Savran. New York: Theatre Communications Group, 1988, 288–305. Copyright ©1988 by David Savran. Used by permission of Theatre Communications Group.

Born and raised on The Hill, a black slum in Pittsburgh, August Wilson dropped out of school in the ninth grade, dividing his time between the street and the public library. There he first encountered the works of black American writers, which he read voraciously, supporting himself as a cook and stock clerk. With the twenty dollars he earned writing a term paper for his sister, he bought a used Royal typewriter and began to compose poems and stories. Deeply aware of both the changing texture of race relations in America and the violence circulating within the black community, he turned to writing as a way of effecting social change. In the late sixties he cofounded a black theatre in Pittsburgh but did not secure a production of a play of his own until the late seventies, after he moved to St. Paul, Minnesota. In 1981 *Ma Rainey's Black Bottom* was accepted at the O'Neill Theater Center. It opened on Broadway three years later to critical acclaim, followed by *Fences*, which won the 1987 Pulitzer Prize, *Joe Turner's Come and Gone* (1986) and *The Piano Lesson* (1987).

   All four plays are part of a series in progress, each work set in a different decade of the twentieth century. With this project Wilson is writing a new history of black America, probing what he perceives to be the crucial opposition in black culture: between those who acknowledge and celebrate the black American's African roots and those who attempt to deny that historical reality. *Ma Rainey,* for example, set in 1927, centers on the conflict between two of the legendary blues singer's sidemen, Levee and Toledo, the former brash, self-destructive and charismatic, always willing to accommodate the white man, the latter thoughtful and politically aware. "We done sold ourselves to the white man in order to be like him," Toledo says. "We's imitation white men." Levee never understands, however, and he remains incapable

19

of expressing his discontent to those who are oppressing him. Instead of dealing with his anger and pain directly, he turns on one who could help him, knifing Toledo for stepping on his shoe.

Joe Turner's Come and Gone, which takes place in 1911, performs a ritual of purification, setting African religious tradition against American Christianity. It documents the liberation of the spiritually bound Herald Loomis, who years before had been pressed into illegal servitude by the bounty hunter named in the play's title. In the course of the play the details of everyday life in a Pittsburgh boarding house give way to the patterns of African religion and ritual. With the help of Bynum, an African healer, a "Binder of What Clings," Loomis effects his own liberation. He recognizes that his enslavement has been self-imposed; this man "who done forgot his song" finds it again. Bynum explains to him: "You bound on to your song. All you got to do is stand up and sing it, Herald Loomis. It's right there kicking at your throat. All you got to do is sing it. Then you be free."

Wilson's 1950s play, *Fences*, an examination of the nature and dynamic of inheritance, is his most structurally conservative work, centered upon the steadily escalating conflict between Troy Maxson and his teenage son, Cory. Following the well-made play model, the first act climaxes in Troy's revelation of the events that have been crucial in shaping his life: his break with his father and the murder that put him in the penitentiary for fifteen years, wiping out the possibility of a career as a baseball player. The second act ends with Cory's reconciliation with the shadow of his father, now dead. As Cory's mother explains, "That shadow wasn't nothing but you growing into yourself. You either got to grow into it or cut it down to fit you. But that's all you got to make life with." Rose has come to understand the dogged persistence of the past, in all its irony: "Your daddy wanted you to be everything he wasn't . . . and at the same time he tried to make you into everything he was."

Each of Wilson's plays is modeled on the well-made play, developing conflict step by step to a crisis that hinges on the disclosure of a crucial and traumatic incident from the protagonist's past. However, Wilson is subtly and powerfully transforming the problematic protagonist inherited from Ibsen and Miller. In *Ma Rainey* and *Fences* the central character is revealed to be both victim and victimizer, intellectually astute yet spiritually or emotionally crippled. His ambiguous moral status allows Wilson to use him to undermine and question, in a concrete and visceral way, the workings of oppressive systems—institutionalized racism in *Ma Rainey*, the mechanics of patriarchy in *Fences*.

In all of Wilson's dramas, the conflict between African and European plays itself out not simply on the level of character and theme, but formally as well, in a tension between the strictures of the well-made play and an impulse toward jazz-inspired improvisation and poetic form. Consistently Wilson fractures the narrative line with ingenious theatrical devices: in *Ma Rainey*, the songs; in *Fences*, Gabriel's extraordinary ritual dance; in *Joe Turner*, the Juba dancing and exorcism. Each play mixes European and African elements, keeping them intact, to create not a homogeneous synthesis but a complex and plural whole. It is as if each play, both formally and thematically, reflects Wilson's vision of a more equitable and respectful society, one that will not simply integrate African Americans by forcing them to renounce their cultural heritage and their history, but will encourage them to build upon and celebrate their past.

March 13, 1987—West Bank Cafe, New York City

DS: What were your early experiences in theatre?

AW: I was a participant in the Black Power movement in the early sixties and I wrote poetry and short fiction. I was interested in art and literature and I felt that I could alter the relationship between blacks and society through the arts. There was an explosion of black theatre in the late sixties—theatre was a way of politicizing the community and raising the consciousness of the people. So with my friend, Rob Penny, I started the Black Horizons Theatre in Pittsburgh in 1968.

I knew nothing about theatre. I had never seen a play before. I started directing but I didn't have any idea how to do this stuff, although I did find great information in the library. We started doing Baraka's plays and virtually anything else out there. I remember *The Drama Review* printed a black issue, somewhere around '69, and we did every play in the book. I tried to write a play but it was disastrous. I couldn't write dialogue. Doing community theatre was very difficult—rehearsing two hours a night after people got off work, not knowing if the actors were going to show up. In '71, because of having to rely so much on other people, I said "I don't need this," and I concentrated on writing poetry and short stories.

Then in 1976 a friend of mine from Pittsburgh, Claude Purdy, was living in L.A. He came back to Pittsburgh and came to a reading of a series of poems I'd written about a character, Black Bart, a kind of Western satire. He said, "You should turn this into a play." He kept after me and eventually I sat down and wrote a play and gave it to him. He went to St. Paul to direct a show and said, "Why don't you come out and rewrite the play?" He sent me a ticket and I thought, "A free trip to St. Paul, what the hell?" So I went out and did a quick rewrite of the play. That was in November '77. In January of '78, the Inner City Theatre in Los Angeles did a staged reading of it.

DS: What's it called?
AW: *Black Bart and the Sacred Hills*—a musical satire. In 1981 we did a production in St. Paul at Penumbra Theatre, for which Claude Purdy worked. When I moved to St. Paul I got a job in the Science Museum of Minnesota as a script writer—they had a theatre troupe attached to the museum. That was the first job where someone was actually paying me to write. We dramatized tales of the Northwest Indians—how Peyote got his name, how Spiderwoman taught the Navahoes to read—which were very popular. Then I started doing Profiles of Science—I went around to all the curators asking who can I write a play about. The biology guy suggested William Harvey, who discovered the circulation of the blood, so I wrote a one-man show on Harvey, one on Charles Darwin, one on Margaret Mead. I was writing scripts without knowing that I was becoming a playwright. Then I found out about the Eugene O'Neill Theatre Center's National Playwrights Conference and wrote a play called *Jitney!* that I sent in along with *Black Bart*. They sent them back. Then I submitted *Jitney!* to the Playwrights' Center in Minneapolis. They accepted it and gave me twenty-five hundred dollars.

I remember walking into a room there containing sixteen playwrights and thinking, "Wow, I must be a playwright." The Playwrights' Center was a very helpful experience. We did a reading of *Jitney!* and I felt encouraged. So I wrote *Fullerton Street*, which was set in the forties. We did a staged reading of it and I sent it off to the O'Neill and they sent it back. I sent *Jitney!* to them again because I thought, "You guys didn't read this play," and they sent it back a second time. I was forced to look at it again and I thought, "Maybe it's not as good as I think it is. I have to write a better play but how the hell do you do that?" I felt I was writing the best I could. A workshop of *Fullerton Street* had been very helpful, so I felt confident. *Jitney!*—okay, it wasn't quite big enough. *Fullerton Street* was epic and too unwieldy. I decided to try for something right in the middle. I sat down and wrote *Ma Rainey's Black Bottom* and sent that off to the O'Neill and they accepted it.

DS: When you first started writing plays, what playwrights influenced you most strongly?

AW: None, really. Baraka wrote a book called *Four Revolutionary Plays* which I liked—I liked the language, I liked everything about them. In my early one-acts I tried to imitate that and then I discovered I wasn't him and that wasn't going to work. Other than Baraka, the first black playwright I found who wrote anything that even approached what was, to my ear, realistic dialogue for black folks was Philip Hayes Dean. I directed his play *The Owl-Killer* for the theatre in Pittsburgh. I don't want to judge it as a play, but I thought the dialogue was good. Likewise, *The Sty of the Blind Pig*. I haven't read Ibsen, Shaw, Shakespeare—except *The Merchant of Venice* in ninth grade. The only Shakespeare I've ever seen was *Othello* last year at Yale Rep. I'm not familiar with *Death of a Salesman*. I haven't read Tennessee Williams. I very purposefully didn't read them.

The first professional production I saw was *The Taking of Miss Janie* by Ed Bullins in New York. I think it's his best work but I didn't really care for the play. But something happened when I saw *Sizwe Bansi Is Dead* at the Pittsburgh Public Theater in 1976. I thought, "This is great. I wonder if I could write something like this?" Most of the plays that I have seen are Fugard plays, so he's probably had an influence on me without my knowing it. Among the fourteen or so plays I've seen have been *Blood Knot, Sizwe Bansi, "Master Harold" . . . and the boys* and *Boesman and Lena*.

DS: I'm surprised to hear that you know so few plays. I'm struck by how linear your plays are, how traditional the protagonist-antagonist opposition is and how smoothly they build to a final confrontation. Especially in *Joe Turner*. It's like Ibsen.

AW: The foundation of my playwriting is poetry. Not so much in terms of the language but in the concept. After writing poetry for twenty-one years, I approach a play the same way. I think Robert Duncan said form equals content. So each play is specific, each is different, each has its own form. But the mental process is poetic: you use metaphor and condense. I try to find a metaphor to carry the work.

I approach playwriting as literature, as opposed to a craft—though craft is important. It occurred to me one day that when I sit down to write, I am sitting in the same chair as Ibsen, Shaw, Miller, Beckett—every playwright. You're confronted with the same problems: what to do with this space and how to articulate your ideas in two hours of public time, moving characters about in an environment designed specifically for them. It gives you a sense of power, sitting in this hallowed and well-worn chair. I get comfortable and write from the feeling that I'm free to do anything I choose to do, to create this thing called literature.

DS: What was the most important experience in your training as a playwright?

AW: The O'Neill. I first went with *Ma Rainey* when it was a fifty-nine page, ill-organized script—some people say it's still ill-organized—and was fortunate enough to work with Michael Feingold as my dramaturg. The important thing I learned was to rewrite. Not just patchworking here and fixing there, but exactly what the word means—re-writing. When you write, you know where you want to go—you know what a scene, a particular speech is supposed to accomplish. Then I discovered that it's possible to go back and rewrite this speech, to find another way to say it. In a poem you rewrite six or seven times before you end up with what you want. But I didn't think of theatre as being like that. And I learned to respect the stage and trust that it will carry your ideas. The intensity of the O'Neill process—working in four days, working fast—was also good experience. It comes down to problem solving. But there's no one correct solution.

The O'Neill made me more conscious of what theatre is about. There's nothing like encountering the problems of costume, lighting, set design—What do you mean by this? Where is this? Where is the window?—which make you more aware of the totality of what you're doing. I discovered with *Fences*, for example, that I had a character exiting upstage and coming back immediately with a different costume. That's really sloppy but I was totally unaware. I never thought, "The guy's got to change his costume." I've become conscious of things like that and it's made me a better playwright. But I don't want to lose the impulse, the sense, as with *Ma Rainey*, that anything goes, that you may do whatever you desire to do. Maybe I wouldn't have written *Ma Rainey* as I did, had I been aware of the problems with casting and with the music.

DS: In *Ma Rainey* the instruments the characters play become metaphors. Toledo the pianist sounds a broad compass of experience and Levee the trumpet player expresses individual subjectivity more aggressively.
AW: With the trumpet you have to blow and force yourself out through the horn. Half-consciously, I tried to make Levee's voice be a trumpet. I was conscious when I was writing the dialogue that this is the bass player talking, this is the trombonist talking. Levee is a brassy voice.

DS: How do you start a play?
AW: I generally start with an idea, something that I want to say. In *The Piano Lesson* the question was, "Can one acquire a sense of self-worth by denying one's past?" (I think I place myself on one side of the question.) So then, how do you put this question on stage, how do you narrate it? Next I got the title from a Romare Bearden painting called *The Piano Lesson.* His painting is actually a piano teacher with a kid. I wanted a woman character as large as Troy is in *Fences.* I wanted to write it for Mary Alice to challenge her talent. I think she's a wonderful actress and there are not many roles for black actresses of that magnitude. From the painting I had a piano, and I just started writing a line of dialogue and had no idea who was talking. First I had four guys moving the piano into an empty house. I discarded that because people would be offstage too much, getting other pieces of furniture.

Someone says something to someone else, and they talk, and at some point I say, "Well, who is this?" and I give him a name. But I have no idea what the story line of the play is. It's a process of discovery. While writing *The Piano Lesson* I came up with the idea of tracing the history of the piano for a hundred and thirty-five years, with the idea that it had been used to purchase members of this family from slavery. But I didn't know how that was going to tie in. I knew there was a story, but I didn't know what the story was. I discovered it as the characters began to talk: one guy wants to sell the piano, the sister doesn't want to. I thought, why doesn't she want to sell it? Finding all those things helped me to find the story. I put off writing the history of the piano—one character tells the whole story—until I found it out in the process of writing dialogue. As it turned out, the female character is not as large as I intended. I'm not sure the play's about the idea I started with. I think the central question ended up being "How do you use your legacy?"

I write in bars and restaurants. At the start of the day, I take my tablet and I go out and search for a play. I get some coffee and sit down. If I feel like writing something, I do. If I don't, I go about my day. I've started writing a play called *Two Trains Running*, set in the sixties. I have no idea what it's about. I started with a line of dialogue. I was in rehearsals in New Haven and this line came to me. I said, "Not now, please, I'm busy," but I had to go with it. It may or may not end up in the play. But having discovered it, I know something central to the character who is speaking. The story and the character will grow out of that one line of dialogue.

Then I will place the character within the sociology of the sixties, keeping in mind that I am trying to write plays that contain the sum total of black culture in America, and its difference from white culture. Once you put in the daily rituals of black life, the play starts to get richer and bigger. You're creating a whole world in the process of telling your story, of writing this character. Once you place him down in his environment, you have to write about his whole philosophical approach to life. And then you can uncover, from a black perspective, the universalities of life. Some questions will emerge that man has been asking himself ever since he's been on the planet. One of my favorite lines in *Joe Turner* is, "Why God got to be so big? Why he got to be bigger than me?" I think this is one of the first questions man asked himself when he found out that he wasn't God. Why am I not the biggest thing in the universe? Romare Bearden said, "I try to explore, in terms of the life I know best, those things common to all culture." You discover that the black experience is as valuable, rich and varied as anybody else's and that there's been so little written about it.

Blacks do not have a history of writing—things in Africa were passed on orally. In that tradition you orally pass on your entire philosophy, your ideas and attitudes about life. Most of them were passed along in blues. You have to make the philosophy interesting musically and lyrically, so that someone will want to repeat it, to teach it to someone else as soon as they've heard it. If you don't make it interesting, the information dies. I began to view blues as the African American's response to the world before he started writing down his stuff. James Baldwin has a beautiful phrase—"field of manners and rituals of intercourse." An African man has a whole different field of manners. All cultures have their mythology, their creative motifs and social and political organizations. To my mind, people just gloss over these things in the black community without really examining it and seeing what's there.

DS: I'm interested to hear you talk about history. One line from *Ma Rainey* could, I think, stand as an epigraph to your work: "The white man . . . done the eating and he know what he done ate. But we don't know that we been took and made history of."

AW: We're leftovers from history—history that happened when there was a tremendous need for manual labor, when cotton was king. But history and life progress, you move into the industrial age, and now we're moving into the computer age. We're left over. We're no longer needed. At one time we were very valuable to America—free labor.

DS: So what you're doing with your series of plays is rediscovering history, rewriting history.

AW: Yes, because the history of blacks in America has not been written by blacks. And whites, of course, have a different attitude, a different relationship to the history. Writing our own history has been a very valuable tool, because if we're going to be pointed toward a future, we must know our past. This is so basic and simple; yet it's a thing that Africans in America disregard. For instance, the fact of slavery is something that blacks do not teach their kids—they do not tell their kids that at one time we were slaves. That is the most crucial and central thing to our presence here in America. It's nothing to be ashamed of. Why is it, after spending hundreds of years in bondage, that blacks in America do not once a year get together and celebrate the Emancipation and remind ourselves of our history? If we did that, we would recognize our uniqueness in being African. One of the things I'm trying to say in my writing is that we can never really begin to make a contribution to the society except as Africans.

If you took Africans and said, "Here's all the money and resources you need, solve the problems of society," things would be totally different. The social organization would be different. We'd probably all live in round houses, as opposed to square ones. I don't think society would be as consumer-oriented. Now, if you can't buy anything, you're worthless. You don't count if you can't consume. I don't think it would be that kind of society because of the differences in our values and our attitudes toward ownership.

To make inroads into society, you have to give up your African-ness. You can be doctors, lawyers, be middle-class, but if you want to go to Harvard, you have to give up the natural way that you do things as blacks. Let me give you an example. I was in a bus station in St. Paul. I saw six Japanese-American guys having breakfast at the counter. They chatted among themselves and then the check came and they—I'll make a joke here—they all reached for their American Express cards. It was nice and they embraced and there was a slight bow and off they went.

What would be the difference if six black guys came in and ordered breakfast? The first thing they'd notice is the jukebox. This is very important: it never entered the mind of those Japanese guys to play the jukebox. Six black guys walk in, somebody's going to the jukebox. He's gonna drop a quarter. Another guy's gonna say, "Hey Rodney, play this." And he's gonna say, "Man, get out of here, play your own record. I ain't playin' with you." Another thing I notice, none of the Japanese guys said anything to the waitress. But a black guy would say: "Hey, mama, don't talk to him. Look, baby, where ya from? Why don't you give me your phone number?" A guy gets up to play another record, somebody steals a piece of bacon off his plate: "Don't mess with my food. Who took my food?" It comes time to pay the bill, it's only two dollars: "Hey, man, lend me two dollars. I ain't got no money. Come on, man, give me a dollar."

If you're a white observer you say, "They don't know how to act. They're loud. They're boisterous. They don't like one another. The guy won't let him play a song. They're thieves. He stole a piece of bacon." The Japanese have their way of eating breakfast. Blacks have their way. If you bring in six white characters, an entirely different dynamic would go on. White society tells Africans, "You can't act like that. If you act like that, you won't get anywhere in society. If you want to make progress, you have to learn to act like us. Then you can go to school, we'll hire you for a job, we'll do this, that and the other." I don't see that said to other ethnic groups. Asians are allowed to maintain their Asian-ness and still participate in society. That suppression of blacks does not allow you the impulse, does not allow you to respond to the world without encumbrance. I try to reveal this and to allow my characters to be as African as they are and to respond to the world as they would.

DS: How closely do you work with Lloyd Richards?
AW: Generally I will meet with him an hour before rehearsal and talk about what happened yesterday and what we're going to do today. I don't talk to actors in rehearsal. I talk to Lloyd and he understands and communicates my concerns to the actors. Other than that, I just look at the way things are

going and I listen. Some things might strike my ear wrong. I might find a
certain scene doesn't build the way I thought it did. So I make changes when
necessary and come back the next day with new pages.

DS: How extensive are these changes?

AW: Usually the changes are minor. For example, in *Ma Rainey* Levee had
to put his shoes on and there weren't lines to cover that action. That's
the only thing I can remember actually adding to the script in the rehearsal
process.

    Fences was a bit different because we were cutting a four-hour play down
to two hours and ten minutes. Sometimes in watching it I'd say, "We cut this,
but I need it back." One part I cut out for the Yale and Goodman productions
I put back because I needed a moment between father and son that was not
a conflict. Cory asks Troy, "Hey, Pop, why don't you buy a TV?" And Troy
tells him that the roof needs tarring. He's teaching him a lesson about
priorities. "If you don't fix the roof, the water's going to run all over your
brand-new TV. So if you had twenty dollars, what would you do?" You need
that moment to balance the conflict. Rehearsals were more cutting and
adding to shape it, as opposed to major rewriting.

    I do a major rewrite before the O'Neill Conference and then, after the
two-day staged readings, I've got a bunch of notes and ideas and I do another
major rewrite and that is generally the play that we go into rehearsal with.
I don't mind cutting. I'll say, "If that's not working, what do you need? Let's
put something else in here," because this is theatre. Nobody writes a perfect
play by just sitting down and writing. You find out what's there when the
actors begin to move around in the space.

    With *Joe Turner* people had been saying before rehearsals that we should
see Loomis find his song. After a read-through I knew that moment was
missing. We went into rehearsal and it remained an unsolved problem. Then
I came up with the idea of ending the first act with him on the floor unable
to stand up. When he stands at the end, you can read that as him finding his
song. That's one thing I discovered in rehearsal that was crucial to the play.
I never would have found it sitting at home.

DS: Is there a favorite among your plays?

AW: Not really, it's like comparing your kids. They're all mine. Although I
always consider the last thing I've done the best. So I think *Piano Lesson* is

my best play. After that, it would be *Joe Turner* and then *Fences*. I think I was able to get more things through in *Joe Turner*. Among my plays, *Fences* is the odd one, more conventional in structure with its large character. I kept hearing *Ma Rainey* described as oddly structured and I thought, "I can write one of those plays where you have a big character and everything revolves around him." I like *Joe Turner* for the ideas and for Loomis's accepting responsibility for his own salvation and his own presence in the world. Those kinds of statements are not present in *Fences*. So of those three, I like *Joe Turner* best. I hope that it shows a growth, a maturing.

DS: I find that sexual politics comes into more prominence in *Joe Turner*, when Bynum says, "When you grab hold to a woman, you got something there. You got a whole world there."
AW: A way of life kicking up under your hand.

DS: There and in your other plays I get a sense of the interconnection between racial politics and sexual politics. Can you describe your goal in portraying black men?
AW: I'm trying to write an honest picture of the black male in America. I try to present positive images, strong black male characters who take a political stand, if only in the sense of Loomis in *Joe Turner*: one, Joe Turner's come and gone, it ain't gonna happen no more; two, I don't need anyone to bleed for me, I can bleed for myself. I can accept responsibility for my presence in the world. The idea of responsibility is crucial because, I believe, white Americans basically see black males as irresponsible, which I think is incorrect. They say, you should be responsible in the same way we are, without understanding that we have different ideas of responsibility.

I try to position my characters so they're pointed toward the future. I try to demonstrate the spirit of the character. For instance, in *Ma Rainey*, Levee's a very spirited character who does a terrible thing. He murders someone. He's going to spend the next twenty years in the penitentiary. But he's willing to confront life with a certain zest and energy. It's the same with Troy. He wrestles with death. I try to make them heroic. I've experienced it and I'm just trying to uncover it, pulling layer after layer from the stereotype.

DS: In reading *Fences*, I came to view Troy more and more critically as the play progressed, sharing Rose's point of view. We see that Troy has been crippled by his father. That's being replayed in Troy's relationship with Cory. Do you think there's a way out of that cycle?

AW: Surely. First of all, we're all like our parents. The things we are taught early in life, how to respond to the world, our sense of morality—everything, we get from them. Now you can take that legacy and do with it anything you want to do. It's in your hands. Cory is Troy's son. How can he be Troy's son without sharing Troy's values? I was trying to get at why Troy made the choices he made, how they have influenced his values and how he attempts to pass those along to his son. Each generation gives the succeeding generation what they think they need. One question in the play is, "Are the tools we are given sufficient to compete in a world that is different from the one our parents knew?" I think they are—it's just that we have to do different things with the tools. That's all Troy has to give. Troy's flaw is that he does not recognize that the world was changing. That's because he spent fifteen years in a penitentiary.

As African Americans, we should demand to participate in society as Africans. That's the way out of the vicious cycle of poverty and neglect that exists in 1987 in America, where you have a huge percentage of blacks living in the equivalent of South African townships, in housing projects. No one is inviting these people to participate in society. Look at the poverty levels—$8,500 for a family of four, if you have $8,501 you're not counted. Those statistics would go up enormously if we had an honest assessment of the cost of living in America. I don't know how anybody can support a family of four on $8,500. What I'm saying is that 85 or 90 percent of blacks in America are living in abject poverty and, for the most part, are crowded into what amount to concentration camps. The situation for blacks in America is worse than it was forty years ago. Some sociologists will tell you about the tremendous progress we've made. They didn't put me out when I walked in the door. And you can always point to someone who works on Wall Street, or is a doctor. But they don't count in the larger scheme of things.

DS: Do you have any idea how these political changes could take place?

AW: I'm not sure. I know that blacks must be allowed their cultural differences. I think the process of assimilation to white American society was a big mistake. We don't want to be like you. Blacks living in housing projects are isolated from the society, for the most part—living as they choose, as Africans. Only they don't realize the value in what they're doing because they have accepted their victimization. They've marked themselves as victims. Once they recognize that, they can begin to move through society in a different manner, from a stronger position, and claim what is theirs.

DS: A project of yours is to point up what happens when oppression is internalized.
AW: Yes, transfer of aggression to the wrong target. I think it's interesting that the two roads open to blacks for "full participation" are entertainment and sports. *Ma Rainey* and *Fences*, and I didn't plan it that way. I don't think that they're the correct roads. I think Troy's right. Now with the benefit of historical perspective, I can say that the athletic scholarship was actually a way of exploiting. Now you've got two million kids who think they're going to play in the NBA. In the sixties the universities made a lot of money off of athletics. You had kids playing for free who, by and large, were not getting educated, were taking courses in basketweaving. Some of them could barely read.

DS: Troy may be right about that issue, but it seems that he has passed on certain destructive traits in spite of himself. Take the hostility between father and son.
AW: I think every generation says to the previous generation: you're in my way, I've got to get by. The father-son conflict is actually a normal generational conflict that happens all the time.

DS: So it's a healthy and a good thing?
AW: Oh, sure. Troy is seeing this boy walk around, smelling his piss. Two men cannot live in the same household. Troy would have been tremendously disappointed if Cory had not challenged him. Troy knows that this boy has to go out and do battle with that world: "So I had best prepare him because I know that's a harsh, cruel place out there. But that's going to be easy compared to what he's getting here. Ain't nobody gonna whip your ass like I'm gonna whip it." He has a tremendous love for the kid. But he's not going to say, "I love you," he's going to demonstrate it. He's carrying garbage for seventeen years just for the kid. The only world Troy knows is the one that he made. Cory's going to go on to find another one, he's going to arrive at the same place as Troy. I think one of the most important lines in the play is when Troy is talking about his father: "I got to the place where I could feel him kicking in my blood and knew that the only thing that separated us was the matter of a few years."

Hopefully Cory will do things a bit differently with his son. For Troy, sports was not the way to go, the white man wouldn't let him get away with that. "Get you a job, with your hands, something that nobody can take away from you." The idea of school—he doesn't know what that is. That's for white folks. Very few blacks had paperwork jobs. But if you knew how to fix cars, you could always make some money. That's what Troy wants for Cory. There aren't many people who ever jumped up in Troy's face. So he's proud of the kid at the same time that he expresses a hurt that all men feel. You got to cut your kid loose at some point. There's that sense of loss and separation. You find out how Troy left his father's house and you see how Cory leaves his house. I suspect with Cory it will repeat with some differences and maybe, after five or six generations, they'll find a different way to do it.

DS: Where Cory ends up is very ambiguous, as a marine in 1965.
AW: Yes. For the average black kid on the street, that was an alternative. You went into the army because you could learn how to do something. I can remember my parents talking about the son of some friends: "He's in the navy. He *did* something"—as opposed to standing on the street corner, shooting drugs, drinking wine, and robbing stores. Lyons says to Cory, "I always knew you were going to make something out of yourself." It really wounds me. He's a corporal in the marines. For blacks, that is a sense of accomplishment. Therein lies one of the tragedies of blacks in America. Cory says, "I don't know. I put in six years. That's enough." Anyone who goes into the army and makes a career out of it is a loser. They sit there and are nurtured by the army and they don't have to confront life. Then they get out of the army and find there's nothing to do. They didn't learn any skills. And if they did, they can't find a job. Four months later, they're shooting dope. In the sixties a whole bunch of blacks went over, fought and died in the Vietnam War. The survivors came back to the same street corners and found out nothing had changed. They still couldn't get a job.

At the end of *Fences* every person, with the exception of Raynell, is institutionalized. Rose is in a church. Lyons is in a penitentiary. Gabriel's in a mental hospital and Cory's in the marines. The only free person is the girl, Troy's daughter, the hope for the future. That was conscious on my part because in '57 that's what I saw. Blacks have relied on institutions which are really foreign—except for the black church, which has been our saving grace. I have some problems with it but I recognize it as a central social organization and sometimes an economic organization for the black community. I would like to see blacks develop their own institutions that respond to their needs.

DS: That religious element is so important in *Joe Turner*. At the end of that play, when Loomis "shines," the moment of fulfillment and salvation has such strong religious overtones—both African and Christian—as well as social and political ones. How do you see the relationship between the religious and the political?

AW: I think blacks are essentially a religious people. Whites see man against a world that needs to be subdued. Africans see man as a part of the world, as a natural part of their environment. Blacks have taken Christianity and bent it to serve their African-ness. In Africa there's ancestor worship, among kinds of religious practices. That's given blacks, particularly southern blacks, the idea of ghosts, magic and superstition—for example, the horseshoe as a good-luck symbol. It's not the shape, it's the iron, the god of iron which protects your house. Relating to the spirit worlds is very much a part of African and Afro-American culture.

I try to approach people with an anthropologist's eye. That's why I make constant references to food. If you study culture, you want to know what people eat, what their social organization is. In my plays you can see what the economics are—that's an important part of any culture. In *Fences*, for example, Gabriel goes to work every day. He goes and collects his fruits and vegetables to sell and he's trying so hard to be self-sufficient, even though he's gravely wounded. He's my favorite character because he still wants to contribute and work. I'm trying to illuminate the culture, so that you're able to see the "field of manners and rituals of intercourse that can sustain a man once he's left his father's house."

What I want is that you walk away from my play, whether you're black or white, with the idea that these are Africans, as opposed to black folks in America. Yet I have found a tremendous resistance to that. I talked with an audience at Yale Rep after *Joe Turner* and I actually lost my temper. I said, "How many recognize these people as Africans?" There were two hundred people sitting there and about eight raised their hands. I'm very curious as to why they refuse—I have to say it's a refusal because it's so obvious. So many people blocked that, wanting to recognize them as black Americans. I was really surprised to find that.

DS: Do you read the critics?

AW: Sure. Do I value them? I have mixed opinions about critics. I've been fortunate to have gotten mostly good reviews. If you have six hundred people at a play, you have six hundred different opinions. But critics should have an informed opinion and therein lies their value—they can bring a lot, not to a particular play, but to the development of theatre. The bad reviews that I've gotten are the ones I study. I think the guy's misread the play and I want to know, how did he see it this way? I'm trying to communicate to everyone. If I missed communicating with someone with an informed opinion, then I try to look at it through his eyes and see how he arrived at his opinion. I don't place a whole hell of a lot of value on the critical response. I'm glad when anyone who sees my work says, "I really enjoyed that." A critic's saying that is no different from an ordinary person walking up and saying that to me.

DS: How do you see the American theatre today?

AW: I'm relatively new to theatre. I can speak most about playwriting because I've been a participant at the O'Neill for four years. I'm a member of New Dramatists. For the most part, I've been disappointed in the work, even from some very talented playwrights. First, it's the influence of television. A whole generation of playwrights has been raised on television. I think it's a bad influence on theatre, which in many ways is almost an archaic art form. I'm fearful it may go the way of opera, which is an elitist art, one that doesn't engage the larger society.

Theatre engages very few people. I don't think it has to be that way. I think it should be a part of everyone's life, the way television is. But it's not. It's moving the other way. As it costs more and more to produce plays, you see fewer and fewer. Fewer playwrights are given the opportunity to fail. You can learn immeasurably from a failure. You should at least be given the opportunity to bat—if you strike out, you strike out. The cost of production, the price of tickets, all of these things further remove theatre from the people and make it an elitist art form, which I think is wrong. But I don't know how you correct it.

The second main problem is society's attitude toward playwriting. It's not considered a part of literature. What has been missing from the new plays I've seen is metaphor. The story often reads like a TV sitcom—it's slight, there's no character development. Writing for the stage is very different. If playwriting was reconnected to the idea of literature, I think you would begin to see better plays. If you're giving the audience the same thing they're getting on TV, there's no reason to come to the theatre.

If every regional theatre would select a playwright and commit themselves to doing a play of his or hers every year, by the third year you're going to have a better playwright. There's nothing like writing a play knowing that it's going to be produced and working to reward the faith that's been placed in you. New plays are looked at in a disparaging way. A theatre will do its fifth Shaw in five years on the mainstage without even considering whether a new play deserves more attention than a staged reading or a second-stage production. You say "new play" and people run the other way. Theatres should be encouraging and nurturing, providing a home for playwrights and providing audiences with an alternative. Of course they say there isn't the material there. I'm saying if you work with what you have, five years from now you're going to have different and better material.

The playwright has a responsibility to the audience. I'm asking people to hire a babysitter, get dressed, find the car keys, find a place to park, pay money—more than it costs to go see a movie. When they get there, I should have something to say to them that's worth all their trouble. I discovered my responsibility sitting in the theatre at Yale, watching the audience. You can't do that with workshops or staged readings. Playwrights are not like fiction writers. They need living bodies. One thing I'll never forget is my confrontation with a set designer at the O'Neill who asked me a thousand difficult questions about the play. Unless you go through that process, you're working in a vacuum.

I'm not sure what to do about production costs. I do think the American people would subsidize the theatre if it was made a part of their life.They subsidize television, simply by watching it. Maybe we have to have commercials in the theatre. There has to be some financial basis to allow all the people involved in the production to make a living.

DS: What are your goals for the future?
AW: What's important for me is to write plays, as opposed to movies or television. After *Ma Rainey* I was offered work on this and that movie. But I want to establish myself as a playwright first. I hope to write one play a year and finish my series. I'm working on the sixties play now. I have my forties play. I'll either rewrite it or throw it out and come up with a better idea. Then

I'll do contemporary plays. But I've enjoyed the benefit of the historical perspective. I have an idea for a novel that I've been tossing around. A novel, for me, was always a vast, uncharted sea. It was like being lost on the ocean. So was a play, for that matter, at one point. So I feel confident coming from plays and I'd like to try my novel. I still write poetry.

DS: You said that when you first got interested in theatre, you thought it could be an effective political tool. Do you still think it can be?
AW: Absolutely. All art is political. It serves a purpose. All of my plays are political but I try not to make them didactic or polemical. Theatre doesn't have to be agitprop. I hope that my art serves the masses of blacks in America who are in desperate need of a solid and sure identity. I hope my plays make people understand that these are African people, that this is why they do what they do. If blacks recognize the value in that, then we will be on our way to claiming our identity and participating in society as Africans.

And one other thing: the blues is the core. All American popular music, especially in 1987, is influenced by the blues. This is the one contribution everyone admits that Africans have made. But the music has been pulled so far out of context that it's no longer recognizable. Any attempt to claim it is met with tremendous resistance. The music is ours, since it contains our soul, so to speak—it contains all our ideas and responses to the world. We need it to help us claim this African-ness and we would be a stronger people for it. It's presently in the hands of someone else who sits over it as custodian, without even allowing us its source.

DS: When Loomis finds his song, he can stand up again.
AW: Yes.

Cool August: Mr. Wilson's
Red-Hot Blues

Dinah Livingston / 1987

From *Minnesota Monthly*, 21 (October 1987), 25–32. Reprinted by permission.

The ashtray on the table at Bailey's Bar & Grill is full of August Wilson's dead Marlboros. He has smoked five of them in the past hour. "With all the pressure on smokers these days, do you ever think of quitting?" I ask. "No," he says. His smile fades. "I think antismokers have become obnoxious, and I don't tolerate obnoxiousness from anyone."

The smile returns, and Wilson relaxes. "Oh, I mean, when I'm a little short of breath goin' up the stairs, I think, 'Well, maybe I oughta quit.' But I would never stop because people *told* me to."

This afternoon he has been at home working on his new play, *The Piano Lesson*, with Berniece and Wining Boy and Boy Willie and Lymon and Sutter's ghost tumbling onto paper as fast as his pen can set them down. *The Piano Lesson* starts rehearsals at the Yale Repertory Theater in New Haven, Connecticut, on October 26. Three weeks earlier, *Joe Turner's Come and Gone* opens at the Arena Stage in Washington, D.C., bound for a Broadway debut in March. *Ma Rainey's Black Bottom* recently concluded a long run at the Penumbra Theater in St. Paul—the only Twin Cities theater that has ever staged his work.

August Wilson is on a roll. He won the Pulitzer Prize in April for *Fences*, his fiery drama of father-son conflict. In June the play won four Tonys, including Best Play. Now Wilson is negotiating with Paramount Pictures to bring *Fences* to the screen. People have begun to recognize him on the streets of St. Paul. "It's nice," he says.

Lloyd Richards of Yale Rep, who has directed many of Wilson's plays, has called Wilson "a major playwright—not for the black theater or the green theater or the blue theater, but for the American theater." Wilson writes about freed slaves, gypsy cab drivers, jazz players. He writes about the men he admired the most when he was growing up in a Pittsburgh slum—the black "warriors" against white society who ended up in the penitentiary—and about the women who supported them. Often his dialogue soars with the lyric rhythms of a lifelong poet. Just as often, it burns with anger.

In Wilson's plays, black people are only as successful as white people allow them to be. When Troy Maxson, the hero of *Fences*, is promoted from garbage collector to garbage-truck driver, it is clear that he has gone as far as he can go. The blues singer Gertrude "Ma" Rainey rakes in money for white record-company executives who won't invite her to their homes. The fury of Levee, a young jazzman in *Ma Rainey*, explodes into a diatribe against the "white man's" God: "God ain't never listened to no nigger's prayers. God take a nigger's prayers and throw them into the garbage. . . . In fact—God hate niggers. Hate them with all the fury in his heart."

August Wilson is forty-two years old. His father was a white man, a heavy drinker who seldom visited his children. Ask Wilson what the white part of his heritage means to him, and he says: "The cultural environment of my life has been black, and I've always considered myself black." His eyes say: Next question, please. His ambition is to "trace the odyssey of the black male in American society" with a play set in each decade of this century; he has written six of them already. They are plays of absolute conviction and passionate intensity, expressing hatreds that Wilson himself disavows: "I don't write from a well-spring of bitterness."

Wilson has lived in St. Paul for almost ten years, and he says he's here to stay. By proclamation of Mayor George Latimer, May 27, 1987, was August Wilson Day. More recently, Wilson replied to a City Council tribute with a paean to his adopted city. "In St. Paul," he said, "I found a city that encourages dreams. . . ."

During three meetings with me this summer, Wilson talked about his roots, his plays, and his image of black life in America. He smiled easily—a sheepish, disarming smile that reveals a dimple half-hidden by his grizzled beard. He chuckled often. He speaks with a husky workingman's voice, pouring out equal measures of street talk and refined eloquence. Wilson appears to remember it all: the names of his grade-school classmates, the date he first set eyes on St. Paul, his poems and his plays—which he can recite, word for word, months and years after he wrote them. During our second meeting, at the offices of *Minnesota Monthly*, he ran out of Marlboros and borrowed three cigarettes from a colleague of mine. A couple of days later, he repaid his debt with a brand-new pack and a shy grin of thanks.

Minnesota Monthly: What drew you to St. Paul?
August Wilson: My good friend Claude Purdy was out here. He was directing Penumbra's first show, a play called *Eden* by Steve Carter. It was November 1977. The first time I came to St. Paul was November 13, 1977.

Claude had sent me a ticket; I'd written a musical satire for him, and he asked if I'd come out and rewrite it. I stayed here ten days; did a rewrite of the play; went back to Pittsburgh, where I was living at the time. In January of '78, he called and said he had a theater in Los Angeles that wanted to do a staged reading of the play.

I stopped in Minnesota on the way to the staged reading. When I came back, I ended up staying here two weeks, and it was during that time that I met the woman who later became my wife. We were driving down Summit Avenue, and they had the elm trees, and I thought, "Boy, this is really a nice place. I'm gonna move up here." I kind of said it aloud and without thinking. It was the first time the idea had entered my head, and I thought, "Why not?" And on March 5, 1978, I moved from Pittsburgh to St. Paul.

When I got here, I said, "Where's the street where the trees were?" And they told me how to get to Summit Avenue. When I got there, they were cutting down the trees; they had Dutch elm disease. And I remember standing there and thinking, "Is this an omen? Shall I go back to Pittsburgh?" Anyway, I decided to stay. I thought it was a nice, comfortable, relaxing place—a nice atmosphere to work.

MM: And were you right?
AW: Absolutely—no question about it. It's like paradise.

MM: You've mentioned one special place in St. Paul that welcomed you— Dixie's, when it used to be Esteban's.
AW: I lived right on Grand, not too far from Esteban's. I stayed home most of the time, but I started going out Wednesdays at eight o'clock. I started going up to Esteban's, and I would sit there and write.

I kind of got to know the manager, a guy named Chip; the bartender, Norman; and some others. It was really the first place that I felt like I became one of the regulars. And I got to know some of the other people who came

in quite often. They were very much interested in what was going on
with my plays.

So I would come in sometimes, and it would be eleven o'clock at night,
and there would be these people sitting around with the lights turned down
low. They'd say, "August is here, and he's writing"—so they'd turn the lights
up. That really made me feel welcome. It was a good place.

And then it changed and became Dixie's, and I've been there maybe two
or three times since. I can't stand to go there, because it's no longer the same
place. I can't go there because I've got this affection for what used to be
there—for Esteban's.

MM: I think you've said you're basically a loner, and you aren't interrupted
by friends coming in to shoot the breeze.
AW: Sometimes you are; sometimes it's even a welcome interruption, if
you're working on something and you stop to talk to someone and you take
a little break. That's probably another part of the reason why I write in bars:
Writing's a very lonely, very solitary occupation.

MM: Are you inspired by what you see and hear in bars?
AW: I don't know if it's inspiration. It may be just the general atmosphere of
the bar. Sometimes I'll be at Sweeney's, and they'll put on a good tape, and
the music is inspirational. It's music I like, and I'm off on a roll, writing
something.

MM: What kind of music?
AW: I like jazz, blues. Sometimes they put on fifties or sixties
rhythm-and-blues—something I recognize. I try to place a year to it: what
year it came out, what I was doing when I first heard the song, and whatever
the song may mean to me. And then somehow I find the inspiration to
keep working.

MM: Did you run into a lot of bigotry in Pittsburgh when you were
growing up?
AW: Oh, sure. Pittsburgh, and I'm sure anywhere else in the country.

I was born in '45, so I grew up in the fifties and sixties. We lived in a mixed
neighborhood—mostly a mixture of Syrians, Jews, and blacks. The street
I lived on . . . indeed, there was a *community* of people, and I remember

coming home from school, and all of the parents would be sitting on the stoops, talking and exchanging recipes, talking about what they were cooking for dinner, talking about their kids. That was a nice neighborhood, in the sense that anyone in the neighborhood was your social parent. Any one of the adults could tell you to do anything, and you did it quicker than if your mother told you to do it—because if Miss Pearl or Bella or Julie or Sadie said to do something and you didn't do it, and they told your mother, it was twice as difficult.

That neighborhood was called the Hill District, and we were living in two rooms—my mother and six kids. Then we moved to a rented house in a neighborhood called Hazelwood. There's a steel mill there, Jones & Laughlin Steel, where a lot of people worked. When we moved in, someone threw a brick through the window that said, "Nigger Stay Out." There was a big story on the front page of the paper. And knowing my mother, that just made her more determined. So we moved there.

I went to a parochial school: St. Stephen's. They had just started letting blacks in the school. I was the only black in my eighth-grade class.

Then I went to Central Catholic High School, where I was the only black in the school. Every morning there would be a note on my desk: "Go Home, Nigger"—things like this—which up until the time I was fifteen I had not really encountered or even been aware of.

MM: I think you've said that your parents' generation protected their kids from a knowledge of racism.
AW: They sheltered us from a lot of the indignities they suffered. I think it's wrong, but there are some things you don't want to tell your kids. You don't want to tell your kid: "You can go to Woolworth's and buy something, but they won't give you a paper bag."

MM: They wouldn't give you a paper bag?
AW: No, they didn't give blacks bags; you had to carry your purchases out without a bag. I find it very interesting that even today you have to ask for a bag. You can buy, say, some dish soap, and they expect you to carry it out of the store. You have to ask, "May I have a bag, please?"

Now I get a bag for a pack of gum: "Could I have a bag, please? Thank you!" I'm makin' up for all the bags I didn't get. You've gotta give me a bag when I buy something. I don't care what it is.

MM: I remember reading about one thing that happened to you in school: You did a paper on Napoleon that was supposed to be too good for a black boy to have written. What happened, if it's not too painful?
AW: No, it's not painful at all. I don't mind telling the story; I like to tell the story.

I went to Central Catholic High School in ninth grade. It was a very difficult time, to say the least. The principal on various occasions had to send me home in a cab. He would, like, walk me through these forty guys who were waitin' to beat me up, and put me in a cab and send me home. What he failed to realize was . . . he didn't send a cab to pick me up in the morning, and I had to come to school by myself the next morning. So I got in a lot of fights.

I got tired of it. So one day—it was April—I went down to the principal's office and said, "I'm gonna quit." He went and got my English teacher, Brother Dominic, and they tried to talk me into staying, and I said, "I don't want to stay." And so I left. I just walked out.

My mother wanted me to be a lawyer. That fall she said: "Well, O.K., if you're not gonna be a lawyer, go down there and learn how to fix cars or something."

So I went to Connelly Trade School. I couldn't get into auto mechanics, because that class was filled up, and I couldn't get into auto body. They put me in sheet metal. I was in the sheet metal shop making tin cups. I was not good at it. I was sitting there making sheet cups or mechanical drawings and all this stupid kind of thing.

We had [regular classes] half a day on some days, and I was looking forward to that—and I walked into the classroom, and they're doing, like, fifth-grade work. Half the kids could barely read. I said, "This isn't working out." So I decided that I didn't want to go to Connelly Trade, and I didn't want to make any tin cups, and I didn't want to be an auto mechanic.

Right across the street from where we were living in Hazelwood was a public school: Gladstone High School. I decided I was going to go to Gladstone. One of the tenth-grade subjects was the history class—one of my favorite classes. The teacher was a black teacher, and he was one of those black teachers who did not like black people. Mr. B favored the white students over black students.

I had a run-in with him, 'cause one day I heard Carolyn Forsaith and Barbara Miller—who were two of Mr. B's favorite students . . . and one day one said to the other, "Did you do your homework?" And she said, "No, did you do yours?" And she said, "No." And Mr. B called the roll, and they both said, "Yes." And he called my name, and I hadn't done my homework. I said, "Yes." And he told me to bring it up. I said, "If you tell Carolyn Forsaith and Barbara Miller to bring theirs up, I'll bring mine up."

He said, "Just bring it up." And it really disturbed me that he would ask me to do this and not them. It ended up with me demanding that they tell the truth.

We had to do a term paper, and I selected Napoleon because I liked Napoleon. We used to pick apples when I was a kid—fourteen, fifteen. There was an abandoned apple orchard in the neighborhood, and we would go and pick apples. Everyone had a name. Ba Bra was Tarzan. Earl was Daniel Boone; he was a scout. I was Napoleon, because I was the leader; I made the decisions. Everyone looked to me: "What do we do now?" kind of stuff.

So I wrote this term paper. I read all these books on Napoleon, and I wrote my paper. I was real proud of it. I turned it in, and the next day Mr. B asked me to stay after school; he wanted to talk to me about my paper. And I thought, "Hey, that's cool. He saw I did a good job."

And he wrote "A+," and then he wrote "E." And he said, "I'm going to give you one of these two grades." I told him, "That doesn't make much sense to me. What are you talking about?" He began flipping through the paper, and he asked me where I did my research, and I said, "Well, I've got a bibliography here." And he said, "Wellll—you have some older sisters, don't you?" I said, "Yeah, I have three of them." "Wellll—is it possible that *they* could have written this paper?" I said, "To be honest, I write *their* papers." I remember telling him, "As you know, most of the students will go right to the encyclopedia and copy whatever's there. I have attempted to do some research here and come up with some different things. I think it's *enough* that I say I wrote the paper."

He leaned back in his chair and took his pen and drew a circle around the "E" and handed me back the paper. And I took the paper, tore it up, threw it in the trash basket, and walked out.

I did not go to school the next day—or any day after that. I got up the next day and . . . right outside the principal's office was a basketball court. And I got my basketball and went out and shot basketballs. Did that for about two weeks. As I look back on it, I think that I wanted the principal, or someone, to notice that I wasn't in school and to say, "Well, what are you doin' shootin' basketballs? What's the problem? What's going on here?" But no one ever said a word. The principal never came out; Mr. B never came out. Nobody said, "There's a kid out there shootin' basketballs. He should be in school."

I ran into Mr. B one time years later. Nikki Giovanni was in Pittsburgh reading some poems. I remember Mr. B came to me and very patronizingly put his hand on my shoulders and said, "Well, August, maybe one day you'll be up there reading poems." And I thought, "Well, Nikki Giovanni is O.K., but I'm as good a poet." God, I'd read at I-don't-know-how-many universities by this time. And Mr. B never knew. He wasn't gonna find out. I looked at him, and I thought, "Get away from me. You don't know what the hell's going on."

I heard he got on the Board of Education. We used to tease him about this: He would come in and take off his sport jacket and put on a smock—what was actually a stock boy's smock, because, see, Mr. B was very ambitious. He taught school, and in the summer he worked as a soda jerk, and he worked in a stock room as a stock boy. He was determined to be successful in America. And he was determined to work hard, because that's what it took to be successful. So he was not above teaching tenth-grade history and in the summer making ice-cream cones. He wanted to make it. He wanted to be somebody.

MM: Were you born a Catholic?
AW: No. There was a wonderful woman in the neighborhood named Miss Sarah Degree. She saw us playing in the front one time, and she said, "Where you live? I want to go talk to your mother." And she talked to my mother, and she asked if she could take us to church on Sunday. And my mother said yes, because Miss Sarah took everybody's kids to church on Sunday. Sunday morning, you would see Miss Sarah coming down the street with forty kids. And she had 'em all in a line, and she would take 'em all to church. We started going to church with Miss Sarah.

MM: Was she white?
AW: No, Miss Sarah was a black woman, and every Catholic I knew that lived in the Hill District was a Catholic because of Miss Sarah. If there was ever a saint, it was Miss Sarah. She passed away last year. She was in her nineties, and God bless her, she was still goin' to church.

I've been threatening to write the bishop of the Diocese of Pittsburgh
a letter, because we need to honor her in some way: Miss Sarah Degree
Gymnasium, or Miss Sarah Degree House for Wayward Women. She was
just a wonderful woman. There's no question: If she was white, they'd have a
Miss Sarah Degree Child Care Center or something. I swear I believe that;
maybe I'm wrong, but I believe that wholeheartedly. God, she probably
didn't even have a decent burial. But that's the way it goes.

For Miss Sarah, everything was the Church and God. She had a thousand
statues in her house. When my mother had my youngest brother, we stayed
with Miss Sarah for the week or so that my mother was in the hospital. We
had Sunday School every day. At six o'clock, there's Miss Sarah teachin' us
about the Bible. We had to sit there in this hot room in the middle of the
summer with Miss Sarah and this huge chart that she got from somewhere,
teachin' us stories from the Bible and makin' us say the Rosary every night at
seven o'clock.

MM: Was your church integrated?
AW: Yes. The church was integrated, *except* . . . no, we have to be honest
about these things. There was Holy Trinity, a huge, big, beautiful church with
big steeples—a gorgeous, gorgeous church. Then there was St. Bridget's,
also in the same neighborhood. And then over here a little tiny, tiny church
that does not look too much different than a garage—a two-story garage—
because they did have steps going down. It was called St. Benedict the Moor's.
We went to St. Bridget's Church. But we were considered members of St.
Benedict's parish because St. Benedict's was a black church. All the blacks
were members of St. Benedict's, irrespective of where they went to church.

Now—things change. They tear down St. Bridget's Church. They tear
down St. Benedict's. The only one that's left is Holy Trinity. All the white
people are gone, so it's all black. And they name the church Old Holy Trinity
St. Bridget St. Benedict the Moor. After much discussion about the matter,
they decided to just name it St. Benedict the Moor. And they put up this
statue of St. Benedict. The church sits on the dividing line between the
downtown and the Hill District—and they had the statue with its back
turned to the blacks and its arms opened to downtown. Every single person
in the neighborhood, whether they were Catholic or not, noticed that and felt
insulted that we got a black saint and he's turned his back on us and opened
his arms up to the white folks downtown.

This was in 1969—and they have promised so many times. It is 1987, and it is *still* facing downtown. I think the Diocese of Pittsburgh ought to spend $12,000, $15,000, whatever it costs to send some men to unscrew the base of that statue and turn the damn thing around.

MM: Your mother sounds like a very proud, impressive woman.

AW: She had a sixth-grade education, but she was a very good reader. She taught all of us to read, and she would read us books. I'd always gotten straight A's, and all the teachers had told her that I could be anything I wanted to be; it was up to me. So she was trying to impress this upon me.

She was also a very impressive woman personally. I remember when Morton Salt had a contest on the radio. Apparently they had just come out with the slogan "When it rains, it pours"—and if you could name the product, you got a brand-new Speed Queen washing machine. And my mother heard this on the radio. We didn't have a telephone, so she had to write the number down for my sister, give her a dime, tell her to run to the store, and call this number, and say "Morton Salt." And I remember my sister standing there confused, trying to figure out why—and my mother said, "God damn it, just go *do* what I told you. Go to the store, call the number, say 'Morton Salt.'" So my sister ran out of the house, down the steps, went to the store, and said "Morton Salt." My mother's home listening to the radio, and "Hey, we got a winner!"

When they found out that she was black, they wanted to give her a certificate to the Salvation Army, where she could go down and get a used washing machine. And she told them exactly what they could do with their certificate, and she didn't want no used washing machine because she was due a brand-new washing machine like they said on the radio.

All of her friends were telling her that was stupid. They said, "Daisy, go get the used washing machine. Then you won't have to be wringin' out them clothes on your hand." She said, "No." It wasn't until about two or three years later we got a brand-new Speed Queen washing machine from Herb Glickman.

Herb Glickman was one of the guys who'd go around knocking on the doors willing to give black people credit. See, if you're on welfare, you can't get credit, can't buy no washing machine. But Herb Glickman, God bless him, who himself did not have the money to pay for a washing machine . . . he'd go get some customers, and he'd go down to the store and say, "Look, I want to buy five washing machines, and let me owe you"—because he *could* get credit. And then he would come around, and he would charge you— and of course he'd charge you, naturally, a little more than he'd pay for it. But he was willing to take a dollar a week or a dollar a month, so you could pay him on credit.

Then, I remember, the insurance man used to come: Gordon. I didn't like Gordon; I didn't like Herb either. Whenever these guys came, they were takin' money out of the house. So when I saw Gordon, that meant I couldn't get no nickels. If I said, "Ma, can I have a nickel to buy a Popsicle?" it was like the nickel had gone to Gordon already and there wasn't no nickels. So every time I saw him, I knew: He come to get some money, which is gonna make it harder on me.

MM: Was he white?
AW: Oh sure. All these people were white. There was literally an army of whites who would come through that whenever you saw 'em in the community, they were takin' money out of the community. They'd come through knockin' on doors. Gordon was goin' around gettin' his little money; Herb was goin' around gettin' his money; other people were goin' around. But they always came. And it was about getting this little bit of money from these little poor people.

Herb . . . he wasn't a bad guy at all. As you get older, you understand it: He was a businessman; he was just a guy that could get credit. He would buy the merchandise for $39 and sell it to you for $49, because he was willin' to take the risk of you payin' him. He was willin' to come every week and get $2 until you finished payin' him. So he earned every dime of that extra that he charged. And had it not been for him, there was a whole lot of blacks who wouldn'ta had *nothin'*. We wouldn'ta had no radio. We wouldn'ta had no washing machine. We wouldn'ta had God knows what else without Herb Glickman—and people like him. He was an honest man—and a hard-working man, at that.

MM: You don't feel bitter about people like that?
AW: No, I don't feel bitter. I feel grateful.

Where you get bitter is things like, for instance: The house my mother lived in is a rowhouse, and all of these houses are identical. My mother bought one of those houses. And two doors down the street is a white woman, Mary Bartirome. Mary had her house insured. And Mary is payin' $40 a month. The same insurance company charged my mother $300 for the same thing that they're charging Mary $40 for. What the hell's the difference? I mean: here's a house, here's a house; you charge this much insurance.

MM: You've used an interesting phrase about middle-class blacks when their parents would send them to the movies. They'd say, "Don't show your color."
AW: It means "Don't act out." It really means "Don't be yourself." It means "Go down there and try to act the best you can, like you see white folks acting." It was really used as "Be good." But you see, if you say showing your color is bad, you're saying, "Don't go down there and act like a nigger; don't go down there and act black." Why would you tell a black kid that? How else are they supposed to act?

MM: Can we talk a little about how you became a playwright?
AW: I started writing poetry. Then when I was twenty, I wrote a term paper for my sister, who was going to Fordham University. And she gave me $20. I went down to McFarren's typewriter store, and they had this old Royal typewriter in the window that I had my eye on, and it was $20. Twenty dollars in 1965 was a lot of money. I could live two weeks on $20. I walked out of the store with it, and then I realized I didn't have bus fare home. So I had to carry this thing home, up a steep hill.

I didn't know how to type. I sat right down and typed up a couple of poems. And this is work, because it took, like, a half-hour to type five lines, because I didn't know where the keys were.

I remember I bought a typewriter tablet—twenty-five sheets, or something like that. I could not *imagine* having five hundred sheets of paper, or what the hell anyone would ever do with that much paper. And I remember when I bought my first ream of paper: "I'm really a writer now. That's five hundred sheets of paper, five hundred poems. I might not write five hundred poems in my *life*." It was really a big deal.

I fell in with a group of artists—painters—and they put on art shows. I was invited to read my poetry at art shows. I even did a fashion show once; I got paid $50, which was a lot of money—in 1966, this was—to recite some poems at this fashion show with two guys playing violins in tuxedos. And I wore a black turtleneck.

Then, around 1967, there was this art gallery, Halfway Art Gallery, in Pittsburgh. It was a place to congregate. We put out a little magazine called *Signal*. Then we changed the name to *Connection*. I was the Poetry Editor. Then we decided to name ourselves the Center Avenue Poets' Theater Workshop. We had poetry readings and gallery jazz sessions and the whole bit. We talked about doing theater, 'cause theater was part of our name. I had never seen a play before.

In '68, Rob Penny wrote a play; he said, "Hey, look what I did!" I said, "Let's do it." We both looked at each other and said, "How?" "I don't know; let's do it. Let's start a theater."

Some guy said, "Let's name it Black Horizons." Then they said, "Who's gonna direct it?" I said, "I'll direct it."

I had no idea how to direct a play. I went to the library and got books on how to direct a play, which was very difficult stuff. I mean, I didn't understand all that stuff they were talking about. It didn't apply to what I was doing: "You act like him"; "Come on in"; "Move over"; "Come through that door"; "When you say your lines, you go back around the bar over there"; "O.K.—let's do it." It worked.

I went around to businesses, churches—saying, "Be our sponsor." Got $25, $10. Put their name in the program like I seen people do. And we put on this play. And people came to see it; we charged fifty cents. We were surprised how many people came. And the people liked it. We were a good theater company. We did good work, 'cause I insisted that we do the best we could do.

Around '73, '75, I wrote a couple of one-act plays. One was called *The Coldest Day of the Year*. An old man and an old woman meet on a park bench. The first line of dialogue is . . . the guy walks up and she's sitting there, and he says, "Our lives are frozen in the deepest hate and spiritual turbulence." She looks at him, and he says, "Terror hangs over the night like a hawk. The wind bites at your tits." She says, "It was cold yesterday." He says, "No, today is the coldest. You said so yourself."

And they begin to talk. And he saw her on the corner yesterday, and she was waiting for someone. And he says, "He didn't come?" And she says, "No, he didn't come." "And you came back today?" "Yes, and tomorrow as well." He says, "I know about such things. One day you'll get tired of waiting and nobody coming, and then you'll go yourself." She says, "Perhaps." The bus comes. And he has given her his coat. It's made of wool from the sacrificial

lamb. She starts to give him back his coat, and he says, "No, keep it. I tell
you what. I'll pretend that I'm he and that I came. I'll pretend I knew you
in your youth, when your breasts didn't sag against your belly, when you
were a trembling flower in the spring wind, and I came to pick it. Or when
you were a blackberry bush and I was a bear searching among the briars.
And maybe I'll sing a song for you." So they begin to talk, and he begins
to become this guy she was waiting on, and he begins to play this game.
They dance, they sing, they play this game. He says, "You lied in the dark"—
whatever that means. She says, "I never lied." He says, "You were the target,
I was the arrow, and fate was the bow." He says, "Tell me, did I hit the target?"
She says, "Come and find out."

He says, "I want you forever, lady. I want to touch heaven with you, and
I've been in training." That's one of my favorite lines.

The first part of it was mostly her story, and then he gets to tell his story.
She says, "There's a story you wear in your face like a mask. Tell it to me." He
says, "I'm not much with fancy words and all."

That's my favorite play. I've written better plays, but there's something
about that one that I like a lot. I like the language. There's a charm about it,
I think.

MM: You're a self-taught playwright, aren't you?
AW: Sure. I never took any classes in playwriting. I never read any books
on it. I never read any books on writing, period. I always thought, "You *do* it.
You learn by doing."

MM: What have you learned about playwriting from Lloyd Richards?
AW: Lloyd's a wonderful person, of high integrity—an excellent director.
I don't know what more anyone could ask for.

Yale Rep is a great place to work. We do the work that is necessary for the
play to realize its potential without any regard to what may happen to it after
we finish working on it. We don't work with Broadway in mind. If you start
off working with the idea that you are going to prepare this play for the
commercial theater, then you are not serving the play; you're serving what
you project to be the market.

I've learned from Lloyd to trust the space that we call the stage. I've
learned to respect it and realize that what you put up there is important, and
that you have a responsibility for what you put up there, and that every one

of those words on the page are going to get said, and they'd better be the words that you want said.

I just had a meeting with him. I took the rewrite of *The Piano Lesson*. And I discovered that I have a tendency to say the same things two or three times. These are things that I want to be sure that the audience *gets*. So Lloyd says, "Once is sufficient. You'd be surprised at how much the audience picks up. You don't have to beat 'em over the head." Having worked with me, he knows that whatever the problems of the play . . . tell me, I can handle 'em.

MM: Tell me a little about *The Piano Lesson*.

AW: All of the male characters in this play, with the exception of the preacher, Avery, are a certain kind of black male. Every single one of them has been in a penitentiary—out on the Parchment Farm. They're all outlaws, in a sense. None of them has really committed a crime that you would put someone in a penitentiary for. Behind all of them, men like that, who I'll call warriors, there are women who support them, who nurse them, who feed them, who comfort them. And without those women, they couldn't exist. Berniece is one of those women. But she never knows when she's gonna go to another burial. That's what those women do: They always bury their men.

Berniece is tired of it. She does not want to be one of those women who supports those men. That's what the play is about. And there is Avery offering her a bridge to safety, which is the church. But you see, Avery is not Berniece's kind of guy. Her intention to marry Avery is a betrayal of her sisterhood. It's also a betrayal of all the men in her life that she's loved and that have loved her. It's a betrayal which I hope that the audience will recognize they do not want her to make.

I think this is my best play. I think I was able to articulate my ideas in a real dramatic fashion. And I've been able to get more action in the play than I have in my other plays. I'm real excited about it.

MM: It sounds wonderful.

AW: Yeah. I think I found the one perfect metaphor—which is the music, the piano. One of the things I started out with was the idea of putting this piano on stage, and the audience has to sit there and look at it. It looks strange. And then you begin to find out more, and more, and more. Every time you look at it, you see something different. You learn it was stolen. You learn this happened, and that happened. And every new piece of information you find out about the piano, the piano changes. Hopefully, your attitude toward the piano keeps changing, which makes the piano get bigger and bigger and bigger and bigger, and it becomes more and more and more important.

MM: Is it going to be a real piano?
AW: No. No.

MM: What are you going to do?
AW: Theater, man, theater.

What they'll do, probably, is get an old piano, from somewhere, and they'll make a shell and put the shell over it, and color it and make it look like wood. They're wonderful. They can make anything. You'll look at it, and it's gonna look just like a piano.

We've got a house for *Fences*. People go, "Is that a real house?" It looks real, man. It's got running water back there in the kitchen. We got an ironing board behind the door. Nobody sees it; it's just behind the door. But the set designer, he's got spices up on the shelf—spices and canned goods—'cause the actors in there, it's like a kitchen to them. It has everything a kitchen has, complete with ironing board behind the door. You know, it's . . .

MM: Magic.
AW: It just blows me away, that they would take all that great attention to detail—somethin' that the audience can't see.

MM: At the end of *Fences*, you show that in many ways Cory Maxson resembles his father, Troy. Is that one of your themes: that there's a kind of continuity from generation to generation?
AW: Sure, I think so. I've got a poem I wrote for my grandfather that ends with the line "I'm walking toward you in his shoes." One of the questions [in *Fences*] was "Are we our fathers' sons?" And if in fact we are our fathers' sons, must we become our fathers? Are the tools that they have given us to participate in the world . . . are they sufficient for our survival and progress?

MM: Where do you get the ideas for your plays?
AW: *Joe Turner's Come and Gone* came from a painting by the artist Romare Bearden. It showed a man coming down the stairs of the boardinghouse reaching for his lunch bucket, a woman with her purse apparently going

out, and a child sitting at a table drinking a glass of milk. And in the center
of the painting was this man with a hat and coat who was sitting in this
posture of abject defeat.

I wanted to find out who this man was, so I began to write a short story
called "The Matter of Mill Hand's Lunch Bucket"—which was the title of the
painting. After about twelve pages, I abandoned it and began to write a play.
I did not quite understand what the play was about until I was listening to
a song by W. C. Handy called "Joe Turner's Come and Gone," in which
Handy said that the story of the blues could not be told without the story
of Joe Turner.

Joe Turner was the brother of Pete Turner, who was the governor of
Tennessee who would press Negroes in peonage. The men would be late
coming home from work, and someone would say, "Oh, haven't you heard?
Joe Turner's come and gone. He had a chain with forty links on it." And so
the women around Memphis made up this song: "They tell me Joe Turner's
come and gone, he's got my man and gone. He came with forty links of
chain, he's got my man and gone." So that is what I realized happened to this
figure in the painting, who became Herald Loomis: He'd been caught by
Joe Turner and pressed into peonage.

So it can be a line of a blues lyric, a painting, an image. *Fences* actually
started with Troy standing in the yard with the baby in his arms, and the first
lines I wrote was "I'm standing out here in the yard with my daughter in
my arms. She's just a wee bitty little ole thing. She don't understand about
grownups' business, and she ain't got no mama." I didn't know who he
was talking to. I said, "O.K., he's talking to his wife." O.K., *why* is he telling
her this? So then I had to invent a series of circumstances that would allow
him to stand in the yard with a baby in his arms and say those words to her.

MM: How did you learn to write poetry?
AW: You learn by doing. I certainly read a lot of poets and imitated all the
poets who are out there. There's no substitute for the actual practice of the
writing. I've written thousands upon thousands of poems.

MM: I've read that you were influenced by Dylan Thomas and John
Berryman.
AW: I like John Berryman a lot—what he used to call psychic shorthand,
and the way he would turn and twist a line. Thomas was probably an early

influence. But I don't think he's really influenced my writing as much as he influenced the idea of what a poet is.

MM: You've mentioned Derek Walcott.
AW: In my opinion, he's the best poet alive writing. In the entire world.

MM: What does he write about?
AW: Love. Honor. Duty. Betrayal. *Life.*

MM: Those are the great themes.
AW: Sure. I think they should be every writer's themes. I want to say there's only one story: It's the story of the human condition. And every writer writes about it. And you can't fool people, because they know if you're being honest about it. Because they know the story too well. And I think part of the writer's job is to present the story in a way they've never seen it or thought of it before.

MM: Do you still get flaming mad when you think of the ways blacks have been treated throughout history? That fuels your drive to write, doesn't it?
AW: Well, I don't know if that fuels the drive to write as much as my artistic agenda, which is, as James Baldwin called it, "a profound articulation of the black experience." And as he further defined it, it's this ritual of intercourse that can sustain a man once he's left his father's house. What I'm trying to do is to place those values of the black experience on stage in what I call "loud action"—simply to demonstrate that they exist and that they are capable of sustenance, and to point out some avenues of sustenance. That's what fuels my work—more so than any bitterness or angriness. I don't write from a wellspring of bitterness. I write from a very positive viewpoint of black life and black experience.

MM: Do you think that thirty years ago you could have been such a success as you are now?
AW: I certainly couldn't have written my plays without Lorraine Hansberry, and Ed Bullins, and Ron Milner, and Amiri Baraka, and all of those playwrights who have preceded me. Because they did their work, that enables me to do mine.

I don't know. What was the situation like thirty years ago? In some ways, of course, it was a different society. But I don't think the situation for blacks in America has changed since World War II. That's the last time we had jobs.

MM: Well, what about younger blacks? Aren't they more upwardly mobile?
AW: How could they be upwardly mobile? They don't have jobs. Society has no use for them. Society has no jobs for them. Their fathers didn't have jobs. So they don't have nothing. They're left over from history. You see, cotton is no longer king, and there's no longer a need for these thirty-five million people that are in this society. There are no avenues for them to fully participate other than music and sports.

MM: Aren't they entering the professions in greater numbers?
AW: Oh, they probably are, but it doesn't really affect the lives of thirty-five million blacks in America because you have a few lawyers and a few doctors and a few professional people. They actually make up a teeny, teeny—very, very small—percentage of blacks in the country. Most blacks live in poverty, misery still in 1987. Most blacks live in housing projects, areas set off from the rest of the city—America's version of South African homelands.

MM: The situation for blacks in South Africa is unspeakable. Is it that bad here?
AW: Sure. No question.

MM: Well, they're not totally segregated in their own little townships.
AW: Well, yes, in a sense they are. Look at the Robert Taylor Homes in Chicago. They're isolated and separated. In Pittsburgh they're isolated and separated. And look at the welfare hotels in New York. You have thousands of people living in them. And they're paying these guys twelve hundred dollars a month for a little room. I mean, it's just terrible. Babies fall out the window. There's no screens. There's no heat. There's no air. There's nothing. The elevators don't work. That's where blacks live.

MM: Do you think young black people are sufficiently in touch with their heritage?
AW: Well, they're not losing touch with their sensibilities, which are African sensibilities—which is the way that they respond to the world. That is very strong.

MM: What are African sensibilities?

AW: The whole philosophical system is different. For instance, Europeans look at man as apart *from* the world. In African sensibility, man is a part *of* the world. That's a very basic philosophical difference which influences how you think, how you live, how you respond to the world around you.

Given the resources of the nation, and the task of solving the problems, we would come up with different solutions to transportation, to housing, to whatever, because it's a different mind at work. I always like to say that if we were in charge, we would all live in round houses.

You see, blacks in American society have had to respond to the way Europeans respond to the world in order to survive in the society. And they have not been allowed their cultural differences. I think that if we move toward claiming the strongest parts of ourselves, which is the African parts, so that we can participate in the society as Africans, we would be all the stronger for it.

MM: You've written a one-man show on Malcolm X. Is he one of your heroes?

AW: Oh, sure. Without question. Malcolm was a very important historical figure in the black experience.

MM: Were you a Black Nationalist during the sixties?

AW: Sure. I still consider myself a Black Nationalist. That's what I call myself. At the advent of the Black Power movement of the sixties, I began to see that blacks were looking for ways to alter their relationship to this society and to alter the shared expectations of themselves as a people. I felt it a duty and an honor to participate.

MM: What are the main tenets of Black Nationalism?

AW: Self-determination, self-respect, and self-defense.

MM: Well, how do you get self-determination if you're oppressed?

AW: I wish I knew the answer. That's what the whole thrust of the sixties and Black Power was about: to gain self-determination and self-respect and self-defense. That's what they're fighting for in Nicaragua. But I'll shut up about that. There's people fighting for that all over the world. Wherever there are oppressed people, the idea is to gain self-determination.

MM: By overthrowing the government?

AW: No. I don't think that anybody ever advocated overthrowing the government. What it means is to alter the relationship of yourself to the society you live in. Acquiring some power, for instance, is a way of altering your relationship with society without overthrowing anything.

MM: You've called the blues "the book of black people." What does that mean?

AW: I think that what's contained in the blues is the African American's cultural response to the world. We are not a people with a long history of writing things out; it's been an oral tradition: passing information, knowledge, ideas, and attitudes along orally. In order for the information to survive, you have to tell it in such a way that it's memorable—so that someone else hearing the story will want to go and tell someone else. That's a way of ensuring its survival. One way to make that information memorable is to put it in a song. Music provides an emotional reference to the content of the song.

The thing with the blues is that there's an entire philosophical system at work. And I've found that whatever you want to know about the black experience in America is contained in the blues.

They couldn't stop 'em singing and passing along all their information in songs. This is what I've found the blues to be. So it is the Book. It is our sacred book. Every other people has a sacred book, so I claim it as that. Anything I want to know, I go there and I find it out.

MM: Which blues artists mean a lot to you?

AW: All of them.

MM: You weren't always able to support yourself with your writing, were you?

AW: No. As a matter of fact, very few people can. I've been fortunate enough to get grants from the Jerome Foundation, the McKnight Foundation, the Bush Foundation, the Guggenheim Foundation, the Rockefeller Foundation. Prior to that, I worked at The Science Museum of Minnesota as a script-writer. Then I worked for the social-service organization called Little Brothers of the Poor. I worked as a cook, cooking lunch for the staff of about ten people, and I did that maybe two-and-a-half years. It was really one of most pleasant experiences I've had—one of the best jobs I've had. I was working

four hours a day, which gave me time to write. I wrote *Ma Rainey* when
I was working there.

  I was free. Whatever I wanted to cook on a particular day, it was up to me.
There was no schedule—as long as I had lunch ready by, like, one o'clock. So
some days I would come in at twelve and order pizza. And I would make a
salad, order pizza, you know. . . .

MM: Do you want to write novels someday?
AW: I don't know about plural, but I have an idea for *a* novel, sure. It's
called *Elder Green*. It's the story of an anthropologist who is listening
to a blues song called "Elder Green," becomes intrigued by the song, and
decides that he is going to uncover the roots of the song. And he sets off
to find Elder Green. The only clues he has are the clues in the song. He gets
to go down and uncover, using his anthropology, black culture in America.

MM: Do you write pretty fast?
AW: I do. Just sit down and do it if you're going to do it.

MM: How has your life changed since you've become successful?
AW: I don't think it's changed much. I still live in the same place, I still do the
same things that I was doing before. I can afford to buy my cat 9 Lives.

MM: At the Tony Awards, you gave your wife credit for standing by you.
AW: She's certainly been a support to me through all those years—especially
when I said, "Hey, look, I want to quit my job at The Science Museum,"
where I was making a fairly decent salary, to go make $88 a week at Little
Brothers here, because I wanted some time to write. I could not have done it
without her.

MM: Do you see yourself as St. Paul's newest celebrity? Or as a celebrity at all?
AW: No, I don't. I see myself as a playwright who happens to live in St. Paul,
a place I enjoy living.

MM: Do people recognize you on the street?
AW: More so now than before—since the publicity and my picture in the
paper. Some people do. It's always fun. People come up and say, "I saw your
play in New York, and I really enjoyed it." It's nice.

MM: One article said that on the opening night of *Ma Rainey* on Broadway in 1984, you took pictures of the celebrities.

AW: I would like to correct that. That is certainly not the case. I absolutely did not take any pictures at all of anybody. I don't know how that got started, unless I may have had my sister's camera in my hand and someone saw me with it. My sister took a lot of photos. I didn't take a photo of *anyone*. I wouldn't. For instance, I was just in New York, and Sidney Poitier came to see the show. He was backstage, and I coulda walked backstage and said, "Hey, hi! I wrote this, man!" He's a nice guy, and I'd like to meet him sometime, but I wasn't gonna run backstage because Sidney Poitier was there.

MM: Are you ever afraid of running dry as a creative artist?

AW: I have a lot of ideas. Since I am working out of a four-hundred-year autobiography, which is the black experience, I could write forever. I will never run out of material, because there's so many things that need to be said that haven't been said about those four hundred years.

MM: And you don't run out of that passion, that enthusiasm, for doing it?

AW: Oh, no. It's important work, and it needs to be done, and I think it's valuable work. It's fun doing it, too. I get a great kick out of writing.

August Wilson: Playwright

Bill Moyers / 1988

From *Bill Moyers: A World of Ideas—Conversations with Thoughtful Men and Women About American Life Today and the Ideas Shaping Our Future.* New York: Doubleday, 1989, 167–80. Copyright © 1989 by Public Affairs Television, Inc. Used by permission of Doubleday, a division of Random House, Inc.

Everyone has to find his own song, says August Wilson, and he found his in the blues. From music and literature he has shaped a philosophy of life and some of the country's most compelling drama. Wilson broke onto Broadway in 1984 with *Ma Rainey's Black Bottom* and won the Pulitzer Prize in 1987 for *Fences.* He is at work on a cycle of plays that will resurrect black voices from every decade of this century.

Moyers: Your plays are set in the past—*Joe Turner* in 1911, *Ma Rainey* in 1927, *Fences* in the 1950s. Do you ever consider writing about what's happening today?
Wilson: I suspect eventually I will get to that. Right now I enjoy the benefit of the historical perspective. You can look back to a character in 1936, for instance, and you can see him going down a particular path that you know did not work out for that character. Part of what I'm trying to do is to see some of the choices that we as blacks in America have made. Maybe we have made some incorrect choices. By writing about that, you can illuminate the choices.

Moyers: Give me an example of a choice that you think may have been the wrong one.
Wilson: I think we should have stayed in the South. We attempted to transplant what in essence was an emerging culture, a culture that had grown out of our experiences of two hundred years as slaves in the South. The cities of the urban North have not been hospitable. If we had stayed in the South, we could have strengthened the culture.

Moyers: But wouldn't it have been asking a great deal of people for them to stay where they were the victims of such discrimination and oppression?

Wilson: I'm not sure, because the situation existed very much like that in the North, too. We came to the North, and we're still victims of discrimination and oppression in the North. The real reason that the people left was a search for jobs, because the agriculture, cotton agriculture in particular, could no longer support us. But the move to the cities has not been a good move. Today, in 1988, we still don't have jobs. The last time blacks in America were working was during the Second World War, when there was a need for labor, and it did not matter what color you were.

Moyers: And now you feel surplus to the economy and to the society.

Wilson: Yes. There's a character in *Ma Rainey's Black Bottom* who says that blacks are left over from history. I think that's true.

Moyers: What do you see happening today that you might be writing about twenty years from now?

Wilson: Strange as it may seem, I don't look at our society today too much. My focus is still on the past. Part of the reason is because what I do, I get from the blues, so I listen to the music of the particular period that I'm working on. Inside the music are clues to what is happening with the people. I don't know that much about contemporary music, so if I were going to write a play set in 1980, I would go and listen to the music, particularly music that blacks are making, and find out what their ideas and attitudes are about the situation, and about the time in which they live.

Moyers: If you went to the ghetto in Newark, where I spent time filming a documentary for CBS, you would hear rap.

Wilson: Rap comes straight out of the black tradition. It's an extension of what we used to call the toast. Here's one: "The *Titanic* is sinking, and the banker comes up and says, 'Shine, Shine, save poor me, I'll give you all the money that you can see.' 'Say, there's more money on land than there is on sea,' and Shine swam on." This kind of thing was very common in the forties and the fifties as part of black folklore and culture.

Moyers: Why were blues so important? Is it *Ma Rainey* who says that you sing the blues not to feel better but to understand life?

Wilson: The blues are important primarily because they contain the cultural responses of blacks in America to the situation that they find themselves in. Contained in the blues is a philosophical system at work. You get the ideas and attitudes of the people as part of the oral tradition. This is a way of passing along information. If you're going to tell someone a story, and if you want to keep information alive, you have to make it memorable so that the person hearing it will go tell someone else. This is how it stays alive. The music provides you an emotional reference for the information, and it is sanctioned by the community in the sense that if someone sings the song, other people sing the song. They keep it alive because they sanction the information that it contains.

Moyers: Another variation on the oral tradition, carried from one generation to the other. Do you remember the first time you heard the blues?

Wilson: I do. Very specifically, I remember Bessie Smith. I used to collect 78 records that I would buy at five cents apiece, and I did this indiscriminately. I would just take whatever was there, ten records, and I listened to Patti Page and Walter Huston. I had a large collection of the popular music of the thirties and forties. One day in my stack of records there was a yellow label that was typewritten, which was kind of odd, and I put it on, and it was "Nobody in Town Can Bake a Sweet Jelly Roll Like Mine." It was Bessie Smith, of course. I had one of the old 78s where you had to keep putting the needle in, and I recall I listened to the record twenty-two straight times. Just over and over. I had never heard anything like it. I was literally stunned by its beauty. It was very pleasing, but it was very much different than Patti Page singing whatever she was singing. There was an immediate emotional response. It was someone speaking directly to me. I felt this was mine, this was something I could connect with that I instantly emotionally understood, and that all the rest of the music I was listening to did not concern me, was not a part of me. But this spoke to something in myself. It said, this is yours.

Moyers: You said earlier that music is a way of processing information. What was the information the blues brought to a kid named August Wilson?

Wilson: —That there was a nobility to the lives of blacks in America which I didn't always see. At that time I was living in a rooming house in Pittsburgh.

After I discovered the blues, I began to look at the people in the house a little differently than I had before. I began to see a value in their lives that I simply hadn't seen before. I discovered a beauty and a nobility in their struggle to survive. I began to understand the fact that the avenues for participation in society were closed to these people and that their ambitions had been thwarted, whatever they may have been. The mere fact that they were still able to make this music was a testament to the resiliency of their spirit.

Moyers: Which everyday life squashed.

Wilson: Attempted to squash because the spirit was resilient and strong and still is.

Moyers: As you talk, I think of those moments in *Joe Turner* when the characters are absolutely struck dumb because, as you wrote, "They ain't got words to tell." And I think of those black teenagers in the ghetto—Newark in particular. Many of them will be dead by the time they're thirty. They don't have words to tell their story. The blues don't speak to them. It's mainly rap. Do you think August Wilson could write a play about those kids?

Wilson: Sure. I'm a part of them in a sense. We come out of the same tradition, the same culture. I haven't actually stopped to look at what is happening with them, their particular life—but there's no question I could, because it's me, also.

Moyers: Does rap music have anything in common with the blues? I don't think of rap as beautiful, although I do think of the blues as beautiful.

Wilson: Oh, sure, without question. It has something in common with the blues. It's part of the tradition. They're defining the world in which they live, they're working out their ideas and attitudes about the world, they're working out their social manners, their social intercourse—all these things they're working out through the rap. And it's alive and vibrant. You have to listen, and a lot of us are unwilling to stop and listen. In the larger society, we are not listening to our kids, black or white. You have to stop and listen. It may be a world that you have to struggle to understand because it's different from the world that you know. For instance, if I go listen to rap, what these kids are doing these days is different from what I did as a teenager, and the way they're working out their social conduct is different from the way we did.

So I simply have to say, okay, I'll buy in on your terms, let me see what you guys are doing, let me understand what's going on with you.

Moyers: You were a dropout, like many of them, but you could read at a very early age, couldn't you?
Wilson: Yes, at four years old.

Moyers: What does it mean to be able to read?
Wilson: To be able to read means you can unlock information. I thought it was absolutely magnificent of the South African kids when they went to war over what language they were going to learn in school, because they understood and recognized the value of language. You cannot liberate yourself by learning the oppressor's language because all the things that oppress you are built into the linguistic environment—and they recognized that. Blacks in America don't have the political sophistication yet to understand the value of language, for instance, or, for that matter, the value of reading.

Moyers: I can't imagine what it would be not to see words come to life on the printed page. Don't you think not being able to read makes a real difference to these kids?
Wilson: Yes, I agree with you in a sense. I can't imagine what the world would be like if I could see words and not understand what they meant. It's simply the fact that the kids are not being taught to read in school. Everyone says this, everyone knows this, and no one does anything about it.

At one time it was against the law to teach blacks how to read. If you knew how to read, they would pull out your eyes, or if you could write, they would cut off your hands. This is fact. I find it interesting that we're not that many years removed from that. Although it's no longer against the law, someone, somehow, still makes sure that you don't know how to read, because if you can read, you can unlock information, and you're better able to understand the forces that are oppressing you.

Moyers: Who reached you? Who brought the poet to life in you?
Wilson: I think it was my mother. She's the one who taught me how to read. Reading was very important to her. She stressed the idea that if you can read, you can do anything—you could become a lawyer, you could be a

doctor, you could be anything you wanted to be if you knew how to unlock the information. So she took me to the library, and when I was five years old, I had my library card.

Moyers: What did you read?
Wilson: I started with *Curious George.* I can remember reading *Invisible Man* when I was fourteen years old. In fact, I read all the books in the Negro section of the library. There were only about thirty or forty books there. I read them all. I read Langston Hughes, of course, and *Invisible Man*, and Dunbar—I don't think I ever took that Dunbar book back to the library.

Moyers: But if you could read, why did you leave high school?
Wilson: I got off on a rocky road in high school. I went to Central Catholic High School in Pittsburgh, where I was the only black. I had a lot of problems in the school. I got in fights a lot. The principal had to send me home in a cab two or three times. After lunch break, we had to walk around the quadrangle. Constantly someone would walk up, step on your shoe, push you—I don't care to recite the litany of all that. It was very difficult. So I left, which was a disappointment to my mother, because she wanted me to go to a nice Catholic college and be a lawyer. She finally said, if you're not going to do that, then go learn how to do something with your hands. So I went to trade school the next year, which would have been my tenth year. She had a brother who was an auto mechanic, so she thought I should be an auto mechanic. But the auto mechanic class was filled, and the auto body class was filled, and so I ended up in a sheet metal shop making a tin cup.

In this trade school, you went to school half a day, but they were basically doing fourth- or fifth-grade work, so I said, "I can't stay here." Then I went to the school that was across the street from where we lived—Gladstone High School. I was bored, I was confused, I was disappointed in myself, and I didn't do any work at the school until my history teacher assigned us to write a paper on a historical personage. I chose Napoleon.

Moyers: Why Napoleon?
Wilson: Oh, I had always been fascinated with Napoleon because he was a self-made emperor. The title of my paper was "Napoleon's Will to Power."

I got the line from Victor Hugo. It was a twenty-page paper. My sister typed it up on a rented typewriter. When I submitted it to my teacher, he didn't think I had written it. He wanted me to explain it to him. I had my bibliography and my footnotes, and I felt that's all the explanation I should give. But he thought one of my older sisters had written it. I told him, "Hey, listen, I write their papers, so I mean, you know, you just have to take my word." Now, in all fairness to him, I hadn't done any work in his class, and all of a sudden, I turn in this paper. Most of the kids would go down and copy right out of the encyclopedia the three or four paragraphs that were in there about whomever. I didn't do that. I threw a little of my ideas in there, and tried to write about Napoleon.

Well, the upshot of that was he gave me a failing grade on the paper. He had written A plus on it or an E, and he said, "I'm going to give you one of these two grades." And when I refused to prove to him that I'd written the paper, other than to say that I had written it, he circled the E and handed it back to me, and I tore the paper up and threw it in his wastebasket and walked out of the school. I was fifteen years old, and I did not go back. However, the next morning I got up and played basketball right underneath the principal's window. As I look back on it, of course, I see that I wanted him to come and say, "Why aren't you in school?" so I could tell someone. And he never came out.

Moyers: Do you ever go back to where you grew up in Pittsburgh?
Wilson: Oh sure.

Moyers: What's happened to it?
Wilson: Same thing that's happened to most black communities. Most of it is no longer there. At one time it was a very thriving community, albeit a depressed community. But still there were stores and shops all along the avenue. They are not there any more. It has become even a more depressed area than it was then. When I left my mother's house, I went out into the world, into that community, to learn what it meant to be a man, to learn whatever it is that the community had to teach me. And it was there I met lifelong friends who taught me and raised me, so to speak. I still have family there. So I go back as often as I can. I go and I stand on a corner, and say, "Yeah, this is me."

Moyers: Have any of those people seen any of your plays? Do they talk to you about them?

Wilson: They do. I go back, and there are some of the guys on the avenue, people just hanging out on the street. They don't know anything—all they know is you did something. They'll walk up and say, "Hey, how you doing, man? We proud of you." It was the fact that someone from that community did something, whatever, that they see you on TV or they hear you wrote a book. Strangers, literally, walk up and say, "I'm real proud of you."

Moyers: What does that say to you about those folks?

Wilson: It says that it could have been any one of them, that there is a tremendous amount of talent that is wasted; that for every Louis Armstrong there are a hundred people whose talent gets wasted; that there are no avenues open for them to participate in society, where they might prove whatever is inside them. Those same people have vital contributions to make to the society. They could solve some of the problems—transportation, housing, whatever. But no one is asking them. They're not allowed to participate in the society.

Moyers: One of your characters said, "Everyone has to find his own song." How do these people find their song?

Wilson: They have it. They just have to realize that, and then they have to learn how to sing it. In that particular case, in *Joe Turner*, the song was the African identity. It was connecting yourself to that and understanding that this is who you are. Then you can go out in the world and sing your song as an African.

Moyers: Do you think those people in Pittsburgh must find the African in them or in their past before they really know who they are?

Wilson: Yes, because it's without question that they are African people. We are Africans who have been in America since the seventeenth century. We are Americans. But first of all, we are Africans. There's no way that you can dispute the fact that we are African people, and we have a culture that's separate and distinct from the mainstream white American culture. We have different philosophical ideas, different ways of responding to the world, different ideas and attitudes, different values, different ideas about style and linguistics, different aesthetics—even the way we bury our dead is different. The way that we participate in life is very much different than white America.

Moyers: Friends of mine who go back to Africa say that they find themselves thinking and being treated as if they were American tourists. They're Americans.
Wilson: Sure. If you take these people back over to Africa, they'll walk around trying to figure out what the hell's going on. There's no way that they can relate to that. But the sensibilities are African. They are Africans who have been removed from Africa, and they are in America four hundred years later. They're still Africans.

Moyers: What happens when you get in touch with that sensibility? The Jews in their Passover celebration always end by saying, "Next year in Jerusalem." They have a fixed place. But what does it mean to say, "Next year in Africa"?
Wilson: Part of our problem as blacks in America is that we don't claim that, partly because of the linguistic environment in which we live. I was in Tucson at a writers' conference, and I challenged my host to pull out his dictionary and look up the words "white" and "black." He looked up the word "white," and he came up with things like "unmarked by malignant influence, a desirable condition, a sterling man, upright, fair and honest." And he looked up the word "black," and he got "a villain, marked by malignant influence, unqualified, violator of laws," et cetera. These are actual definitions in *Webster's Dictionary.*
    This is a part of the linguistic environment. So that when white Americans look at a black, they see the opposite of everything that they are. In order for themselves to be good, the black has to be bad. In order for them to be imaginative, the black has to be dull. So you look at Africans, and you say, "Well, he's a violator of laws, he's unqualified, he is affected by an undesirable condition." This is what black means. We are a visible minority in this linguistic environment, and we are victims of that.

Moyers: What does it mean, then, to go back to Africa?
Wilson: It's not a question of going back to Africa. It's to understand that Africa is in you, that this is who you are, that you can participate, and that there isn't anything wrong with being an African, even though the linguistic environment teaches that black is all these negative things. You understand

that there's nothing wrong with the way that you do things, and there's nothing wrong with the way that you respond to the world—it's simply not the way that whites respond to the world.

Moyers: Some whites are saying today that if blacks in the ghetto are to emerge into the mainstream of American life, they really have to become mainstream Americans.
Wilson: Blacks don't melt in a pot. People hold up the examples of the Irish, of the Germans—these are all Europeans who share the same sensibilities as the mainstream, so it's very easy for them to melt. But we cannot change our names and hide behind the label of being an American, because we're a very visible minority. You can see us coming a block away. When you see us coming, we become a victim of that linguistic environment that says all those things—that we're unqualified, that we're violators of laws, or this, that, and the other. So we have a very difficult time even getting started, and there's no way that we can melt into the pot. We have a culture. Other ethnic groups and other races—the Orientals, for instance—are allowed their cultural differences.

Moyers: Chinatown in San Francisco is a tourist attraction. Harlem is not.
Wilson: We allow the Chinese to have their cultural differences. Not only do we allow them, we salute them for it. But blacks are expected to become like whites, without really understanding that in order to do that, we have to turn our head around almost three hundred and sixty degrees. Our worldviews are drastically different.

Moyers: But if blacks keep looking for the African in them, if they keep returning spiritually or emotionally to their roots, can they ever come to terms with living in these two worlds? Aren't they always going to be held by the past in a way that is potentially destructive?
Wilson: It's not potentially destructive at all. To say that I am an African, and I can participate in this society as an African, and I don't have to adopt European values, European aesthetics, and European ways of doing things in order to live in the world—how is that destructive?

Moyers: But don't you have to adopt American values, American—
Wilson: —We got the American part together the first hundred years that we were here. We would not be here had we not learned to adapt to American

culture. Blacks know more about whites in white culture and white life than whites know about blacks. We have to know because our survival depends on it. White people's survival does not depend on knowing blacks. But we still have our own way of doing things, even though we are Americans.

Moyers: How does an American black today get in touch with the African that's in him?

Wilson: Simply wake up and look in the mirror—because it's there. You look in the mirror, and you say, "This is who I am." The culture is very much alive. Scholars can go back and trace the Africanisms that are alive in the black American culture of today. The way that blacks participate in the world is fueled by their African sensibilities, so that is alive and vibrant and growing. The culture is organic. We're constantly debating the character of our culture. So it's alive—it didn't disappear, it didn't die.

Moyers: Did your mother, for example, talk to you about Africa?

Wilson: No.

Moyers: Did you know anything about Africa?

Wilson: No. What I knew about Africa was that I was a victim, like everyone else. I would go to see Tarzan movies, and I'd root for Tarzan, because this is what we were taught. We certainly didn't want to root for the Africans, because, first of all, they always lost. You know they're always going to lose. And they would do these caricatures of Africans—put bones through their noses and make them look ridiculous. Certainly we didn't want to be associated with that.

Moyers: So how do these blacks living in Pittsburgh, in Detroit, in Minneapolis, or anywhere, get in touch with the African in them without putting on beads or a dashiki? What do they do?

Wilson: I think they simply look in the mirror and recognize that this is who they are. There's an inner strength that comes with recognizing that this is okay, that there's nothing wrong with being African.

Moyers: If you look in the mirror, you see black. You say, though, that being black is much more than the color of your skin, it's a condition of the soul.

Wilson: Sure, I'm assuming that this person who looks in the mirror lives in a black cultural environment which is basically an African culture, or it's an amalgamation of African American culture. It's an adaptation of your African sensibilities to where you find yourself in the world.

Moyers: You had a white father. And yet you chose the black route, the black culture, the black way. Could you not just as easily have chosen the patriarchal way?

Wilson: Well, no, because the cultural environment of my life was black. As I grew up, I learned black culture at my mother's knee, so to speak.

Moyers: Even with a white father?

Wilson: He wasn't around very much. There was no question that I was black.

Moyers: You didn't make a conscious choice, you didn't say, I'm going to choose black.

Wilson: No, that's who I always have been. The cultural environment of my life, the forces that have shaped me, the nurturing, the learning, have all been black ideas about the world that I learned from my mother.

Moyers: The popular image in our culture today is of the black male who's not there, who's irresponsible, who has several children by several women, and who comes and goes—but it's not just a matter of being black.

Wilson: This is true—which is one of the reasons in *Fences* I wanted to show Troy as very responsible. He did not leave. He held a job. He fathered three kids by three different women, due to the circumstances of his life, and he was responsible toward all of them.

Moyers: As he brings that little baby home for Rose to take care of, he's not going to abandon her.

Wilson: Because it's his daughter, it's his flesh and blood.

Moyers: How does it happen that the women in your plays are all so strong, and that they choose to live with these men who are not?

Wilson: The men need support and nourishment, and in the black community, there are always women who can supply that for them. My mother's a very strong, principled woman. My female characters like Rose come in large part from my mother.

Moyers: You said your mother was principled—in what way?

Wilson: For instance, there was a contest on the radio, where they said, "When it rains, it pours," and if you could name the product, you won a brand-new Speed Queen washer. Well, my mother heard this over the radio, and she called my sister and gave her a dime, because we didn't have a telephone, and she said, "Run out to the store, call this number, and say, 'Morton's Salt.'" My sister did, and she happened to be the first one to call up with the correct answer, "Morton's Salt." And they announced over the radio that my mother was the winner of this brand-new Speed Queen washer. But when they found out that she was black, they wanted to give her a certificate to go to the Salvation Army and get a used washing machine. In so many words, she told them what they could do with their certificate. She refused to do that.

Moyers: They wouldn't give her the one she won.

Wilson: They wouldn't give her the new one, the one she won, because she was black. If you were black, you should be willing to take a secondhand machine.

Now, at that time my mother was washing clothes on a scrub board, where she had to heat up the water, because they didn't have hot water. I can remember her girlfriend saying, "Daisy, go ahead, take the machine. You know, why be foolish, you've got to scrub all those clothes." There was no way my mother would take the machine. So it was many years later before she got a washing machine.

Moyers: So she wasn't going to play the game by the white man's rules. She was going to live by her own principles, her own code of conduct and honor.

Wilson: Yes. She did that all her life.

Moyers: One of your characters—was it Toledo in *Ma Rainey*?—hates himself because he has played the game, and has sold out in order to make it in a white man's world.

Wilson: None of my characters hate themselves. Let me say that. Toledo was a forerunner to the African nationalist or black nationalist.

Moyers: In the sixties, you became temporarily a black nationalist.

Wilson: I still consider myself a black nationalist and a cultural nationalist.

Moyers: What's that?

Wilson: That's a good question. I simply believe that blacks have a culture, and that we have our own mythology, our own history, our own social organizations, our own creative motif, our own way of doing things. Simply that. That's what I mean when I say cultural nationalist.

Moyers: What's your opinion, then, of *The Cosby Show*?

Wilson: I watched it maybe once or twice. It does not reflect black America, to my mind. Most of black America is in housing projects, without jobs, living on welfare. This is not the case in *The Cosby Show*.

Moyers: But they are black Americans who have made it. They are successful, their children are going to college, the mother is strong and smart, the father is a professional who is doing very well. They've made it in America.

Wilson: They are black in skin color only. All the values in that household are strictly what I would call white American values. You can search the entire United States, and I think you would be hard-pressed to find that family, despite the fact that there are some blacks who have "made it," who have money and who own their own houses, who are not on welfare, who are educated, and who have jobs that have responsibility to them. We have black doctors, and we have black lawyers. Of the Africans on the planet, we're probably the most educated, but also the most unenlightened, because we don't realize that that's just who we are.

Moyers: Since Africans don't have a Jerusalem, don't they have to say, "Next year in the American dream"? They say, "I have a dream that I can make it in this country." Isn't that the Jerusalem for blacks?

Wilson: Well, maybe, but see, there's another part of Passover. A friend of mine invited me to Passover once, and I was struck by the very first words. It starts off, "We were slaves in the land of Egypt." That's the first thing. "Next year in Jerusalem" comes at the end. But they were constantly reminding themselves of what their historical situation has been. I find it criminal that after hundreds of years in bondage, we do not celebrate our Emancipation Proclamation, that we do not have a thing like the Passover, where we sit down and remind ourselves that we are African people, that we were slaves. We try to run away, to hide that part of our past. If we did something like that, then we would know who we are, and we wouldn't have the problem that we have. Part of the problem is that we don't know who we are, and we're not willing to recognize the value of claiming that, even if there's a stigma attached to it.

Moyers: I was brought up in Texas, where blacks celebrated Juneteenth, the day the Proclamation took effect in Texas.

Wilson: I'm aware of the Juneteenth celebration, but that's in certain parts of the country. It should be celebrated like the Jewish Passover wherever blacks find themselves.

Moyers: What would it say?

Wilson: It would say, this is who we are. We recognize the fact that we are Africans, we recognize the fact that we were slaves, and we recognize that since we have a common past, we have a common present and a common future. There's no progress made in America for blacks unless there's progress for everyone.

Moyers: Do I hear you arguing for separate but equal cultures?

Wilson: The cultures exist. They are separate cultures, in the sense that they are different cultures. I don't know what equal means. When you say equal, you're talking about equal to what?

Moyers: —Equally celebrated, equally recognized, equally considered as a legitimate culture. You see, when I went to *Fences*, I wept. I wasn't an out-sider, even though it was about the black experience in America. I wept at the relationship between the father and the son, at the mother who was so loyal to a disloyal husband, at the importance of tradition, at the role of the com-munity. I was not an outsider there. I felt a part of that experience you were writing about. But you were writing about black America.

Wilson: I was writing about black America—the specifics of the play are about black America. But there is something larger at work. A painter, when asked to comment on his work, once said, "I try to explore in terms of the life I know best those things which are common to all culture." So while the specifics of the play are black, the commonalities of culture are larger realities in the play. You have father-son conflict, you have husband-wife conflict—all these things are universal.

Moyers: So you're not unsympathetic to those blacks who look at the Huxtables in *The Cosby Show* and see there something that they want, something to achieve. You're saying that's not the whole story.

Wilson: That's not the whole story. And of course, you can go into the ghetto in Newark, and ask the people what they want—they want decent homes, they want a nice car, they want whatever the society has to offer someone who is willing to work. If you can trade your talent and get something, this is what they want. They want to be the Huxtables. But there are no avenues for them to do that. The social contract that white America has given blacks is that if you want to participate in society, you have to deny who you are. You cannot participate in this society as Africans. Music and sports are the only avenues that are open for full participation of blacks without any further qualifications—you just have to be good.

Moyers: But the dominant commercial ethos in America is so strong, and there are so many more people who watch television than attend plays, that it seems to me that the Huxtables are winning the battle for the black imagination, and the Ma Raineys and the August Wilsons are losing.

Wilson: Yes, but even blacks who look at *The Cosby Show*, and who want to share some of the wealth, say, of the Cosby family, understand that that's foreign to them. That is not the way they live their lives. That is not the way they socialize. They recognize that immediately as the way white people do it. But they would like to have that and still be who they are and do the things they do. They would probably go out and buy a big Cadillac instead of whatever car the Huxtables might drive, because their sense of style is different. It might be a yellow one or a pink one. It's a question of aesthetics, you see. Without question, they would decorate their house differently. Why? Because their ideas are different. Their culture's different. Basically, we do everything differently. But we still would like to have whatever rewards the society has to offer to someone who is willing to work and who has a talent to sell.

Moyers: You remind me, as you talk, of the fact that both Jews and blacks have been through such great suffering, and yet they kept singing the song of the Lord. And when I think of that, of the faith of both peoples, I think of the character in *Ma Rainey's Black Bottom* who hears that a white mob has forced a black preacher to humiliate himself, and who cries out, "Where the hell was God when all this was going on?" What's August Wilson's answer to that question?

Wilson: It was the wrong God that he was expecting to come and help him, as he later points out. It was the white man's God. He answers the question himself. When the Africans came to America, their religion was stripped from them.

Moyers: Wasn't it the black church that held together the possibility of hope?
Wilson: The church is probably the most important institution in the black community. There's no question of that. But it's an overlay of African religions onto the Christian religion. The original African religions were stripped away from them. They weren't allowed to practice these religions. Amiri Baraka has said that when you look in the mirror, you should see your God. If you don't, you have somebody else's God. So, in fact, what you do is worship an image of God which is white, which is the image of the very same people who have oppressed you, who have put you on the slave ships, who have beaten you, and who have forced you to work. The image was a white man. And the image that you were given to worship as a God is the image of a white man.

Loomis in *Joe Turner* rejects that image of Christianity. We're talking about image, not the religion—there's nothing wrong with the religion. It has great principles if it's practiced. But Loomis rejects the idea that he needs someone else to bleed for him. Christianity says, "Jesus bled for you." Loomis says, "I don't need anybody to bleed for me. I can bleed for myself." He slashes his chest and demonstrates his willingness to bleed for himself, to be responsible for his own salvation.

Moyers: So the God of the slaveholder can't be the God of the slaves.
Wilson: Without question, no. It's two different things.

Moyers: This is why Levee in *Ma Rainey* says that the prayers of the black man should be tossed into the garbage can.
Wilson: That God is tossed into the garbage because you're praying to the wrong God.

Moyers: You keep writing about each of us finding our own song. How do we know when we've found our song?
Wilson: It comes out. You'll sing it, and you'll go, "There it is." It's just a thing you'll know. It will feel right.

Moyers: Do the characters in your plays talk to you?

Wilson: They do, yes. They tell me the whole thing. Sometimes I have trouble shutting them up. It's a matter of where you place yourself. I crawl up inside the material, and I get so immersed in it that as I'm inventing this world, I'm also becoming a part of it. You discover that you're walking down this landscape of the self, and you have to be willing to confront whatever it is that you discover there. The idea is to emerge at the end of the landscape with something larger than what you had when you went in—something that is part of the illumination of the truth. If you're willing to wrestle with your demons, you will find that your spirit gets larger. And when your spirit gets larger, your demons get smaller. For me, this is the process of art. The process of writing the plays is a very liberating thing.

Moyers: Are you able to talk back to these characters?

Wilson: I do, yes, just like I talk to you. They're my partners, my friends. All the characters are part of me. People ask me, "Which one do you identify the most with?" And I say, "Well, I probably make the strongest identification with the male protagonist—but they're all me." Gabriel is me. Rose is a part of myself. Cory, Troy, Loomis, Levee, and Toledo—they're all different aspects of the self. People used to say, "You can only write what you know." I didn't quite understand that. But it's so true. All this is made up out of myself.

Moyers: But a lot of what these characters told you, they made up, didn't they?

Wilson: They did, sure, yeah. They say them, and I just write them down.

Moyers: You once said that the most valuable blacks were those in prison, those who had the warrior spirit in the African sense—men who went out and got for their women and children what they needed when all other avenues were closed to them. Who do you think has the warrior spirit in America today? Who's fighting the battle?

Wilson: Those same people are, for the most part. Since the first Africans set foot on the continent, there has been a resistance. The people who look around to see what the society has cut out for them, who see the limits of their participation, and are willing to say, "No, I refuse to accept this limitation that you're imposing on me"—that's the warrior spirit. These are the same people who end up in the penitentiary, because their spirit leads them.

I think Levee has a warrior spirit. He does a tremendous disservice to blacks by killing Toledo, because he's killing the only one who can read, he's killing the intellectual in the group. That's a loss we have to make up. We have to raise up another one to take Toledo's place. But I still salute Levee's warrior spirit. It's a progression to the wrong target, but I salute his willingness to battle, even to death. All of the characters demonstrate a willingness to battle. Not all of them are in the penitentiary, but some, because of that spirit, find themselves on the opposite side of the society that is constantly trying to crush their spirit.

Moyers: I was going to suggest that maybe the black middle class possesses that warrior spirit today in the sense that they're struggling in a white man's world to make it, to provide for their children, to keep that house, to pay that mortgage, to send those kids to school, to live responsibly. There's a struggle going on there in the black middle class.

Wilson: There probably is a struggle. But the real struggle, since an African first set foot on the continent, is the affirmation of the value of oneself. If in order to participate in American society and in order to accomplish some of the things which the black middle class has accomplished, you have had to give up that self, then you are not affirming the value of the African being. You're saying that in order to do that, I must become like someone else.

Moyers: But it seems a burden to expect middle class blacks to hold on to that mentality where they were put upon and put down, to be thinking all the time about the horrible days, the malignant days.

Wilson: I'm not sure that those were bad days. I guess all I really want to say is that there's nothing wrong with being African, there's nothing wrong with African culture, and there's nothing wrong with the black American culture, which is an African culture. There's nothing wrong with the way that we do things. It's just different. But because it's different, it's frowned upon.

I was in the bus station in St. Paul, and I saw six Japanese Americans sitting down, having breakfast. I simply sat there and observed them. They chattered among themselves very politely, and they ate their breakfast, got up, paid the bill, and walked out. I sat there and considered, what would have been the difference if six black guys had come in there and sat down? What are the cultural differences? The first thing I discovered is that none of those Japanese guys played the jukebox. It never entered their minds to play the jukebox. The first thing when six black guys walk in there, somebody's going to go over to the jukebox. Somebody's going to come up and say, "Hey, Rodney, man, play this," and he's going to say, "No, man, play your own record. I ain't playin' what you want. I'm playin' my record, man. Put your own quarter in there." And he's going to make his selection. He's going to go back.

The second thing I noticed, no one said anything to the waitress. Now six black guys are going to say, "Hey, mama, what's happenin'? What's your phone number? No, don't talk to him, he can't read. Give your phone number to me." The guy's going to get up to play another record, somebody's going to steal a piece of bacon off his plate, he's going to come back and say, "Man, who been messin' with my food, I ain't playin' with you all, don't be messin' with my food." When the time comes to pay the bill, it's going to be, "Hey, Joe, loan me a dollar, man." Right?

So if you were a white person observing that, you would say, "They don't know how to act, they're too loud, they don't like one another, the guy wouldn't let him play the record, the guy stole food off his plate." But if you go to those six guys and say, "What's the situation here?" you'll find out they're the greatest of friends, and they're just having breakfast, the same way the Japanese guys had breakfast. But they do it a little differently. This is just who they are in the world.

Moyers: You've answered my question. I was going to ask you, don't you grow weary of thinking black, writing black, being asked questions about blacks?

Wilson: How could one grow weary of that? Whites don't get tired of thinking white or being who they are. I'm just who I am. You never transcend who you are. Black is not limiting. There's no idea in the world that is not contained by black life. I could write forever about the black experience in America.

Hurdling Fences

Dennis Watlington / 1989

From *Vanity Fair*, 52 (April 1989), 102–13. Reprinted by permission of Dennis Watlington.

One night last October, nearly seven hundred people attended a fund-raising dinner in New Haven in honor of Lloyd Richards, dean of the Yale School of Drama. Biagio DiLieto, the mayor of New Haven, was there, and Benno C. Schmidt Jr., the president of Yale, but 75 percent of the crowd was black, dressed in dinner jackets and high fashion and expressing a mood of gaiety commonly referred to in black parlance as stylin'. Actor Danny Glover spoke, singer Theresa Merritt performed, and telegrams from Sidney Poitier and James Earl Jones were read. The affection seemed torrential for the man who in 1959 had directed the first production of Lorraine Hansberry's *A Raisin in the Sun*, who for twenty-one years has been the artistic director of the National Playwrights Conference of the Eugene O'Neill Theater Center, and who has presented at Yale the three most recent plays by the South African playwright Athol Fugard. Excitement peaked when August Wilson, the playwright seated beside Richards on the dais, rose to speak. "I'm very glad to be here," he said quietly when the clapping stopped, "and I'm grateful for having been given the opportunity to come to Yale and study at the master's feet."

Wilson is forty-three. He met Richards seven years ago, and since then they have developed one of the strongest collaborations in the history of American theater. Wilson's first three plays directed by Richards—*Ma Rainey's Black Bottom*, *Fences*, and *Joe Turner's Come and Gone*—moved from the Yale Repertory Theatre to Broadway, and all three won the New York Drama Critics' Circle Award. *Fences* won the most honors in Broadway history, including a Tony for Richards's direction, a Tony for Best Play, and a Pulitzer Prize. And the *New York Times* said *Joe Turner's Come and Gone* may have been "Mr. Wilson's most profound and theatrically adventurous . . . to date." Their fourth project, *The Piano Lesson*, goes from the Goodman Theatre in Chicago to the Old Globe in San Diego next month, and the playwright has nearly finished number five. He has also started work on the screenplay of *Fences*, which will reportedly star not only James Earl Jones but also Eddie Murphy.

Who is this writer of plays covering black life in America decade by decade who has muscled in on the best Broadway real estate and now threatens to do the same in Hollywood?

I'm in a cab in St. Paul, Minnesota, on my way to a restaurant called Tommy K's. The town, which is predominantly white working-class, has a bland, gray look, and it's cold. During the ride I think to myself, I can understand why Bob Dylan left Minnesota, but what the hell brought August Wilson here?

The playwright's waiting for me in the restaurant, a very ordinary-looking fish-and-burger eatery, and in the course of getting the interview going we fill the place with cigarette smoke. I tell him he's a mystery to most people, because unlike James Baldwin and Amiri Baraka, for example, he has refused to define his feelings publicly. Soft-spoken, aloof, he has kept a low profile and let his awards do his talking for him.

"I'm no mystery," he says. "I'm just one of the hardworking oppressed." I ask him how he figures.

"Black people in general today are oppressed. I place myself squarely with the people. You don't transcend them." He says it with calm resignation, not with any hardened militancy, so I try again. "It would seem like your royalty checks separate you from the majority."

"Royalty checks can't make up for four hundred years of free work, four hundred years without a lunch break," he says, and laughs.

"You don't *seem* like someone who's oppressed," I venture.

"It's not about *feeling* oppressed, it's about *actual* oppression. I think you have to make some connections. I was talking with my daughter, who's eighteen. She goes to Morgan State University. They were having a black forum, and the things they were talking about reminded me of some of the things we used to talk about in the sixties—Timbuktu and all the great African civilizations. There's nothing wrong with that, but you should start by making connections to your parents and your grandparents and working backwards. We're not in Africa anymore, and we're not going back to Africa. You have to understand your parents and understand your grandparents. I like to say I'm standing in my grandfather's shoes."

Wilson, I know, was born in Pittsburgh, and I also know that his father was white. So it's clear which grandfather he is talking about. The fact that the other grandfather resided in the camp of the oppressor is interesting too.

"You're from an interracial background, aren't you?" I ask him.

He says abruptly, "Yeah, my father was white, if that's what you mean."

"How was it, growing up with a white father and a black mother?"

His tone is defensive when he responds. "There's not much to tell. My father very rarely came around. I grew up in my mother's household in a cultural environment which was black."

I tell him that I am married to a white woman, and that our son is cut from the same rare fabric as he is, and this seems to make him more comfortable with me, but he still doesn't elaborate on his answer to my question.

"Did you grow up in the projects?" I ask.

"No, my mother wouldn't allow it."

They lived in an integrated pocket of the mainly black area of "the Hill" in Pittsburgh. When he was twelve, he and his mother and three sisters and two brothers moved from a two-bedroom apartment to Hazelwood, a blue-collar steelworkers' neighborhood which had three streets of blacks.

"Looking back on it, those very important years from twelve to eighteen were spent in a place that had Little League teams and middle-class experiences. You could sleep with your windows open, and a friend could come stick his head in your window to wake you up.

"When I was twelve, I made a discovery in the library, the Negro section, thirty or forty books, and I read them all. After I read Langston Hughes, I became interested in writing. In high school Brother Dominic was one of my favorite teachers. He would always tell me I could be an author, and I needed to hear that. We had to write a poem, and I remember writing:

The black man walks in the dark
Unseen by human eyes
Dark are the night shadows around him . . .

This was 1959, and I didn't say the Negro man, I said the *black* man.
I remember Brother Dominic called me in, and the gist of what he said was
that I should write about something other than blacks. He was well-meaning,
but he was all wrong. He suggested that I should write about more universal
stuff, but that was suggesting that the black experience was outside of the
universal experience. I started writing nature poems, but I got over that."

At nineteen Wilson left home to develop himself as a writer. Instinctively,
he headed for the Hill District, where he met several other aspiring artists.

"I moved into a basement apartment with a group of writers and painters.
It was a great time. In this community of artists, I began to discover who I
was. I began to discover myself as a black man in relation to the world. My
friend Rob Penny—we used to call him Black Rob—turned me on to tapes
by Malcolm X. I really embraced this. It was around that time I bought a
record player for three dollars, and it only played one speed, 78. I used to go
to this place that had stacks and stacks of 78s. I'd buy them ten at a time—
give the man fifty cents and I'm gone. One day there was this typewritten
yellow label and it said, 'Nobody in Town Can Bake a Sweet Jelly Roll Like
Mine—Bessie Smith.' I'd never heard of Bessie Smith. I listened to it twenty-
two straight times, and I became aware that this stuff was my own. Patti
Page, Frank Sinatra—they weren't me. This was me. The music became the
wellspring of my work. I took that stuff and ran with it. The place I was
living in had all kinds of people—ex-convicts, an ex-counterfeiter. One dude
I knew was a heroin junkie. He used to shoot up in the room, but he would
never let me mess with that stuff. Now, I was young and impressionable,
and I probably would have tried it. One day this cat comes in and offered
me some, but my friend grabbed him and told him, 'Don't give August that
stuff.' They looked out for me, because they knew that I wanted to do
something."

As he speaks, I can see that he was a fine candidate for painting a long,
balanced picture of black life. Like a talented white musician who comes to
the Apollo Theatre in Harlem and is inspired to the point of reverence, he
could become a guardian of black culture, even overromanticize it, because
he was free of the usual anger and cynicism.

For the next ten years, he developed his poetry. He became the artistic
director of a small black theater group, and he took on a slew of odd jobs. In
1977 he gave a poetry reading about a character named Black Bart, and a
friend suggested he turn the material into a play. Wilson had only recently

had his first experience with professional theater; he had seen a production of *Sizwe Bansi Is Dead*, by Athol Fugard, John Kani, and Winston Ntshona, at the Pittsburgh Public Theatre.

"'I can't write plays, man,' I said. But my friend Claude Purdy said it was a great character, and he kept talking about it, so between that Sunday and the next Sunday I wrote a play, *Black Bart and the Sacred Hills*. The next Sunday I walk in and say, 'Where's Claude?' They tell me he went to St. Paul to direct a play. I say, 'Where is St. Paul?' I had no idea where it was. Two days later I get a call from Claude. He says, 'I'm out here doing this play. Why don't you come out and rewrite the script for me?' He sent me a ticket, and I went. I stayed about ten days, did the rewrite, and went back to Pittsburgh. Claude called and said they were doing a staged reading of the play in L.A., so I went there, and I stopped in at St. Paul on the way back and met the woman who eventually became my wife. I said to myself, I should move here. So I did that two months later, and I've been here ever since."

"Why St. Paul?" I ask. "Nothing here but ice."

I don't say that I have just asked my black cabdriver if he'd heard of August Wilson and he hadn't. August tells me it's a good town. "As far as the cold is concerned, it drives everyone inside, and in my case, closer to my work."

Wilson married Judy Oliver, his second wife, in 1981. The daughter he spoke of earlier is the only child from his first marriage.

In 1980 Wilson became aware of the National Playwrights Conference and Lloyd Richards. "I sent my first play to the O'Neill because my friend Rob sent me the brochure and wrote on it, 'Do this!' I said O.K. I had no idea who Lloyd Richards was, but a friend of mine who had studied with him in New York told me he was the black dude who directed *A Raisin in the Sun*. It was odd to me, a black cat running this thing. So I figure that's cool, and I sent my stuff."

Over the next few years Wilson continued to send his work to the O'Neill. After five rejections, one of his plays finally caught the fancy of Lloyd Richards. It was *Ma Rainey's Black Bottom*.

Lloyd Richards's parents were born in Jamaica. They immigrated to Canada and then to Detroit in the 1920s. Lloyd's father died when he was nine.

"There was never a time that I wasn't aware of the fact that I had value. We had tremendous family pride."

He went to Wayne State University and was set to attend law school when he decided to change his major to speech. "I was loath to explain it to my mother. I waited until it was irrevocable. Everyone thought it was a rather idiotic choice because there was no future in it."

In the beginning he worked with small theater groups and acted on radio, in *The Romance of Helen Trent* and *Jungle Jim*. His first significant role in New York was in a play called *The Egghead*, written by Molly Kazan, directed by Hume Cronyn, starring Karl Malden. "The young man who was my understudy during that production was James Earl Jones."

Acting led to directing and teaching. In 1959 he directed *A Raisin in the Sun*, a watershed in black theater, and soon after that he was asked to teach at New York University and at Boston University. In 1967 he first participated in the O'Neill Center's National Playwrights Conference, a new group devoted to developing writers for the stage, and the sum of his three professional involvements led to his appointment as artistic director of the Yale Repertory Theatre in 1978 and dean of the Yale School of Drama in 1979. There he was in a perfect position to foster new talent, and soon a play came along that had the right voice.

"I was at work, and my wife called me up and said I'd gotten a telegram. So I said, 'Read it.' It said, 'Your play has been selected for work at the National Playwrights Conference of the Eugene O'Neill Theater Center.' Since then, I can't tell you how many openings I've been to, Broadway openings, and this award, and that award, but nothing has felt like that first telegram that said I was going to the O'Neill."

At their first private meeting to discuss *Ma Rainey*, Wilson recalls, "Lloyd said, 'You've got a lot of work to do,' and I said, 'I ain't ever been scared of hard work.' But then he surprised me when he told me that raising his kids was the single most important accomplishment in his life. That led me into the man. When he told me that, it clued me in to the kind of person he was."

When Richards told Wilson that he wanted to do the play at Yale, Wilson asked him to direct it. "I discovered I didn't know anything about casting, so Lloyd cast it. The first day of rehearsal, the actors read the script, and they had some questions. Before I could get it together, Lloyd started answering the questions. And he knew the answers. I found out that he knew the characters like I did. I was amazed at the answers he was giving. So I visibly relaxed from that moment. I realized, Pops knows what's happening. So I sat back and said, 'Let Pops do it.'"

"He included me in everything that happened. He would say, 'They're building the set over there in the shop. Did you stop by and see what they're doing?' I said no. He said, 'Why don't you stop by?' He wanted me to know how it happened, that it didn't just come from nowhere."

It's rare for a playwright's first real production to wind up on a Broadway stage, but Richards was able to shield and nurture Wilson under the Yale umbrella. By the time the play moved to New York, the polish was evident.

"When we opened on Broadway, the only exchange between Lloyd and me was whether or not we should wear tuxedos. He said, 'If you wear one, I'll wear one.' I said, 'O.K., let's wear one.'"

Lloyd Richards says he loved the characters in *Ma Rainey* because they took him back to the old-time black barbershops, which were cultural meeting places for black males. "You heard unique points of view, and you heard a combination of people—the articulate who had a large vocabulary and the articulate who had a small vocabulary. I say the articulate in each case because in the quest to express a complicated idea with a small vocabulary, one needs to use that in a very selective and special way. He or she ends up speaking very much in metaphor and the poetry of the streets, and the wonderful imagery is used really to explain a complicated idea. Also, there are the educated sitting around that barbershop, who in many respects manifest their education. *Ma Rainey* had both of them. The sounds that made music."

Ma Rainey was nominated for a Drama Desk Award, an Outer Critics Circle Award, and a Tony. Buoyed by its success, Wilson and Richards moved on.

"I'm a great boxing fan, and boxing is like writing," says Wilson. "I look at Lloyd like he's my trainer. Now, Lloyd is old enough to be my father. Having grown up without a father, that has a lot to do with my relationship with him. I always view him in a fatherly way. You know, you want to please Pop. You want Pop to be proud of you. I want to score a knockout. See, I came to learn about theater, but I learned a lot about life."

While *Ma Rainey* was in rehearsals, *Fences* had already been written. As Wilson says, "I never wanted to be a one-play playwright. For the new play, I wanted to explore our commonalities of culture. What you have in *Fences* is a very specific situation, a black family which the forces of racism have molded and shaped, but you also have husband-wife, father-son. White America looks at black America in this glancing manner. They pass right by the Troy

Maxsons of the world and never stop to look at them. They talk about
niggers as lazy and shiftless. Well, here's a man with responsibilities as prime
to his life. I wanted to examine Troy's life layer by layer and find out why
he made the choices he made.

"I should have written *Joe Turner* after *Ma Rainey*, and then *The Piano
Lesson*. *Fences* was the odd man out, in the sense that it was not the kind of
play I wanted to write. But all these people who are used to theater kept
trying to tell me my work should be something different."

All during *Ma Rainey*, they pressured him to write a more commercial,
conventional play, with one main character and others supporting him.
"After telling people that I knew how to write that kind of play, I asked
myself, Do I really know how to write that kind of play? So I wrote *Fences* in
answer to the challenge that I'd given myself."

It grossed $12 million in one year.

"After *Fences*, I went back to what I wanted to write, which was *Joe Turner*.
Fences was just a way to prove that I could do that, and it's kind of ironic that
it is the play that became the big hit. I'm not going to try to write another
Fences. I'm back to what I should have been writing anyway, the ensemble
pieces like *Joe Turner*, *The Piano Lesson*, and this new play I'm working on,
called *Two Trains Running*."

"Don't you feel weighed down by that $12 million albatross?" I ask.

"No, no. I've already written better plays since *Fences*. As far as the
albatross is concerned, I take that shit off my neck."

Like it or not, *Fences* has bestowed virtually every award a playwright can
receive on Wilson, and it has all happened in a short span of time. How has
this affected him?

"I'll tell you a story about those awards and things. There is a group called
the Theatre of Renewal, and they give out the TOR Awards. So when *Ma
Rainey* was happening, people were talking Pulitzer Prize, Tony Award,
Drama Desk Award, this award, that award. Early on in *Ma Rainey*, they
wrote me a letter and said I got this TOR Award. I said, 'What's that?' They had
a ceremony, and I didn't go. They sent me a little trophy about six inches
high. I just threw it in a box with my stuff. It didn't mean nothing to me.
I was waiting on the big stuff. Well, let me tell you, Pulitzer came, and I didn't
get it. Outer Critics Circle, and I didn't get that. No Drama Desk either.
I said, Wait a minute, let me find that. Well, I pulled it out, and it sits on my
desk to this day as a reminder that someone gave me an award and I didn't

appreciate it. I said, August, they're all important, no matter where they come from."

His current play, *The Piano Lesson*, is one more of his historical plays, what he calls his ensemble murals. "I got the title from a Romare Bearden painting. It's a painting of a woman, a piano, and a little girl playing the piano. The woman is standing over her, and I heard the woman in my mind admonishing the little girl: *Now, you, Maretha*, get *your piano lesson*. That's how it started. I wanted to explore the question, Can you acquire a sense of self-worth by denying your past? I don't think you can, and I wanted to show this. I had the idea of this piano. I wanted it to be very visible onstage. I wanted the piano in the course of the play to get bigger and bigger. I figured the more you understand the piano, the more you understand about these people. The piano goes back 137 years, and was used to purchase members of the family during slavery. The play is set in the year 1936."

About his next play, *Two Trains Running*, he says, "You see, I'm working on a four-hundred-year autobiography. I'm as old as the black experience in America. That's a deep whale. The play is about a woman named Aunt Ester, who is 322 years old. She's a repository of the entire experience."

August Wilson is the luckiest playwright of this generation. By the time he discovered the black experience, he already had plenty of healthy self-esteem. With the help of Lloyd Richards, he could develop as an artist who did not feel compelled to turn rifles on the whites in the audience and empty the chambers. He could create true works of black pride, minus the exclamation points. Together, these two are producing the first broad volume of American theater that happens to be black.

Black Aesthetic: A Conversation with Playwright August Wilson

Abiola Sinclair / 1990

From the *New York Amsterdam News*, May 19, 1990, 30, and May 26, 1990, 30. Reprinted by permission of the *New York Amsterdam News*.

(Black America's foremost critic in an exclusive interview with Pulitzer Prize-winning playwright August Wilson on the future of black theatre, and where he is coming from with regard to it.)

The coffee shop of the Edison Hotel clanked and clattered with the sounds of dishes, silverware, Greek, and laughter. Hardly a place to conduct an interview, but great for general conversation. You could get excited and raise your voice, and no one would even notice.

In the rear was a separate table for two, with posters of *The Piano Lesson*, *Fences*, and several other mementos on the wall above it. It was August Wilson's table—a mini-shrine erected in a loving, but matter-of-fact way. It may have been the matter-of-factness that endeared it to Wilson.

He sat at his table in his characteristic cap, smoking, smoking and drinking coffee. He liked it here. How come?

"When I first did *Fences*, I came here to stay. They were very nice to me, the people behind the desk, the mailmen, everyone. They're just good people. The guy who runs the coffee shop, they're just good people," said Wilson, who ordered coffee to go with his cigarette.

He seemed nervous. I tried to put him at ease, inquiring whether he'd like to eat.

"No, I can't eat and talk at the same time. I never could."

I'd threatened him earlier. "This won't be one of those puff pieces, I can assure you." This elicited from him a furtive look, several puffs on his cigarette, and set his foot to tapping. The black world had stood by and watched in amazement as an African American received not one, but two Pulitzer Prizes. We were happy for him. It was good, great. But who was he? Where was he coming from? What was he thinking?

Had he seen many black plays?

"No," said Wilson, without apology. "I almost never go out. I haven't been to the theatre in a few years."

Why? "Well, for one thing, they don't allow you to smoke! But for another, I just like to stay home. I never go anywhere. I haven't been to a movie in years! It's hard to get me to go out."

Theatre is such a gregarious art. You need people. People to put the play up, sets, costumes, lights—actors, a director. People then have to come to see the play, hopefully on a regular basis. Wilson sounded more like a novelist as opposed to a playwright.

"Well, that's why I'm not an actor, I guess," Wilson shrugged. "Theatre has made me more social. Theatre is a more collaborative art. With a novel you can stay home. I don't know why I'm this way. I've been in New York a month now; I haven't seen any plays. There are probably good plays out there, but I haven't seen them."

Sinclair: I wanted to ask you about *Forbidden City*, by Bill Duke, what you thought of it. But . . . well, in any event, you're going to be called upon pretty soon to adopt more of a leadership role in black theatre. I mean, everyone's standing around wondering what to do with you—in terms of—is he strictly a product of Yale? Is that some sort of isolated event? Or, is this person a vanguard person in terms of leadership because the rest of black theatre is sort of in shambles? How do you feel about that, and the direction of black theatre?

Wilson: Okay. One—I'm not a product of Yale, other than the Yale Repertory Theatre offered me a home, said, "you can come here and do your plays, because of Lloyd Richards's being there!" That's why I went up there. If Lloyd had been in Timbuktu, or if someone else had offered me an opportunity to work at their theatre, I probably would have gone there to work. If N.E.C. (Negro Ensemble Company) had offered me an opportunity to work there, I would have. In fact, N.E.C. turned down *Ma Rainey's Black Bottom* and Yale offered me a place.

Sinclair: When I said a product of Yale, I meant that they gave you a nurturing environment. For instance, Shakespeare had some sort of environment at the Royal Theatre which encouraged him to write, knowing the repertory was waiting for his plays, and probably would perform them. As a result of that, he was able to grind out a lot of material. Whereas, if he didn't have that, the question is—would he have produced so many plays?

Wilson: Well, before I'd gotten to Yale, I went to the Eugene O'Neill Playwrights Conference. I had to meet the December first deadline. The play then went to Yale. I did the same with *Fences*. But all of this, *Ma Rainey* and *Fences*, was before my first production of *Ma Rainey*. So, *Fences* was written before *Ma Rainey* was ever produced.

Now I wrote *Joe Turner's Come and Gone* while at Yale and asked Lloyd, "do you want to do this one, too?" He said, "yeah," so here we go. But, yeah, knowing someone will likely do your play and work with you on it is a tremendous impetus. But I've always worked hard to reward that faith that was placed in me. And, when you're working to do that, I think you can do better work. It's hard sitting out there writing plays, not knowing whether they're ever going to be produced. But, on the other hand, when you know your play will be produced, you have a greater responsibility, because someone will get up on stage and say what you've written; so you've got to be sure you are communicating what you want to say. You have a responsibility to be honest.

I always have a sense that I'm standing in my grandfather's shoes. I'm standing in a long line of people: so standing there, I have to speak not only for myself, but the ideas have to make that connection with the line of people. In other words, I have some very valuable antecedents. That, I think any playwright has to be aware of. So, I try to be aware of that, together with my own ideas, and what I'm trying to say—to speak for myself and those who think like I do. That's all I can speak for—all the Africans who are receiving me on the planet and on the shores of North America.

So what does August Wilson think is the agenda for black theatre for the nineties?

Sinclair: As you know, the problem is outlets, and that has decimated the theatrical community. A lot of the workshops get to reading plays, and that's as far as it goes. There's no money to produce them. And most blacks are looking at television and scratching their heads. What do you see as a solution to that, and an agenda for our theatre, if that could be dumped on you?

Wilson: Okay, the problem is not new. We had the same problem back in the sixties. The main problem, and one of the differences between white theatre and black theatre, is white theatre is for the most part, institutionalized. So, there's a tremendous amount of institutional support from the universities that teach theatre, all the way through the four-hundred-and-some regional theatres, providing plenty of opportunity for white playwrights to see their work produced.

Conversely, Julius Nyerere, one of the political leaders and a representative of our culture, said: "The basis for development is not money, the basis is hard work." Now, in order to produce plays, it requires money, but that should not be the basis for the development of our theatre. In other words, we can't sit around saying, "We ain't got no money, so we can't do no plays. They got all the money, so we can't do nothing." There's the idea of hard work.

Sinclair: But, hard work is induced by the possibility of results, and at some point, no matter how hard you work, you have to come up with x amount of dollars, or you ain't . . .
Wilson: (interrupting): But that goes back to the old question of the sixties institutionalization. You've got to get the money from somewhere.

Sinclair: But—we as a people are not financing our art as a representation of our culture. We see art as some sort of luxury or leisure activity, not a representation of our existence. We don't see it as telling our story, as it were. We don't look at it like that. So we don't *protect* it like that. And, we don't approach it that way. I've been in theatre a long time: Robert Hooks's Group Theatre Workshop, Papp's Mobile Theatre, the Frank Silvera Writers' Workshop since its inception. Dramaturge there for ten years, every week. I've had my own theatre, produced plays, written plays, critiqued literally hundreds of plays over the years—some good, most not—but some great.

My feeling, because this is America, and some cat that doesn't even speak English can come here and, say, open a restaurant and make money; and here we still are—scratching our heads—my feeling is, perhaps if we approach art as a business. In a business you sell your product in such a way that people want to *buy* it. Maybe that way, we could get a better handle on things. If we translate that into theatre, perhaps we could get more done, in terms of selling our culture—to ourselves! I'm not even speaking of the outer world yet. We don't know anything about ourselves!

August Wilson smoked a cigarette and drank coffee and also drank in what was said: "Okay," he declared. "But we sold our culture during the

Harlem Renaissance. And again during the sixties. So, I don't know why we still don't know the value of it."

Sinclair: But we don't!

Wilson: Well, one of the reasons why we don't is because we always seem to want to wait until someone else, other than ourselves, puts their stamp of approval on it. We have no system that expands and extends our art. In other words, I've had four Broadway plays. I can't recall one black review, or critical essay or analysis of my work. Whites have written on my work. One white woman writing somewhere did a critical examination of the women in my plays. Now, this is a white woman! I'm not talking about overnight reviewers. I'm talking about people like Addison Gayle, Amari Baraka, who have the basis for critical analysis; who can judge the work as being valuable or not. And, someone black has to put a sanction on it based on the needs of our people and the purposes of black art.

Either you're doing that work that is valuable, or you're not! And someone black has to put the sanction on it! We always wait for whites to say it's good. I was on a panel with Addison Gayle. I gave him all four copies of my plays. He wrote the book *The Black Aesthetic*. I haven't heard or read one single article from him on my work. I'm expecting him to say, "Yes, this is it," or "No, this is not it." I'm not expecting him to just say he likes my work—but I do expect some critical analysis. And, it's got to come from black people. With the exception of Paul Carter Harrison, I haven't had any critical analysis that I need to build on.

Sinclair: Well, in this instance, I think part of the problem—how can I say this—I don't think they know what to make of you. They don't really know you, and they don't want to say anything against you. I think the feeling is . . . okay, the brother, he's made it. We don't know him, but. . . .

Wilson: No, no. What does the work say! I think a critic should have a criteria.

Sinclair: See, we've gotten to the point where we don't criticize ourselves as we should, for fear it will appear that we are tearing down what few little successes that we have, in an area that has been totally decimated, as I've told you.

Wilson: I see what you're saying. But what that does is it allows whites to put all the sanctions, to continue to legitimize.

Sinclair: Also, our legitimization has never really meant anything, with a few notable exceptions: *The Wiz*, a few other instances.
Wilson: Well, then we'll have to make it mean something.

A rat the size of a teenaged kitten skimmed across the floor of the Edison Coffee Shop and scooted behind the counter—a man with a stick in hot pursuit! Wilson sipped his coffee unflinchingly. "That's Gertrude," said another voice from the kitchen, laughingly.

"Damn! I dreamed of rats two nights ago," said Wilson. "I dreamed I was eating a pastrami sandwich and sat it on the dresser and lay down to take a nap, and about fifty rats climbed in the opened window trying to get my sandwich."

"Oh yeah!" I said. "That kind of dream usually means trouble. People after you, but behind your back with it."

"Shit!" scoffed Wilson. "That don't mean nothin' to me. That's been the case all my life. But I know what I gotta do!"

August Wilson was born April 27, 1945, in Pittsburgh, Pennsylvania, to a German father and a black mother, Mrs. Daisy Wilson.

But Mrs. Wilson alone raised three boys and three girls in a two-bedroom apartment in the Hill section of Pittsburgh. The family later moved to Hazelwood, a steelworkers' neighborhood.

"Unionism in America has generally helped blue collar whites," Wilson observed, "but white unions have shut out blacks consistently, especially in the trades. Domestic fights, drinking were often due to the fact that a black man could never earn a decent wage for the same work as a white man—if he was lucky enough to get work at all. They'd hire you on at the steel mills for five months. If you stay six months, they'd have to take you into the union. So, the white foremen, all across the board, would lay you off halfway into the fifth month. Then if they liked you, and you didn't make waves, they'd hire you all over again.

"This could and did go on for years. One cat, they did that to him for thirty years. So he worked all that time for a beginner's wage. No pension. No retirement. You can't say nothin' on your job. You have no rights. Meanwhile, whites are putting their relatives on. Their wives' relatives. Family from overseas. That was Pittsburgh. When the steel industry slowed down, laying off all the whites, *they* wanted the government to do something! It had been like that for blacks the whole time."

In an environment like that, being a poet and writer was an unusual choice. Wilson left home at nineteen, after being encouraged by a teacher, Brother Dominic, to write his poetry. But Dominic tried to steer Wilson away from his heritage—from being black. Wilson tried writing nature poems. He soon gave that up and returned to his own roots.

"I've worked hard all my life—from the time I was eight years old. Hard work was no problem. I worked for my uncle for a dollar a day. At the end of the week I had five dollars. A lot of money for an eight-year-old. But I wanted to write."

Wilson went to live in an artists' commune back in the Hill District of Pittsburgh. There he met other artists and writers and began to develop a sense of himself. They'd read poetry and have jazz concerts on the weekend. He discovered Langston Hughes, read the forty or so books by black authors at the local library, and found Bessie Smith on old 78 rpm records.

"The music influenced me more than anything," said Wilson. "That music, that was me! Patti Page, Frank Sinatra, they weren't me. That music became the wellspring of my work."

He'd written lots of poetry and several plays, taking assorted odd jobs to support himself. He and Claude Purdy, a good friend, hung out together there in Pittsburgh: Claude encouraging him, and vice versa. He wrote a play, *Black Bart and the Sacred Hills*, based on a poetry character of his. When Claude Purdy got a theatre deal out in St. Paul, Minnesota, he sent for Wilson. Later, Purdy went to Los Angeles and sent for Wilson again.

It was Purdy who told Wilson to submit his plays to the Eugene O'Neill Playwrights Conference. After five rejections, one play caught the eye of director Lloyd Richards: *Ma Rainey's Black Bottom*.

Wilson: I remember back in the sixties, we'd put on plays in Pittsburgh. The white press would never come out. The black papers would send someone out who was totally unqualified, but at least we'd get a write-up. Then, the one play, the white press gave it a review. Suddenly, here come all the black people coming to see the play. The white press had legitimized it. So, here we go. They came out because it was legitimized in the *Post-Gazette*. I remember (Amiri) Baraka standing up and shouting "You can't begin to move towards self-determination until you begin to legitimize yourself."

Sinclair: It's very difficult to critique community theatre. Don't think it's easy. Because what happens is, if you give them a bad review they are jeopardized in terms of getting a grant. It's so intricate. You have to realize when you criticize, you have the power of life and death in your hands. I've had to soften a criticism for fear it would be used against an institution that was under attack and had their funding cut for no apparent reason.

Black theatre is *entitled* to funding, but the games that are played—especially here in New York State where a disproportionate amount of money goes to white theatre and art institutions—it's bad. With no relief. So, if I come up and say—"That play sucks!" That could cost them maybe twenty to thirty thousand dollars next season, you understand? So, it's all of these things that undermine our positive and necessary critical assessment of our direction. It's really a serious problem, because many of our theatres need a good hard critical assessment, minus the intimidation of biased funding sources looking for excuses to undermine our theatre.

What you need to do is come in and try to help us with this. Now, I know you're not a gregarious person, but this time it's time for us to get a group of critics together. By critics, I don't mean reviewers, but those individuals who stand at the precipice of our disaster or self-determination, in terms of determining what is total black aesthetic.

Wilson: Yeah. You need a group of people to determine what is the value of this, as it relates to black people. What is our criteria? Because, the criteria of blacks and whites has got to be different.

The conversation had Wilson. Me also. He was involved, talking freely and listening intensely. When the curve ball came around the corner, I didn't even see it. It came sailing by so naturally.

Wilson: So, how do you see my plays?

Sinclair: Unnh . . . Your plays, in my opinion . . . your plays . . . I see you as a latter-day Zora Neale Hurston. Yes, that's it. Because, what she did was bring a humanistic warmth to our history, without necessarily relegating it to the past. In other words—it's still current, but it has the flavor of something that happened before, and before that, and before that.

Wilson: In other words, it gives you the value of black culture as it is. So, let's explore the value of black culture, and relate that, so you can see there is no idea outside of black life. Black life is large enough; there is no idea that it cannot contain that is not already a part of it—so that you have a whole—complete. This is not a "sub-culture!" You have a whole complete world view—a whole complete cultural philosophy, religion, mythology, history—whatever Maulana Karenga says the criteria for culture is. That's what in fact we have. And as far as the agenda that we were talking about is concerned, I think it needs to be explored. I think it was Baldwin who called for "a profound articulation of the black tradition" which he defined as "that field of manners and rituals of intercourse that could sustain a man once he's left his father's house."

So that when you leave your parents' house, you are not naked. You have acquired from them ideas of justice and morality. You've acquired eating habits, concepts of pleasure and pain; you have a solid ground to stand upon. So, when you go out into the world you are complete. You don't need anybody else's thing to make you whole.

So, when we as black people have this, we can better relate to this society. We need to be self-sufficient in terms of who we are. Black people—and I see many of them saying it now—we are not willing to give up who we are in order to participate in this society.

Sinclair: Some of us are saying this, and some are not; and of course, you're not going to have everyone saying the same thing. But what I see is—too many blacks in important positions are vacillating on this—not because they're *white struck*—but because what's missing is what you've described. When they are bombarded every day with another culture, and it's not even a question of culture, but everyday existence, they have no backup, no backbone—nothing to moor them to any kind of dock in terms of their lives, so they just go drifting on out there . . . and proud of it! Because, at least they can show you, well, I've got this, and that; and they pin their whole existence on something that they have, and try to make that their assets—something they can pass along even. And it isn't.

Wilson: Boy, you know that's a battlefield loss. But for every one of those, there are thousands who are willing to say "no" to this social contract which reads: If you are willing to deny who you are, you can participate in this society; and here, we got a bunch of people to show you who have been willing to do that.

They have been trying to stamp out our culture for a long time. They took away our languages, and religions. The mistake they made was to continue the slave trade, so fresh blacks kept coming over, keeping the culture alive. Blacks have been struggling over the centuries to say, "I am of value, of worth as a person—that my ideas about the world, my attitudes, whatever there is of worth to me, I'm willing to die for that."

Sinclair: Yes, but this aesthetic is not a conscious one that I can see. I've spoken to too many of those people you talk of. Living in the projects, on the margin. You ask them about history, about the culture. The first thing they tell you is "I ain't no African . . . I ain't. . . ."
Wilson: They know they ain't African, but they know they ain't European either! There has to be an inherent feeling of self-worth.

Sinclair: No? Not African. Not European. So, the big question becomes, what are you? That becomes the question. And no answer leads to problems. That's where your drugs come in, your decay.
Wilson: (Pausing, because the conversation was going at almost breakneck speed.) Well, there was an old man in a bar in San Diego, an old drunk man, who used to always say, "We us! We be us!"

Sinclair: Well, the African American experience is my field of expertise, especially in the arts—and in theatre in particular. The history of our theatre will tell you a lot about us by the way; from slavery, the minstrel period, musicals, to now. But the sums that enhance the appreciation of "us" are still left wanting. If you only concentrate on the American experience and leave off the African experience, our accomplishments have been staggering. Not only in the field of music, arts, theatre, etc., but science, invention. Do you realize the number and quality of patents African Americans hold? Even in the field of medicine—blood plasma, transfusion, Charles Drew; the light bulb—Lewis Latimer; the train coupler—A. J. Beard; the elevator—A. Miles. (Pat. No. 371,207 Oct. 1887)—And black folks know nothing of even this. So we is "us!" What then does that mean?
Wilson: Well, that's our job. Me and you! We got our work cut out for us. Can't say we ain't got nothing to do!

And so it was. August Wilson and me, whiling away the afternoon at the Edison Coffee Shop. There's enough material for two more articles this size. I'll probably peddle it to a magazine. We talked about everything: Eddie Murphy, Spike Lee, Robert Townsend, Mike Tyson. We bet a bottle of champagne on the Douglas/Tyson fight. I picked Tyson. They never caught

Gertrude, the rat. Just as well. Keep the phonies out of the place. Later, we walked up Sixth Avenue and Wilson told me a funny story, and gave me a kiss on the cheek. He also gave $5,000 to the Frank Silvera Writers' Workshop earlier this year. He inspired me to work even harder, and his new play *Two Train's Running* is headed this way.

August Wilson: An Interview

Vera Sheppard / 1990

From *National Forum: The Phi Kappa Phi Journal*, 70 (Summer 1990), 7–11. Copyright by The Honor Society of Phi Kappa Phi. By permission of the publishers.

Vera Sheppard: Congratulations on your second Pulitzer Prize, this time for your latest play on Broadway—*The Piano Lesson*. When you were young, did you ever dream of becoming famous, or are you surprised that your work has become so respected and admired?

August Wilson: Well, I don't think one starts off with that idea. I have been writing since 1965, and I always assumed that by the time I was forty I would be a better writer than I was when I was twenty. Fame and that sort of thing never entered into my mind. It was a question of enjoying the work for the work's sake.

VS: You have been quoted as saying that you don't do any research for your plays, yet I get the impression that you know a lot about African American history. Do your incidents showing the treatment of blacks simply grow out of a general feeling you have for the past?

AW: Well, of course I have read some of the history of Africans in America. I think where I get most of my information from is all of these walking history books, the people themselves who have gone through various experiences. In Pittsburgh, there is a place called Pat's Place. I was reading *Home to Harlem*, and Claude McKay had mentioned that their railroad porters would stop in Pat's Place, a place where he hung out. And I thought, well, I know where that's at. I went to Pat's Place and, sure enough, there were these elders of the community standing around, and at that time I was twenty-three years old and it was a time when life had to be continually negotiated. I was really curious as to how they had lived as long as they did. So I stood around in Pat's Place and listened to them. They talked philosophy, history; they discussed whatever the topic of the day was—the newspapers, the politics of the city, the baseball games, and invariably they would talk about themselves and their lives when they were young men. And so a lot of what I know of the history of blacks in a very personal sense I picked up standing there in Pat's Place.

VS: That's probably why you include so much storytelling in your plays. I was going to ask you where this device comes from. You have answered it; it grows partly out of your youth.

AW: It is certainly a part of the culture also. As I got older, I discovered that the stories are all designed for a purpose, and that is to reveal ways of conduct which the community has put sanctions on. When you hear a story, you learn what is expected of you as a man, say, in the black community. I can remember when I arrived at twenty years old on the avenue where all the young men hung out, for instance, there was a story about this lawyer named Al Lichtenstein. These were undoubtedly tall tales about what a fantastic lawyer this guy was. But what they were telling you was that the chances are that, as a young black male, you were at some time going to need a lawyer. I said well, okay, if I ever get in any trouble, I know what I will do—I will get Al Lichtenstein, and the judge will just throw the case right out because he will see that I have Al Lichtenstein as my lawyer.

VS: Each of the plays so far has been set in a different decade. You have indicated that your future works will cover the remaining years, but that this was not your original intention. How and when did the idea of creating a cycle of plays occur to you?

AW: I did not start out with that idea in mind. I wrote a play called *Jitney!* that was set in 1971, and then I wrote a play called *Fullerton Street* that was set in 1941, and then I wrote *Ma Rainey's Black Bottom* which was set in 1927. And I said, well, I have written plays set in three different decades; why don't I continue to do that. It gave me an agenda, a focus, something to hone in on, so that I never had to worry about what the next play would be about. I could always pick a decade and work on that.

VS: And *Ma Rainey* was the first play that was a great hit.

AW: That was the first play. I kept sending my plays to the Eugene O'Neill Theater Center's National Playwrights Conference, and they kept sending them back to me. I had submitted a total of five scripts to them, and they rejected them all, and eventually I wrote *Ma Rainey*. It was accepted, and we had a production at Yale Repertory Theatre which we moved to Broadway in 1984. Yes, that was my first breakthrough.

VS: Maybe you remembered a story that you had overheard where they made the point that you must have persistence.
AW: Well, I got that from my mother. I always saw myself as a warrior in life—you suffer wounds and defeats and what not, and you get up and you continue. So I was determined that if it had taken twelve plays, they would have just had to keep sending them back to me because I was not going to stop writing. No matter what.

VS: And that is a theme in some of your plays, too—to keep on going.
AW: I think so. The whole history of black America demonstrates the resiliency of the human spirit. I certainly bear witness to that from hundreds of years.

VS: I understand that you are not an avid reader of dramatic literature because you feel that it might destroy your own expression, that you do not want to borrow from anyone else.
AW: Well, I started writing poetry in 1965, and I read anything and everything that was out there. As a consequence it took me until 1973 before I could find my own voice as a poet, before I could write a poem that was *my* poem, that was not influenced by John Berryman or Amiri Baraka or anyone else. So when I started writing plays in earnest in 1979, I had not read the body of western theatre that is Ibsen and Chekhov and Shaw and Shakespeare and O'Neill and Williams. I had read Ed Bullins and Baraka and the black playwrights of the sixties, but I thought, I do not want to go back and read all of the ones I have not read because I will just do it my way—I will just say this is my idea of a play.

VS: Your plays are quite traditional in structure; in fact, they are very well-structured. In other words, you are not avant-garde.
AW: Well, I guess not, but that is the manner in which I write. It is an intuitive way of telling a story.

VS: Do you think of your plays as tragedies in the classic sense?
AW: I would certainly hope so—I aspire to write tragedies. I don't know if I have or not, but that is what I sit down to write. Tragedy is the greatest form

of dramatic literature. Why settle for anything less than that? My sense of what a tragedy is includes the fall of the flawed character; that is certainly a part of what is in my head when I write.

VS: So, we can't expect you to be producing comedies in the near future?
AW: No, there is a great deal of humor in human life, and I think I find the humor, but the overall intent of the plays I write is very serious.

VS: You have a preference for putting long monologues into your plays. What do you think the effect of these long storytelling passages should be on the audience?
AW: I just hope the audience listens. There is a black person talking and he is talking a lot, and I think that we have not heard black people talk. Society views black life in a glancing manner, and no one ever stops to ask them, What is on your mind? These are common, ordinary characters who have long speeches, and I want the audience to listen to them.

A reviewer said that the subject matter of *The Piano Lesson*—the legacy of black America, what you do with your legacy—should only take an hour and a half instead of three hours. So you can do that in an hour and a half because it is black and therefore unimportant. But you take the Jewish legacy, and you need more than nine hours to tell the story about the Holocaust in the film *Shoah*.

I think the long speeches are an unconscious rebellion against the notion that blacks do not have anything important to say.

VS: It is interesting that you mentioned the Holocaust because I had thought of the Holocaust, too, in connection with your work. We always hear that we mustn't forget, and it seems to me that you are trying to keep the memory of black people's suffering alive. Are you doing this consciously? Or are you just reminiscing in order to tell your stories?
AW: I think it is important that we understand who we are and what our history has been, and what our relationship to society is, so that we can find ways to alter that relationship and, more importantly, to alter the shared expectations of ourselves as a people. The suffering is only a part of black history. What I want to do is place the culture of black America on stage, to demonstrate that it has the ability to offer sustenance, so that when you leave your parents' house, you are not in the world alone. You have something that

is yours, you have a ground to stand on, and you have a viewpoint, and you have a way of proceeding in the world that has been developed by your ancestors. It was James Baldwin who called for a "profound articulation of the black tradition," which he defined as that field of manners and rituals that sustains a man once he has left his father's house. And I said, Ah-hah! I am going to answer that call. I am going to show that this culture exists and that it is capable of offering sustenance. Now, if in the process of doing that, you have to explore the sufferings of black America, then that is also part of who we are. And I don't think you can ignore that because our culture was fired in the kiln of slavery and survival.

VS: Then you are not so interested in pointing out, "Yes, we have suffered: Let us not forget." But you want to go further—to talk about the reaction to the suffering and the spirit that one can still maintain.
AW: Absolutely. I think my plays are a testament to the resiliency of the human spirit. And that no matter what, we are still here, the culture is still alive, it is vital, and it is as vibrant and zestful as ever.

VS: The character of Troy in *Fences* has that resiliency of spirit.
AW: Yes, I think what impressed me most about Troy was his willingness to engage life, to live it zestfully and fully despite the particulars of his past, despite the way his mother abandoned him, the way he was put out of the house by his father at fourteen, the way he spent fifteen years in the penitentiary—none of that broke his spirit. And he died with his boots on. When he struck out early at the plate, he said: "Death is nothing but a fast ball on the outside corner." Well, he only swung, and he missed. But he was in the batter's box when he died.

VS: And Toledo in *Ma Rainey* gets killed, but he certainly has put up a wonderful fight verbally trying to point out an attitude one ought to take as a black person. Do you think that certain segments of the black population are resisting the idea of looking for their roots?
AW: I think that is certainly a part of black American culture, particularly over the past forty years, when white America issued a social contract that said you can participate in the society if you are willing to deny the fact that you are African: that you cannot bring your Africanness inside the door. I think that the fundamental question that has confronted blacks since the

Emancipation Proclamation is, Are we going to adopt the values of the dominant culture, or are we going to maintain our cultural separateness and continue to develop the culture that has been developing in the southern United States for some two to three hundred years? I think that is the question. Ultimately the people are going to decide one way or the other about how we are going to proceed. For the vast majority of black people the origins are the plantations of the South. Those are our roots, and that is our culture, so one best pay tribute to that. I always say, I am standing in my grandfather's shoes. I want to place myself in that long continuum that goes all the way back to the first African who set foot on the continent. The African who arrived chained and malnourished in the hold of a 350-ton Portuguese vessel—he has not vanished from the face of the earth; he is here, in whatever manifestation, alive in the thirty million black people who are in this country now.

VS: And you might as well be proud of your origin, rather than deny it?
AW: Well, to deny it is to deny your parents and your grandparents and in that sense to deny your self.

VS: You have said that black culture is very different from white culture and that it is important to acknowledge the differences. What is the worldview of the black person as opposed to the white person? I know that is a huge question.
AW: That is a huge question, but I think it is answered very simply. The basic difference in worldview between blacks and whites can be expressed as follows: Western culture sees man as being *apart from* the world, and African culture just sees man as *a part of* the world.

VS: Would you explain that further?
AW: Well, for the white man, nature exists to be conquered. Whereas, for Africans, they see themselves as part of everything, the trees, all of life on the planet. Because Africans are not Europeans, they have different ways of looking at life; there are different things they value. We decorate our houses differently than white people do; we have different rituals that are attendant to burying our dead; our courtship rituals are different. We value and prize linguistic ability. That is one of the values of our culture—the ability to rap. We entertain differently, we party differently, we have a communal sense that I suspect is partly based on our shared history; our sense of style is different, our manners differ from those of Europeans.

VS: You say, Vive La Difference!

AW: Without question. There is nothing wrong with the way anyone does anything. It is only when one culture tries to impose its culture on others and says that your life is deficient unless, for instance, you know Mozart and Beethoven and all the rest of that culture.

VS: You mention rapping. It is true that black language can be very poetic when compared to white speech, and your characters, while they sound very realistic and believable, also sound poetic. Are you re-creating and refining what you have overheard?

AW: Not that I have heard consciously, other than the years that I spent standing at Pat's Place: The rhythms and the manner in which those men talked.

VS: I heard Lloyd Richards say during an interview that your dialogue reminds him of the way people talked in his presence when he was young.

AW: Being an artist, I guess, and being attentive to language, you discover certain things. But it took me a long while before I could value the way blacks spoke. In my earlier attempts to write plays, I felt that in order to make art out of this, I had to change the language, and so I was trying to force words into the characters' mouths that simply did not fit because I did not value the way they spoke. But once I stopped and began to listen in my head to the speech rhythms, I uncovered inferences in black dialogue—a lot of things are done by implication. When you give the language, you are giving the thought patterns as well. There is an impeccable logic in the use of metaphor that I noticed as I was standing around at Pat's Place. So I simply was trying to recreate that sense of style or that sense of interior logic within the characters.

VS: Black speech (in your plays) seems less abrupt and more detailed. Somebody will say something, and a person will answer at length and embellish what he is saying.

AW: Oh sure. For instance, in *The Piano Lesson* you have the question (AW begins to declaim dramatically), "What time Berniece get home?" The answer is not, "Berniece get home at five o'clock." The answer is "You up there sleep. Berniece leave out of here early in the morning. She's working out to support herself cleaning house for one of them big shots down at the steel mills. They don't like you to come late. You come late, they won't give you car fare. What kind of business you got with Berniece?" And they say, "My business, I ain't asked you what kinda business you got." "Well, Berniece ain't got no money, if that's why you tryin' to get hold to her. Now if she go ahead and marry Avery, he workin' everyday, and if she go ahead and marry him, she be doin' alright. But as it stands, Berniece ain't got no money."

VS: Maybe you should have become an actor, too!
AW: So the answer to, "What time Berniece get home?"—well, the implication in that is that I am going to borrow some money from Berniece. So you get not only the question, but you get the whole history of what she's doing, why she won't give you car fare, whom she should marry, why she should marry him, and all the rest of that. But if it was in fact like white speech, it would be, "What time does Berniece get home?" And the answer would be, "Berniece gets home at five o'clock."

VS: And in white speech, the listener would get impatient with the long answer; but the black person is happy to hear it.
AW: Well, you are getting so much more than just the answer to the question.

VS: How did you make the transition from writing poetry to writing plays?
AW: I still write poetry. I still consider it the highest form of written language arts, and I aspire to write great poetry, actually. But it was a friend of mine who talked me into writing a play. I gave a poetry reading, and I had a character in my poems called Black Bart, and my friend said, hey, you could make that into a play, and I thought, no, I don't know how to do that, but he kept after me about it, so from one Sunday to the next, I sat down and wrote this play for him. And I did not immediately become a playwright. But I was intrigued with the idea that I was able to take these forms and make something larger out of them. And that was in '77, and I have continued to do that.

VS: Are you publishing your poetry?
AW: At some point. This may go back to the first question you asked. I have written a lot of short stories and a lot of poetry, but I never sought sanction outside the sanction I would place on my own work. I never sent my poems or my stories off to be published. For me, it was the sheer joy of writing them. But I have been asked by six or seven publishers, and yes, I do plan to publish them.

VS: What is more important about your plays—their uniqueness in depicting the black experience or their universality? What audience do you have in mind when you write?

AW: I write for an audience of one. For myself. I think I have to satisfy myself as an artist first before I write for any particular other audience. So I look at my work as a piece of art, and I have to be satisfied with it. I don't write for black people or white people; I write about the black experience in America. And contained within that experience, because it is a human experience, are all the universalities. I am surprised when people come up to me and say, well, *Fences* is universal. Of course it is! They say that as though the universals existed outside of black life. It was Romare Bearden, the artist, who when asked about his work, said, "I try to explore in terms of the life that I know best those things which are common to all culture." And I thought, Ah-hah! That is also what I aspire to do. When you look at Troy Maxson and his wife Rose and you see that Troy is having an affair with another woman and has fathered a child by her, it does not matter that these are black people; this is a human experience that has been duplicated many, many times by all cultures, and all people throughout the world can understand and recognize that.

VS: You mentioned your mother having been a strong woman and a good influence on you. Do her characteristics have something to do with the fact that you have quite a few female characters that are the strong ones in the family—the reasonable and nurturing ones—while the husbands are less so?

AW: I suspect so. I grew up in a house without a father, in a single-parent household with my mother. In answer to that, I am cautious in writing women characters; I am respectful of them as I would be of my mother. That is, I try to write honest women, I try to place myself in their shoes, I try to look on both sides. I write honestly whatever I find, but I am cautious of being respectful.

VS: There is a lot of symbolism in your plays, and there are many allusions to the supernatural. Would you please address that.

AW: Symbolism is one of the tools of art, and I think it helps in creating metaphors and taking a very large experience and focusing it down to something more manageable. So in *Joe Turner*, for instance, the seven years that the character Herald Loomis spends in bondage with Joe Turner can in fact represent the two to three hundred years of slavery in America. The bones rising out of the ocean are symbolic of the Africans who were lost during the middle passage, who in the course of that play are resurrected and washed upon the land. And Loomis has to make the connection that in actuality this is who he is. The idea of ghosts, the conjure man, these are all part of the culture of black America. They can be directly traced across the ocean to the continent of Africa. And I think that these are things that have survived after 349 years here in America—the supernatural, our sense of self as a part of the world, as a part of the rest of nature. So if you are going to write about black culture, you have to understand that.

VS: Would you explain your characters' relationship to God. There are references in your plays that seem to indicate that God has forsaken the black man.
AW: Well, it depends on what God you are talking about. When Africans were brought to this country, they were denied their language, their gods, customs, and all the rest. Toledo in *Ma Rainey* says, "We forgot the names of the gods." But I have a very simple viewpoint toward that—when you look in the mirror, you should see your God. If you don't, then you have somebody else's God. Because there is not a people on the planet who have a God that does not look like them. Everyone throughout the world, the Chinese, the Europeans, the Eskimos, the Indians—everyone has a God that resembles him or herself.

VS: Yes, and Jesus doesn't look like the black person.
AW: Well, that image of Jesus doesn't—the image that we know. So what happens in *Joe Turner* is that Loomis rejects not just the idea of God, but the idea of salvation coming from outside himself. He says, "I don't need anyone to bleed for me, I can bleed for myself." So it is an acceptance of his responsibility for his own salvation, and by way of that, an acceptance of his responsibility for his own presence in the world.

VS: Your plays have songs in them—*Ma Rainey*, of course, is full of music—and you have said that you get inspiration from listening to the blues. How does this work for you?
AW: Well, the blues are without question the wellspring of my art. It is the greatest source of my inspiration. I see the blues as the cultural response of black America to the world that they found themselves in. And contained within the blues are the ideas and attitudes of the culture. There is a philosophical system at work, and I simply transferred these things over to all the ideas and attitudes of my characters: these come directly from blues songs.

VS: From the lyrics of the blues?

AW: It is the lyrics, but the music also provides you with an emotional reference for the information that is contained in the songs. So it is both. I don't think you can separate them. But I do think that the blues are the best literature that we have as black Americans. It is very profound art.

VS: It is often quite sad.

AW: That is a misconception of what the blues are. The blues are life-affirming music. Unfortunately, what happened is that when the idea of recording came about, White people went down with their recorders, gave these guys a bottle of whiskey and three dollars, and had them sing twelve or fifteen songs, took the songs back to Chicago and sat down and decided which of these twelve or fifteen songs had any worth or value to them. They set themselves up as the custodians of the music, and also as chief interpreters.

VS: And it is the white judgment that focused so much on the negative aspect.

AW: That is exactly my point. The blues are life-affirming music that guides you throughout life; the blues teach you the morality of the culture. These are very valuable things that are being passed along. The blues are rooted in life—they deal with "Hey Mama, it look like Mattie, but she walking too slow. Go put on your night gown. Let's lie down. Last chance I get to be 'round here."

Whereas, white music is talking about the moon and stars, and hey, there, you with the stars in your eyes. It is an entirely different kind of music.

VS: I understand that you also get inspiration from paintings. Is that so?

AW: I have gotten inspiration from the artist Romare Bearden. *Joe Turner's Come and Gone* was written when I was looking at a painting of his called *Mill Hand's Lunch Bucket*. It was a boarding house painting, and in the center of this painting was this man sitting in this chair with his coat and hat on, in this posture of abject defeat, and there is a man reaching for his lunch bucket. There is a child who is drinking a glass of milk, and there is a woman standing with a purse as if she is about to go shopping. And I looked at that, and I said, "Everyone is going to leave. The man is going to work, and the woman is going shopping, and the kid is going to drink the milk and go out, and this man is going to be left there in this posture. And what he needs most is human contact." And then I began to wonder who he was and why he was sitting there like that, and I said, "I am going to animate this boarding house and make the boarding house come alive and give these characters names and find out who this guy is and what is his story." He became Herald Loomis and I got to know his story, but as I was writing the play, I was listening to an album called *W.C. Handy Sings and Plays His Immortal Hits*, and one of the songs on there was a song called "Joe Turner." "They tell me Joe Turner's come and gone, got my man and gone, and with forty links of chain, got my man and gone." And so I said, "Oh, I see, this is what happened to this character." And then ultimately I changed the name of the play from *Mill Hand's Lunch Bucket* to *Joe Turner's Come and Gone*.

VS: It is marvelous what happens to an artist in the creative process. You look at a picture and there is a play.
AW: Yes, and *The Piano Lesson* was also titled after a Bearden painting. There is a painting of a little girl playing the piano with a woman standing over her—her piano teacher (but that became her mother), and so the mother and the little girl at the piano were in the play. So Bearden's art in particular has been influencing me because of the manner in which he treats black life—in all of its richness and fullness in a formal artistic language, and he connects it to the great traditions in art, whether they are Dutch or whatever. But his subject matter is the black experience in America.

VS: I have a question about the frustration that is experienced by the characters in your plays, which then results in violence. This relates to what is happening in society now, doesn't it?
AW: Well, I have to go back to the violence in *Ma Rainey's Black Bottom*, the only play that I say has violence in it. It is obviously a transference of violence to the nearest target. You know, throughout the course of the play Toledo has been set up as a substitute for the white man. There are comments that he reads too many books—just like the white man. That he has forgotten how to laugh and have a good time—just like the white man. So he is being set up as a standard for a stereotype.

VS: In *Fences*, the characters take up the bat.
AW: Yes, there is a fight between the father and son. I don't think it comes out of frustration. Here again is a rite of passage, a ritualistic kind of rite of

passage, in which the son struggles with the father and plays the father, in some cultures in order to become a man himself. Loomis slashing his chest in *Joe Turner's Come and Gone* is far from being self-mutilation. You can look at it that way, but it is his demonstration of his willingness to accept responsibility for himself, to bleed for himself.

VS: So it is symbolic violence.

AW: Yes, it stands as a magnificent gesture because they see the man taking full control of his life. It is a severing of the bonds that have been binding him. And that one symbolic, ritualistic, and blood-letting rite is also a part of many people's culture. The crucifixion itself could be viewed as a blood-letting rite. All of those things are purposeful. I would not call any of them violent acts.

VS: As your plays are performed in various cities, you often revise them. What is it like for a playwright to keep work in constant progress like that?

AW: I have been very fortunate in that the plays have gone through a process. I have submitted them to the O'Neill Theater Center's National Playwrights Conference. Since *Ma Rainey*, each one I have submitted has been followed with an invitation to participate in the conference. We do four days of rehearsal and a very intensive workshop in which they hire actors and directors and a dramaturg, and you sort of stand the play up on its feet. And from those two stage readings I get ideas about how I could make the play better. I try to come up with a draft suitable enough for going into rehearsal. When we open the show at the Yale Repertory Theatre, we do not open it in the spirit that this is an incomplete or unfinished work. When we perform in other cities, I watch the performance and continue to revise.

VS: So it becomes a collaborative effort?

AW: Yes, it is a collaboration between all of the theatres who offer Lloyd Richards and me a place to work. You could not sit and watch a play a hundred times and not find out more things about it. The playwright sitting at home alone is never going to get everything right.

VS: Lloyd Richards has directed all of the major plays. Do you want to talk a little about your relationship with him?

AW: Yes, Lloyd has directed them all. When we worked together on *Ma Rainey's Black Bottom*, I did not know him very well, and I got off the train in New Haven with my script, uncertain what was going to happen. We went into rehearsal, and we read the play. The actors had a couple of questions which I was prepared to answer, and Lloyd liked what I wrote, and he was also prepared and gave the answer, and he was 100 percent correct. Not only was he correct, but he gave me insights into characters I had not had. I visibly relaxed at that point. I said, "Okay, Lloyd knows what is going on." Now we have gotten to the point where there is not a lot of talk about the plays. It is an intuitive, almost nonverbal kind of communication.

For instance, I sent Lloyd a copy of *The Piano Lesson*, and he said I think you have one too many scenes in there. And I said I will take a look at that. End of conversation. Then I read the play. What could he be talking about? And then I found the scene. To this day, he has not pointed out the scene to which he was referring. But it was one I discovered that I could do without. What happened was that Lloyd let me find it, myself, the way he let the actors find it.

VS: I find it interesting that in a sense it is your humility that creates these wonderful plays. I can imagine that there are playwrights who would say, "Well, this is what I wrote—this is it—and you are going to put it on."
AW: I am not that kind of writer. A play is just words on paper. If it does not work, you just put some more words on paper. I have never been the kind to think that it is written in stone, so to speak.

VS: It is fortunate that you ran into Lloyd Richards, that he happened to be there just when you needed him, and you "clicked."
AW: Without question. Lloyd has been important not only as director of the plays, but important to my whole career, and important to my understanding of theatre. I have learned a lot about theatre over the past six years in working with him. He is a very generous man and a very giving mentor in that regard. The fact that we have done these four plays together makes them all seamless—having the same two artistic sensibilities at work on the play.

VS: The plays, taken together, form a whole.
AW: They have a unity and seamlessness to them which would not have been there had I had four different directors. We might have had four disparate kinds of plays. So I am very grateful that it worked out as it did.

VS: What is the status of black theatre companies in America today?

AW: They are not institutionalized. I find that white theatres are supported by institutions throughout the country, from the universities on down. We don't have that kind of institutional support for black theatre.

VS: Is it a good thing to have black theatre companies and white theatre companies, or would you like to see more of a meshing of the two?
AW: I think it is a very good idea to have separate theatre companies. Black concerns and white theatre concerns are very different. If we need some white actors, we will come over and get you guys, and if you need some black actors, you should come over and get us.

VS: As long as none of us get stereotyped! What do you think is the agenda of black theatre today?
AW: I don't think the black theatre has an agenda. It should be an exploration of the culture. Not that long ago it was a crime to teach blacks to read and write in this country. Cultural developments take time—we are in desperate need of writers, simply because we are coming out of an oral tradition. We need to strive for a development of written art that is comparable to the uniqueness of jazz and blues.

VS: I hear you have written a screenplay for *Fences*. Is it coming out soon?
AW: I have been battling for two years with Paramount Pictures who purchased the rights to the movie. The battle has centered on the question of hiring a black director. They have committed themselves to hiring one. If they actually follow through, I would consider that a big victory.

VS: You need a black director to produce it in the best possible way; a white person could not do it as well?
AW: We have proof of that from other films that whites have directed and that ended up unabashedly patronizing. And I certainly would not want that to happen to *Fences*. So for me it is crucial that the exploration of the culture be by those who share in it, those who come from it, no matter how well-intentioned others may be.

VS: There are many stories in your plays that tell of injustices committed against blacks. But what I think is so refreshing is that you don't come across to me as being very angry or militant. You point it out, but you are not strident about it. And I think that makes it even more effective.

AW: I think if you look at black life, you don't have to stand up and shout and indict racism. The ten thousand lynchings in Mississippi will do that very eloquently by themselves. Racism is a problem in the society; it exists. You don't have to kill white people on stage ultimately for effect. In the sixties I founded a black theatre group, and those were the kinds of plays that we did. I look for a more inward exploration of who we are, and once we understand that and understand the relationship that we have to society, then we can seek ways to alter that relationship.

VS: Lloyd Richards said that black theatre nowadays does not have to be all protest anymore.
AW: Yes, I must say the only reason I can do what I do is because the playwrights in the sixties did what they did. So I place myself in that long tradition. I just wrote a play about 1968 that did not deal with any of that because it had been done.

VS: Yes, *Two Trains Running*. What is the theme of that play?
AW: It takes place in a restaurant in 1968. The restaurant is across the street from the meat market and a funeral home, and every morning this man comes and stands in front of the meat market and says to the owner when he comes to work, "I want my ham." And the owner says, "Take a chicken." Nine years earlier he had painted the guy's fence for him, and the owner told him, "If you paint my fence, I will give you a chicken. If you do a good job, I will give you a ham." Well, the man thinks he did a good job, and the owner did not. So his response was to come every morning for nine years. What has happened to him in the nine years is that he has lost all sense of who he is. All he can say is, "I want my ham." He just wanders around in the community telling anyone and everyone, "I want my ham." There is an off-stage character Aunt Ester who is 322 years old. And Aunt Ester is a repository of the entire black experience and wisdom.

VS: It is good that you did not have to show her at that age, that she was offstage!
AW: Absolutely, the make-up person would have had a tremendous job. But your experience is alive, your legacy is alive. All you have to do is tap into it. So at various points the characters in the play have to go see Aunt Ester in order to solve their problems. And she tells them a very simple thing, and

that is: If you drop the ball, there is no need to run to the end zone, because there is not going to be a touchdown. You have to go back and pick up the ball. And so in these characters' lives, they have to go back and pick up the ball where they dropped it in order to proceed on. That is in essence what the play is saying.

VS: In a way you write morality plays.
AW: Something of that sort, I suspect.

VS: What do you envision you will be writing in the future, when the cycle has been completed up to the nineties?
AW: I go back and do it again—I'll do another cycle!

VS: You have offered much information—just like your storytelling characters—thank you!

August Wilson Explains His Dramatic Vision: An Interview

Sandra G. Shannon / 1991

From *The Dramatic Vision of August Wilson*. Washington, D.C.: Howard University Press, 1995, 201–35. Copyright © 1995. Reprinted with the permission of Howard University Press. All rights reserved.

August Wilson granted me the following interview while he was in Washington, D.C., for the November 1991 premiere of *Two Trains Running* at the Kennedy Center. Extremely personable and undeniably committed to his art, Wilson carefully outlined his answers to my questions about his growth from poet to playwright, about the cultural and political agendas underlying his plays, and about his role as a black writer.

The conversation that follows represents the uncut version of the same interview published in the Winter 1993 issue of *African American Review*, 27 (539–59) as "Blues, History, and Dramaturgy: An Interview with August Wilson."

Shannon: The following lines come from your poem "For Malcolm X and Others," which was published in the September 1969 issue of *Negro Digest*:

> The hour rocks a clog,
> The midnight term,
> In bones no shape before
> has warmed in such
> That loves these cold as dead,
> As stone; a flock of saints
> Run ground as thieves.

In another poem entitled "Muhammad Ali," you write:

> Muhammad Ali is a lion.
> He is a lion that breaks the back of wind,

Who climbs to the end of the rainbow with three steps
and devours the gold,
Muhammad Ali with a stomach of gold.
Whose head is iron.

What do these two poems suggest about your early years as a poet?
Wilson: One idea was that I was writing obscure poetry certainly first. It
actually took me from '65 to '73 before I could actually write a poem that I
felt was written in my own voice. The Muhammad Ali poem, however, is
modeled after an African praise song in which you give praises of any kind:
"Muhammad is a lion. He's a lion that bounces into the rainbow with three
steps and devours the gold. Muhammad Ali with fists of diamonds. His fists
are bullets. Muhammad Ali. . . ." You can say virtually anything you care to
say. It's just one praise after another. The Malcolm X poem—I have no idea
what it means.

Shannon: Early in your career you made a gradual shift from writing poetry
to writing plays. How has being a poet affected your success as a playwright?
Wilson: Well, I think that it has been important to my writing. It's the
bedrock of my playwriting. Primarily not so much in the language as it is in
the approach and the thinking—thinking as a poet, one thinks differently
than one thinks as a playwright. The idea of metaphor, which is a very large
idea in my plays and something that I find lacking in most other contemporary plays. So it's been very helpful. I think I write the kinds of plays that I do
because I have twenty-six years of writing poetry underneath all of that.

Shannon: I'm fascinated by the combination of memory, history, and myth-
making and the blues in your work. Do you perceive your role as an historian, as a prophet or healer, or perhaps something else?
Wilson: Well, I just say playwright. Of course, I use history. I use the historical perspective. My work benefits from looking back because we can look and
see—for instance, in *The Piano Lesson*, you can see the actor, the character
going down a road that, given the benefit of a fifty-year historical perspective,
we can see whether that is the correct road or not because we've learned.
We know how all this turned out. So, history is certainly an important part
of my work, and I try to actually keep all of the elements of the culture alive
in the work, and myth is certainly a part of it. Mythology, history, social

organizations—all of these kinds of things—economics—all of these things that are part of the culture, I make sure—I purposefully go through and make sure each element of that is in some way represented—some more so than others in the plays, which I think gives them a fullness and a completeness—that this is an entire world.

Shannon: What is your reasoning behind writing a four-hundred-year-old autobiography in ten plays? At what point did you decide upon this strategy?
Wilson: Well, actually, I didn't start out with a grand idea. I wrote a play called *Jitney!* set in '71 and a play called *Fullerton Street* that I set in '41. Then I wrote *Ma Rainey's Black Bottom*, which I set in '27, and it was after I did that I said, "I've written three plays in three different decades, so why don't I just continue to do that?" Also, the assumption everyone makes is that any writer's work—it's not just my work—they assume it's autobiographical, that you're writing about yourself. None of the characters, none of the events in the play are events in my life. None of the characters are modeled after me. Because I feel if you write your autobiography, you don't have anything else to tell. So I thought when people would ask me that, and I'd say, "Well, you know I got a four-hundred-year-autobiography." That's what I'm writing from. There's a whole bunch of material. You never run out of stories. I think—

Shannon: But you're part of the story?
Wilson: Oh, absolutely. I'm definitely a part of the story. It's my story. I claim it—all four hundred years of it. I claim the right to tell it in any way I choose because it's, in essence, my autobiography; only it's my autobiography of myself and my ancestors.

Shannon: Mr. Wilson, as you know, I am in the midst of writing a biocritical study of your work. During my research I have come across quite a few titles and have acquired the scripts of several never-before-published works. For example, you wrote several brief scripts for the Science Museum of Minnesota. The plays that I have read include *An Evening with Margaret Mead, How Coyote Got His Special Power*, and *Eskimo Song Duel*. Could you talk briefly about that experience?
Wilson: Well, it was a good experience. If nothing else, it was the first time that I was getting paid for writing. Someone was actually paying me—it was good money as I recall—to sit down and write these things. There wasn't,

though, a whole lot of creativity necessary to document a northwest Indian tale for this group of actors to act out on the anthropology floor. I never could understand why they were willing to pay me so much money to do that. There weren't very many projects assigned to do because you would do a project that cost money to get the costumes and to actually rehearse the actors to actually put them on the floor. So once they had two or three things on the floor, they didn't want to have anything else. They could have fired everybody and said, "Okay, that's it." To try to make it interesting, I came up with this idea called "Profiles in Science," and I was going to write a one-woman or one-man show about various scientific characters, which I did—one on Margaret Mead, William Harvey, Charles Darwin. They never did any of them. They never performed them.

Shannon: They had them on file at the library?
Wilson: They had them on file as part of my work, but, here again, to actually do that, they would have actually had to hire a director, and he would have to rehearse it, and they would have had to do whatever—at that time the person was just satisfied to have the three skits, more or less, and these actor cameos. One woman, for instance, was a Guamayan weaver, and we had to write a little spiel for her. She would sit there and explain about the holy weavers of the Guamayan culture. It was a very wonderful idea actually to make that come alive.

Shannon: Mr. Wilson, you discovered the blues in 1965 with Bessie Smith's "Nobody in Town Can Bake a Sweet Jelly Roll Like Mine." In *Ma Rainey's Black Bottom*, you take up the cause of the blues singer. This also seems to be the case in an earlier play called *The Homecoming*. Could you explain your compassion for the plight of the blues singer?
Wilson: Well, you see, it's the singer, but it's also the music. I think that the music has a cultural response of black Americans to the world they find themselves in. Blues is the best literature we have. If you look at the singers, they actually follow a long line all the way back to Africa and various other parts of the world. They are people who are carriers of the culture, carriers of the ideas—the troubadours in Europe, etc. Except in black America—in this society—they were not valued except among the black folks who understood. I've always thought of them as sacred because of the sacred tasks that they had taken upon themselves to disseminate this information and carry these

cultural values of the people. And I found that white America would very often abuse them. I don't think that it was without purpose in the sense that the blues and music have always been at the forefront in the development of character and consciousness of black America, and people have senselessly destroyed that or stopped that. Then you're taking away from the people their self-definition—in essence, their self-determination. These guys were arrested as vagrants and drunkards and whatever. They were never seen as valuable members of a society by whites. In fact, I'm writing a play which deals specifically with that.

Shannon: Your 1977 play called *The Coldest Day of the Year* seems to be about reconciling relationships between African American men and women. What inspired the play? Can you explain the circumstances surrounding its composition?
Wilson: Well, that was undoubtedly inspired by the breakup of my relationship with my girlfriend. I thought I'd write this play. It certainly was not written in the language that I write plays now.

Shannon: Very poetic with lots of figures and metaphors.
Wilson: Yes. Primarily I thought that in order to create art out of black life—because I didn't value the way that blacks spoke—I thought in order to create art out of it, you had to change it. So you had lines like "our lives frozen in deepest heats of spiritual turbulence."

Shannon: Which means?
Wilson: (Chuckle) Well, it has meaning to it. It has a meaning to it. Now, if I was going to write it, I guess the guy would just walk up to her and say, "How you doing, mama? We're out here in the cold."

Shannon: You wrote a similar play in 1973 called *Recycle*, which, as you explained, exorcised "man-woman stuff." What inspired this work?
Wilson: The breakup of my first marriage. Actually, this is the first play I ever wrote, so it has specialness to me. I was examining the cycle aspect of nature, I guess. There's a cyclical kind of thing that goes on in *The Coldest Day of the Year*. But I actually started writing the play one night as I saw this man get his brains blown out. As I was walking down the street and approaching this corner, this guy came out of the bar and was standing looking up and down

the street as though he was trying to decide which way he wants to go, and a hand came out of the bar—it was the bartender I found out later—with a gun. And there was a woman, and he fell on the sidewalk near his car. The woman went over—she was a nurse in the hospital—and she began to beat on this man's chest. She just kept beating him very hard in the chest. And one guy standing there says, "Baby, that man dead. Ain't no need you doin' that. That man dead." Then she just got up and turned and walked away, and I followed her. She went into this bar. She walked in and she said to the bartender, "The niggers are killing one another these days." And he said, "I heard. Is he dead?" She said, "Yeah, he's dead. I beat on his chest." I started out the play with this line. Something happened. Something happened, and I was curious about this woman who beat on his chest almost as if she could have been the murderer—"Yeah, he's dead. I beat on his chest." She didn't say, "I beat on his chest to try to get his heart beating" or anything. She just said, "I beat on his chest." So she got a drink, and I got a drink. I began to write this play. I didn't know what I was going to write about until a guy came by and said to the woman, in essence, "Remember me," and that started the man-woman aspect of the play as though she had murdered him and he is coming back. She looks up and says, "Where did you come from?" He says, "Down the street, lady, or did you forget?"

Shannon: That reminds me of the aspect of reincarnation that comes across in *The Piano Lesson* with Sutter's ghost coming back. Is that an attempt to draw parallels?

Wilson: No, not at all. I would place them in two entirely different categories. The idea of ghosts and the idea of supernatural phenomena in black American life is a very real phenomena that is quite different from someone or what, in essence, may be an accusatory play in which you simply come back to accuse someone for murdering you.

Another little addendum in my mind is who owned the bar. This is a guy named Pope. I use Pope's name in *Fences*. Troy talks about Pope opening up that restaurant down there and fixed it up real nice and didn't want anybody to come in it. There's this guy named Pope, and, in essence, he has this restaurant. I used to go in there all the time, and he used to hate for me to come in there. And as I got a little older, I understood. I come in there and spend ten cents on a cup of coffee. He had this big empty restaurant, and he's waiting for somebody to come in and spend ten cents and want ten cups of coffee for it. So, as a result of that—and I went anyway, even though he didn't like for me to come in there, I still went. But we never talked anyway or anything. Then he bought this bar, and this bar was the most popular bar— I mean Friday and Saturday night, you couldn't even get in the door. I mean there were five hundred people piled up in this store's space when a white guy owned it, and as soon as Pope got the bar, nobody went in there. And so I was almost his only customer at the bar—

Shannon: And he didn't want you to come in.
Wilson: Well, the bar was built different. By this time it was four or five years later, and I guess we both had changed. And I used to go in there, and he remembered me from the restaurant. So now I am his favorite customer— his only customer almost. Of course, there were other people. One night he started talking to me, and it shocked me that Pope would even say anything to me. We started talking about Bessie Smith and Ma Rainey, and he said, "Oh yeah, I remember Ma Rainey coming down to the Star Theater down there on such-and-such street." So he gave me a lot of the history of the neighborhood. And I had gotten to know this guy. We could have been doing this for five years. That was really important to me when Pope started talking to me.

Shannon: Was that the time when you were referred to as "Young-blood"?
Wilson: It was the same era, same time.

Shannon: I think you may have answered this, but which play do you con-sider to be the beginning of your history cycle—*Fullerton Street* or *Jitney!*? As I have not read *Fullerton Street*, could you give me a synopsis of its plot?
Wilson: *Jitney!* was the first one I wrote in terms of order of writing. *Fullerton Street* was a play centered in the forties in which I try to examine the urban northerner. What I wanted to do was to show some people who had come North and encountered the cities and had lost whatever kinds of values they had in the South—almost as if the environment determined that you had to adopt different values in order to survive up here. Domestically a husband and wife whose—the parents of the husband are living in the household with them. It's been six or seven years since they've been up North, and they have become alcoholics living on and waiting for welfare checks. In the South they would not have been living like that.

The important action of the play takes place on the night of the Joe Louis–Billy Conn fight, which they listen to around the radio with a group of male characters who are friends of the husband—the young man Moses, who is like twenty-five or twenty-six years old. After the fight they sit around talking, and they start telling jokes. In this night of telling jokes, what starts off as a joke degenerates into a very vivid description of a lynching they had witnessed when one of Moses's friends was lynched. And I think it was for something for which Moses was the culprit as opposed to his friend, since white folks can't tell one from the other. So he had a special burden of guilt to carry there. It was a very vivid memory, which, from that point in the play, changes his character, and he begins to move closer to at least adopting some new guidelines. So that was supposed to be cowardice. His mother dies—that was the first person I killed off in any of my plays. I remember her name was Mozelle, and I remember when I wrote the scene of Mozelle dying, I was crying, and the tears were falling on the page, and I was trying to write, and the ink was getting all screwed up—

Shannon: You were crying?
Wilson: Oh, yeah! It was like "Mozelle is dead." And I had lived with her for so long.

Shannon: There's a lot of death in *Two Trains*. You seem to have gotten good at that.
Wilson: Absolutely. It surprised me. There's death in all of the plays. When I wrote *Joe Turner*, I said, "Hey, good. Nobody died. No death!" Then I started looking back, and there was Mr. Seth's mother, and there's a ghost in *Joe Turner*. Miss Mabel comes back, and there were constant references to death. I didn't realize it—the two babies. And I thought I had gotten away and wrote a play in which it wasn't—but death is such an integral part of life. You can't have one without the other. So I was very conscious. I mean I wanted to move closer and closer to—I thought this time I wanted to bring the specter of death in the persona of West, the undertaker with his black gloves. I didn't get any menace, any threat in him as he developed into a different character. But I think when I started out, I wanted to have him just as a more menacing kind of presence within the play—sort of like lording over and waiting for each and every one of them, and it turns out he didn't become that menacing character that I originally started to write.

Shannon: Hambone dies, and, of course, Aunt Ester never dies.
Wilson: Aunt Ester never dies. Hambone dies—the first line in the play is when he talks about the second time that 651 came out. He said, "That was LD's number. If he was still living, he'd be in big money." So it starts with LD and reference to the people and Memphis's mother—in a big speech at the end of act I, he tells about when his mother died. Holloway's grandmother. Bubba Boy's woman dies in the play. West's wife died.

Shannon: The mule dies.
Wilson: The mule dies. That's kind of appropriate. He's [Memphis] the only one in the community that's making it—he's a rich man.

Shannon: I like that. The play ends on a good note with him getting more than what he expected for the restaurant.
    What do you think you accomplished in *Jitney!*?
Wilson: I simply wanted to show how the station worked, how these guys created jobs for themselves and how it was organized. There was a head of the station. All of these guys pay their dues; they pay fifteen dollars a month. That gives you the right to use that phone. People know that number, and they call up and order a cab. There were certain rules and things. One of the rules is that you can't drink. Otherwise they won't call your number. They'll call somebody else. There was a lot of competition in jitney numbers. There must be a thousand of them. There's a certain one—COURT-1-9802—which has been a jitney number for about forty-five years. If you go to Pittsburgh now and call "COURT-1-9802," you'll get a jitney. Certain stations have different reputations about whether they come on time or whether the drivers are honest or whatever. But I just want to show these guys could be responsible. They make jobs out of nothing. I think it is very ingenious. Then, of course, in that you had to get into the lives of the characters. It was an attempt to show what the community was like at the time. The important thing was for me to show these five guys working and creating something out of nothing.

Shannon: I found that the Vietnam War is looming, and it has a lot to do with the tone of the play. I went back to some lyrics by Marvin Gaye, "What's Going On?" and I find that what he is saying captures the essence of *Jitney!*
Wilson: That's interesting. That was the only song in the sixties—I used to get so mad at popular rhythm and blues of the day. With all the stuff that was

going on, Stevie Wonder was singing "My Cheri Amore," and the music isn't responding to what's happening except Marvin Gaye. I remember when me and Claude were together, I challenged him to go to the jukebox and find just one song, just one song that had any meaning and wasn't about "I love you. You love me. You done left me." And he went over there—he considered himself lucky to have found "What's Going On?" And I said, "You're right." I can see that that was the only one that I could recall. I think James Brown's "Say It Loud. I'm Black and I'm Proud" was also a very important song which we used in *Two Trains*.

I didn't make the Vietnam War as large a part of *Jitney!* as I could have. And I think it is personal because even though there was a tremendous number of blacks who were killed, that never, for me—there was only one person I had known through a friend of his up in the projects. Their son had gotten killed in the war, and they had a little wake on the lawn. There was the flag, and you went up and paid your respects. Those were the only marks of the war that ever actually touched me or my observation of that community. So it was not a large part. If it had been, then I think it would have become a larger part of my work.

Shannon: Like many other nationalists during the sixties and early seventies, you seem to have been affected by Malcolm X and his unfortunate death. I note that Malcolm X's death looms in the background of *Two Trains Running*. How does his symbolic presence shape the play?

Wilson: Well, it offers an alternative in the sense that in *Two Trains Running* there are three ways in which you can change your life. You have Prophet Samuel, Malcolm X, and Aunt Ester. Originally I was going to have someone who was representative of the idea of assimilation—cultural assimilation to American society and adopting the dominant values of the culture. But I couldn't find any of those characters who were willing to take that view. There were people in the community, of course, but not in my play. I couldn't make any of those characters. So that idea became lost. Originally I thought the rally was going to be a more important part of the play than it is—this Malcolm X rally that was looming over the play. Somehow it stayed in the background as other stories of the characters moved. So actually Aunt Ester has more impact on the play. Two of the characters do go up to see Aunt Ester. So she has more of an impact than Malcolm.

Shannon: At one point in your life, you seemed quite interested in the Muslim religion. What caused this interest, and how did the religion affect your view of the world?

Wilson: Well, I was always—as I think most black Americans—supportive of the Honorable Elijah Muhammad and the ideas. Most people who were sympathetic or simply supportive of his ideas would not join because of the discipline required of the organization. If I look at the Honorable Elijah Muhammad's program, there is the idea of self-sufficiency. The idea of doing for self is the idea that drew me even sympathetically toward him. My first marriage was over religious discrepancies, over the fact that I did not want to join, even though I was sympathetic. But I always had a tremendous amount of respect for him. There was a time after the breakup of my marriage when I went and joined the Nation of Islam in an attempt to save my marriage, which didn't work. So my relationship was such that I still respect all of the teachings, even though I can look at some of them—their attitudes and their feudalistic ideas about their relations with women always can be traced to Islam itself. But I think Elijah Muhammad is one of the most important black men that ever lived in America. I'd put him right up there with Du Bois because he was the one who had an idea. For instance, if you look at the criteria of culture using Maulana Ron Karenga's criteria of mythology, history, religion—we had all those things. But the one thing which we did not have as black Americans—we didn't have a mythology. We had no origin myths. Certainly Elijah Muhammad supplied that. So you could say that he contributed a lot to black American culture—the myth of Yacub, etc. These are things the culture was lacking, and they are forever a part of us. Now whether you agree or disagree, you could always say, "This is how the world started." So I think it's important, if for nothing else than that. I think the ideas that he propagated in the sixties are ideas that we're debating, and we still may emerge following those ideas.

Shannon: The short piece *The Janitor*, which I read in a recent issue of *Antaeus*, is brief but carries a profound message. Can you recall what inspired this work?

Wilson: First of all, I was a member of New Dramatists. They were having a fund-raiser, and they asked all the playwrights to write a four-minute play—not five minutes but a four-minute play. This was kind of difficult. How do you write a four-minute play? So I came up with the idea of the janitor who is someone whom this society ignores and someone who may have some very valuable information, someone who has a vital contribution to make, and yet you have relegated him to a position where they sweep the floor. They do it for some years, and never once do we think to say, "Hey, do you have anything to say about anything? Do you have any contribution to make other than being a janitor or running an elevator or whatever?" So in that sense we really do not take advantage of all of our human potential. And I look at how the Israelis are just absolutely delighted in the fact that they have close to a million Soviet Jews that are coming into the country, and they are looking forward to what those Soviet Jews have to contribute. This is a lot of intellectual power and intellectual potential that is coming in their country, and they're going to use that. And we're sitting over here with thirty-five million blacks who have a lot of untapped potential—thirty-five million. So there's the idea of not taking advantage of your potential. So I thought I'd show this guy here who is sweeping up the floor, and there's this microphone, and he just goes up and starts talking into the microphone.

Shannon: It seems to show that we're caught up in status also—that if you're not of a certain status, then you don't matter. This is dangerous.
Wilson: Absolutely. They're going to get all of these people at this conference to talk about youth—a conference on youth. And all of these people with academic backgrounds and status are not going to say as much in all of their days of seminars and conferences as this man has said there in five minutes. And that was my idea in the play.

Shannon: Can you talk about *Black Bart and the Sacred Hills*? What were you trying to achieve? I'm familiar with the story of Black Bart, the cowboy.
Wilson: This is what I call one of my zany characters. First of all, it is a musical, and it's kind of zany. It's a satire on American society. I have a character, Black Bart, who is a magician. He used to be a cattle rustler. He broke out of jail, and he carved this retreat called the Sacred Hills. And he's making gold out of water. He had the idea he's going to flood the world with so much gold that it was to be despised as "cockroaches in a sweet woman's kitchen." Gold is going to be utterly valueless.

Shannon: How do you put together a plot like that? Where do your ideas come from?
Wilson: I'm not sure. I did this from one Sunday to the next. And I think it was the idea of satire, and the most brilliant satirist I knew was Ishmael Reed.

Shannon: What was it about Black Bart that made you choose him as a character to build the play around?

Wilson: Well, I think Bart actually has his roots in Bynum and Holloway and all of these kinds of characters—many of their roots are in Bart. *Bart* started first as a series of poems in which this character named Black Bart was a magician, but he was also very philosophical—sort of like Holloway and Bynum.

Claude Purdy heard these series of poems and told me, "You should write a play with that character." Then I just started thinking, and the more I thought I came up with the idea of a multicultural satire on American society.

Shannon: Is that fairly long? Is that a fairly long script?

Wilson: It's about three-hundred-something—a lot of pages.

Shannon: I'd like to read that. I'm curious about the title of *Two Trains Running*. Does the title suggest that black people still have choices?

Wilson: I think so. That's very interesting. I've never thought of that. There's only two choices that I see. The question we've been wrestling with since the Emancipation Proclamation is "What are we going to do? Do we assimilate into American society and thereby lose our culture, or do we maintain our culture separate from the dominant cultural values and participate in the American society as Africans rather than as blacks who have adopted European values?" And I think that this is a question that, for the past hundred years, black America has been trying to figure out and debating which way should we go. On the surface it seems as if we have adopted the idea that we should assimilate, and that's simply because one has received more publicity than the other. But if you look at it, you'll find that the majority of black Americans have rejected the idea of giving up who they are—in essence, becoming someone else—in order to advance in American society, which may mean why we haven't moved anywhere. Because that's something— what I see is the majority of the people saying, "Naw, I don't want to do that. I'm me." And because they haven't adopted the values—these are the people in the ghetto; these are the people who suffer; these are the people with—I think white America needs to put some more pressure on in an effort to force them to the idea of assimilating and adopting cultural values and say, "Okay, if you don't do that, then you are going to suffer. And you can look at these people who are here and see that they're doing good. That could be you." They still say, "I don't care. I don't want to do that." They still say "No" even though they are suffering for it. If you go into the black community, you have the culture of black America still very much alive. They still practice the values that their grandparents had, with some exceptions, of course. For instance, black people—we decorate our houses differently. I've always said that I was going to get together some kind of multimedia presentation that will illustrate all these things. Because you can take black gospel and white gospel and put them side by side, and you cannot tell me that these are not different people. And then you take a black person's house and a white person's house—just the way that they are decorated. They have the same things now. They have tables, chairs, and a couch, but our couches got little mirrors on the side. This is what I have studied. I'm working on business cards. I'm collecting business cards, and I am amazed—not amazed. This just proves my point. Black folks will generally give you this business card that is very colorful and highly designed and, according to some white folks, would look amateurish. White folks always have these kinds of cards. I met a guy last night—Bernie Slain. You may know him.

Shannon: Bernie Slain?
Wilson: Yeah, he's got a radio show or a TV show. Bernie Slain. Anyway this guy has got a white card with a big yellow star in the center. And he had another one—this black one with big red letters, and it's got its own special symbols up here. This guy Bernie Slain obviously has a TV show somewhere, so he's doing all right. But still he hands out a card that looks like that.

Shannon: You say that there are differences and that black people ought to acknowledge them. It's not suggesting that one person is better than the other.
Wilson: Oh, absolutely not! It's white America who says, "Our way is better than your way. You're not acting right. You're not doing this right. You're not suppose to act like that." I had a line in *Two Trains* that I took out because it was in the wrong place, and I couldn't make it work there in the speech. He [Holloway] was saying, "It's not how you look; it's how you do. You do ugly. If you change the way you do, we'll let you in the game. Otherwise, you stay over there and suffer."

Shannon: Have you followed the Amiri Baraka versus Spike Lee controversy over the making of a movie on the life of Malcolm X? What are your thoughts about this issue?

Wilson: I think the whole idea of—it's only a movie. We're not talking about something that is going to affect the lives of thirty-five million black people in America. We're talking about a movie about Malcolm X. I think the real issue should have been made fifteen years ago when the guy bought the rights to do Malcolm X and how he sat on the rights to do Malcolm X for twenty years. He's had five, six different people write scripts for him. The guy, Marvin Worth, was simply afraid to make the movie. He told me, "You only get one chance." I said, "Yeah, but you got to take that one chance." My point is why did not Quincy Jones and Bill Cosby and all these people who now say "Malcolm"—why didn't somebody black go and buy the movie rights and say, "Hey, this is one of our icons. We don't want you to have nothing to do with this movie." It should have been in black hands from the beginning. That's what ruined his image. Ain't nobody talking about that. Norman Jewison was going to direct the film. I didn't hear one peep from anybody. I didn't hear Baraka then say, "Hey, a white man is directing a film of Malcolm." The only one that I know that said anything was myself and Spike.

Shannon: Well, it is kind of suspicious now with all of this media frenzy.

Wilson: I think Spike has the right to make whatever kind of movie he wants to make. The people are going to ultimately decide. It's the people who will go in there and say, "Yeah, that's Malcolm" or "Naw, that ain't Malcolm." Mao said, "Let a thousand thoughts contend. . . . The strongest idea will always dominate." So, if you don't like the movie, go make your own. That's what Ralph Ellison said. He said, "The best way to fight a novel is to write another one."

Shannon: You have some very definite ideas on the director's sensibilities in interpreting your work. If you care to elaborate, what is the status of your request that a black director be secured to direct the Paramount release of *Fences*?

Wilson: I said that I wanted a black director—which was from the beginning—I told Eddie Murphy that. Eddie Murphy said, "I don't want to hire anybody just because they are black." Well, neither did I, meaning that I wanted somebody who was black and talented. But I have since learned to look behind that phrase "I don't want to hire anybody just because they are black." And what, in essence, you are saying is that the only qualification that a black person could have is that they are black. "I don't want to hire anybody just because they are black." That means that's the only reason you would have to hire anybody is for their skin color. So when they say that, they just speak ill of everyone. All of those black directors in Hollywood and you say, "I want a black director," and they go, "I don't want to hire nobody just because they are black." I say, "Naw, hire them because they are talented."

Shannon: It suggests that there are no talented black directors.
Wilson: Yes, and the only reason he was going to hire them was that they were black. But they don't know what they're doing, but they are black. So I said when they had lined up Barry Levinson, who's a very nice man. I met with Barry. Barry wanted to do the film. And I went over to Paramount's office and I said, "I don't want Barry to do the film. He doesn't qualify." The qualifications were that he be black, that he had some sensibilities to the culture. This is a drama about the culture. It comes straight out of the culture. And in those instances, I think you should hire—If this were a film about Italian culture, you should hire an Italian director. This is common sense. Now if you have an adventure movie that's not specific to a particular culture, you can hire anybody to direct that.

When I was out there in Hollywood, a black director gave me a lesson. He said, "Man, let me explain something to you. I appreciate what you're doing by wanting a black director, but we've been out here for fifteen years telling these people it don't matter if we're black or not. We're trying to get a job directing *LA Law*, and we've been telling them it don't matter. A black person could direct *LA Law*. A black person could direct these sitcoms. We're trying to get some work. And finally they say, 'Yeah, that's true. Okay.' And they started letting black directors direct episodes of stuff that was noncultural specific like *LA Law*. Here you come along wanting us to say that it does matter. We can't say that." I was saying, "How come I can't get any help from the black directors? How come no black directors are stepping forth and saying, 'Yeah, the boy is right.'" And he said, "We can't say that because as soon as somebody says that, they ain't working no more. So I really appreciate what you're doing, but don't do us no favors."

Shannon: How have you most benefited from your collaboration with Lloyd Richards? What is the current and future status of your working relationship with him?

Wilson: Well, I will continue to work with Lloyd even though he is not at the Yale School of Drama. I've learned a lot about theatre just in the process of working with Lloyd. When I started, of course, I knew very little. I think one of the important things was when I got off the train in New Haven to go to the rehearsal of *Ma Rainey's Black Bottom*, I didn't know Lloyd as a director, and I didn't know how these things were going to turn out. And we went into rehearsal, and we read through the script, and the actors started asking questions. I'm all prepared to answer all these questions, and they ask a question about Toledo, and Lloyd spoke up, and Lloyd answered the question. Not only was it correct, but it gave me some insight. I said, "I didn't know that about Toledo." This went on, but from that moment I visibly relaxed. I said, "Everything's going to be all right. Pop knows what he's doing." It's been that way ever since.

Shannon: I know you said "Pop" jokingly, but do you have a paternal relationship with him?

Wilson: Oh, without question, without question. I think so. Yeah. I have certainly grown up without a father, and he is about twenty-five years older than me. So, yeah, I defer to him in that regard. And another way I look at it since I love boxing is that I am the boxer, and he is the trainer. He's my trainer: "My boy August will get them." So we have had this relationship recently. He'll say, "You've got to throw that left hook a little more." So obviously there is this mentor kind of trainer-boxer relationship. I look at it like that sometimes.

Shannon: Do you ever just marvel sometimes at just how coincidental it was that you and he got together? I mean out of the scripts that he could have chosen, he chose *Ma Rainey's Black Bottom*.

Wilson: Well, I think it's [the] kind of luck that you make happen. He chose *Ma Rainey's Black Bottom* because it was a good script. So that was important. If he hadn't been able to recognize it was a good script—the actual first reader of that script was Michael Feingold, who then passed it on. But then Lloyd recognized it. So that's the first thing. You sort of make luck happen. It almost didn't happen. These producers wanted to do the show on Broadway, and the Dramatist Guild's minimum for an option is $2,500 for a play, but they were offering me $25,000. At that time I was still making eighty-eight dollars a week cooking for Little Brothers. So I called Lloyd up and said, "Hey, I'm going to talk to these people over here." And Lloyd said, "Well, I can understand that." So we went on, and my agent started negotiating this contract with them only to find out six months later that they're talking about making a musical out of *Ma Rainey*. They want me to turn it into a musical. They sent me a contract, just a terrible contract. They had rights to bring in other writers, and I thought, "What's going on here?" And I'll never forget I called one of the guys up on the phone and I said, "Hey, I'm not signing this contract." He said, "Listen. It doesn't matter what the contract says. The important thing is for you to sign it and get to work. A lot of things in this business are done on faith." So I said, "Okay"—

Shannon: But that's hard to take though.
Wilson: —"If it doesn't matter what the contract says, let's make it say what I want it to say." Whereupon I was met with silence. So I called Lloyd and said, "Lloyd." He said, "August, how are you doing?" I said, "Fine. Are you still interested in doing *Ma Rainey*?" Lloyd said, "Well, yeah, but I just want to make sure that these other people—I don't want to step into any muddy water. I just want to make sure that you are through." I said, "I am definitely, absolutely through talking to them." He said, "Well, come up and see me," so I went up and saw him, and we agreed that he'd do it—to put it on that season—and he did it. Now, I guess that my point in all of this is that it almost didn't happen. I'm trying to say it's a happy coincidence, but it's also a coincidence that you make happen yourself at the same time because I could have gone with some other people, and I don't know what kind of crew I would have had. They could have ruined my script, turned it into a musical, and I would have been a one-shot playwright. Something told me—and I think it was the force of Lloyd's personality, his presence and who he was—that I would much rather be associated with this man than be associated with these other people. So I almost made a misstep, but I trusted my heart, and I went with Lloyd.

Shannon: That's interesting because it seems to be the history of African American playwrights to be "one-shot playwrights." And you came so close to that. What advice—what could one do to prevent that? And it doesn't suggest that they are not talented. It boils down to business sense it seems.

Wilson: It doesn't suggest that they are not talented. Of course, I was aware of this when I started writing plays. I looked at all of the highlights and everything, and I was determined that that was never going to happen to me. I said, "I'm not going to follow that road." So I asked around: "What happened to Lonne Elder?"

"Oh, he went to Hollywood."

"What happened to Joseph Walker?"

"Oh, he went to Hollywood."

Shannon: Charles Fuller.

Wilson: Well, Fuller is an example which comes later, but at that time I knew to stay away from that and because I was determined not to be a one-play playwright, I wrote *Ma Rainey*. Then I sat down and wrote *Fences* right behind that, so at the time that I am talking to these people about this thing, by the time Lloyd and I had agreed that we were going to do *Ma Rainey*, I was already on my way up to the O'Neill to do *Fences*. And so after thirty days— you had to wait thirty days after the conference—Lloyd said, "I want to do that one too." So I had a second one. If I didn't have a second play, I'd be still sitting around resting on my laurels, so to speak. But I was already working before we did the first production of *Ma Rainey* at Yale; we knew we were going to do *Fences* the next year. Then no matter what happened, no matter how that went, we were going to do *Fences*.

Shannon: Let me ask you this. How did it feel to have a play on Broadway? What were your emotions?

Wilson: It felt good (pause).

Shannon: But you always kept it in perspective.

Wilson: It felt good, but the theatre we were in—we were in a theatre that was on 48th Street on the left side of Broadway. So you have to go out of your way to get to that theatre. Now they have 44th and 45th Streets, two streets on which there are theatres on both sides. They will not put black plays in some of those theatres. I mean black audiences—all of the people have to rub elbows during intermission when they come out and stand on the sidewalk. And at the end of a black play, there's a whole bunch of black folks standing there rubbing elbows. Go up 48th Street, go up 47th Street, or 46th Street, but you don't get no 44th and 45th. So at the time—I mean it was tremendously exciting. It wasn't like my second play that I had ever gotten produced. It was nice to walk down there. It didn't have my name on the marquee. They don't put—they didn't have Lee Blessing's name on there when he did A *Walk in the Woods*. And I constantly recognized this because—they say, "Well, you've got to wait. It's your first time and all that." That's what they tell playwrights. But I think any playwright—first play, last play, or whatever—should have their name on the marquee identifying him as the person who wrote this play. If your name has no name value, they don't put it up on the marquee; they put the actors' names up there in big letters because it's a business, and that's what it's about. It doesn't matter who wrote the play. It doesn't matter whether the play is any good or not. If you can get a star in there to do the role, you're going to have people come see it. Geraldine Page is in this play. Jason Robards is doing a play that right now has gotten terrible reviews. Here's one of America's premier actors—can't find anything for him to do, nothing worth his talent. So he's in this—I mean the play got some really bad reviews. But people don't care. It's Jason Robards. They go to the theatre to see Jason Robards. They don't care if it's a bad play. So I had a lot of problems with it. They didn't put my name on the marquee; we're on the wrong street—

Shannon: But see I got no inkling of that. I just saw "Wilson on Broadway." That's what trickled down.

Wilson: Yes, but it was tremendously exciting to be there. When we were in Philadelphia prior to that, the cast was in a hotel right across from the theatre. I chose to stay in another one just because it was picked off a sheet. The point that I'm trying to make is that Theresa Merritt (who starred as Ma Rainey in the Broadway production of *Ma Rainey's Black Bottom*) gets locked out of her hotel room. They locked her out because she didn't pay her bill. She was staying in the hotel and had told them, "I'll pay you at the end of the week." They wanted her to pay night by night. And she said, "No, no, no. I paid you last week, didn't I? I've got to wait until I get my money from the company. I'm in this play, and I'm not going to come down here every night and give you fifty-nine dollars day by day by day." So one time she went up to her room, and it was locked. They had locked her out of her room. So they had to call in the middle of the night—it was about one o'clock in the morning—the general manager had to come down there and straighten it out. This is straight out of the play. We went up to her and asked, "Theresa, what did you do?"—which is the exact line that they say to Ma: "Ma, what did you do?" Theresa was livid. "What do you mean what did I do?" Anyway they got her out of there, and she went over to the Hilton, where they had put flowers in her room. The manager said, "Oh, here's Theresa Merritt! Here's flowers. Here's some fruit." He treated her like she should have been treated.

The company in New York was good, but I've got to tell you about when we made the recording of *Ma Rainey's Black Bottom* at Manhattan Records right there in New York in January 1985. The guy that's making—the producer of this recording. We arrived at his studio. He greets us with the words—and I swear to God this is exactly what he said: "You boys come on in. I've got some sandwiches for you." And we looked at one another and said, "This is a line from the play!" He doesn't even know it. He's really trying to be a nice guy. And sure enough he had some sandwiches there. And it's cold in the studio, and Theresa was late. And Theresa walks in and says, "Y'all want to make a record, you better put some heat on around here."

Shannon: She said that jokingly, right?
Wilson: Well, she said that knowing that it was a line from the play, but she was absolutely serious because the studio was cold. And the response was "We're working on it, Ma."

Shannon: Life and art. Of course, Ma Rainey was treated the same way in terms of hotel accommodations, hospitals, and things like that also.
Wilson: This is what I'm trying to point out. The heat never came on. They did bring an engineer up there who looked at the pipes or something and went back in the basement, but the heat in the studio—they recorded the whole thing in their coats, not only in their coats, but they were in their coats and still shivering.

Shannon: That's all so uncanny.
Wilson: The recording booth was nice and warm. I'm in the recording booth. Lloyd is directing the recording. These guys were out there freezing to death. And there's this guy standing around with a few other people. I didn't know who they were. There was this strange guy with this beard standing around. So I get ready to leave—I'm doing the liner notes. We agreed in my lawyer's office with the president of the company. That was one of my conditions. So I'm ready to leave, and I was with Claude, and I said, "Let me see when he

wants these liner notes." So I went back and said, "Mike, when will you need the liner notes?" And he said, "Oh, Mort's doing them." And he points to this guy named Mort Good. And I said, "I don't believe this. Now I'm Levee— Mr. Sturdyvant, you said you'd let me record them songs." And he says, "Well, no. Mort's going to do it." And then he says, "Mort's going to say some nice things about you." I looked at him like he was crazy. And I decided there is no point in me going off on this man and punch him in his mouth, hollering and screaming at him. So I went and called my lawyer and I said—I hadn't signed the contract at that time. And I said, "It's costing them $35,000 to record. It's a waste of $35,000, and I am not signing a contract." So I get a call from the president of the company. "You can do the liner notes. Of course. You know we agreed to that, and there's no problem. You can do the liner notes. And Mort is going to write a little thing on—" I said, "Mort ain't going to write nothing on there." I was adamant by this time that this man's name was going to be nowhere on that album. And see this comes from every blues album that I ever picked up has got liner notes that's done by some white guy. So here was my record, and I was ready to die before I let him. And nobody could see that this was the play being acted out in 1984.

Shannon: Did you have them to pay you in cash?
Wilson: (Laughs) One of these days I'm going to write a story about that. It's just totally unbelievable that this stuff is going on in 1984.

Shannon: That means that you are right on target with the subject matter of the play.
Wilson: And they did this stuff so innocently like "Oh, are we doing something wrong? We thought it would just be nice if Mort just. . . ."

Shannon: To date all of your plays feature men occupying center stage. How do you perceive women's roles in your work? Are you concerned that, so far, women have not been the focus of your plays?
Wilson: No, I am not concerned, and I doubt seriously if I would make a woman the focus of my work simply because of the fact that I am a man, and I guess because of the ground on which I stand and the viewpoint from which I perceive the world. I can't do that although I try to be honest in the instances in which I do have women. I try to portray them from their own viewpoint as opposed to my viewpoint. I try to, to the extent that I am able to

step around on the other side of the table, if you will, and try to look at things from their viewpoint and have been satisfied that I have been able to do that to some extent.

Shannon: I see that. That's the basis of the essay that I gave you—that the women are strong and that if somebody else perceives them as victims, I think that person doesn't read the plays carefully enough because these women choose their routes rather than become victims of men.

Wilson: Yeah, I would agree with that. I try not to portray any of my characters as victims. There was a line in *Two Trains Running* when they are tearing down the building and Memphis is talking about what his business used to be and how he used to sell four cases of chicken a week, but now he's down to one case. "But that's all right," he said. "I ain't greedy. I'll take that. Only they don't want me to have that." I took that line, "They don't want me to have that," out of the script because that makes him a victim of someone else who's doing something to him. They are not doing anything to him personally. It's not like they don't want him to have it. They're tearing down the building. So there was a little suggestion that he would be a victim. And I heard that, and I said, "No, no. I'm going to have to take that out."

Shannon: That reminds me of a conversation between two of the jitney drivers in the play *Jitney!* I think Youngblood is talking, and he's talking about them sending him over to Vietnam. He says, "The white man did it to me." And I think it's Turnbo, who says, "No, the white man didn't do that to you."

Wilson: Well, I try not to—

Shannon: He said, "They didn't know you were black when they sent you over there." And I think Youngblood comes back with the line "They knew I was over there when they were shooting at my ass. They knew that."

Wilson: It didn't make any difference if he was white or black when he was over there.

Shannon: Can you talk for a moment about the restaurant waitress Risa in *Two Trains Running*? What is the meaning of her self-inflicted scars? What inspired you to depict such self-destruction in an African American woman of this decade? What is the larger meaning of her wounds?

Wilson: Well, I wish that I could talk more about her than I can. For me the scarring of her legs was an attempt to define herself in her own terms rather than being defined by men. The closest that I could come up to what kind of psychological motivation that may have been was I think in Holloway's speech: "She makes her legs ugly. That forces you to look at her and see what kind of personality she has." That may be, but basically for me it was her standing up and refusing to accept those definitions and making her self-definition.

I think in almost every play most of my male characters have scars. Levee has a thick scar. Troy has a scar where he was shot. Loomis inflicts scars upon himself.

Shannon: Physical scars?
Wilson: Physical scars. Lymon has it in *The Piano Lesson*. Lymon lost half of his stomach.

Shannon: And Gabriel losing part of his head.
Wilson: Gabriel losing part of his head. The only scarification in *Two Trains* is Risa. Normally it would have been Sterling, but for some reason—People would ask me, "Man, have you got a scar on your chest or something?" It's just unconscious.

Shannon: I know I'm tempted to see some sort of religious parallel in it. I don't know with the nailing to the cross. I don't know. I may be reading too much into that.
Wilson: I'm not sure. It's unconscious whatever it is. But it's no longer unconscious because I recognize it although I didn't purposefully decide. It just emerges. For instance, I didn't decide that death was going to be part of the play. Once you get in there and you're working, you're not even thinking. You're working from another place. It's sort of like this stuff is given to you if you open yourself up for it, and half the time I just accept what I hear. When Boy Willie says, "Sutter fell in the well," I wrote it down. I don't know who Sutter is. But Boy Willie has said, "Sutter fell in the well." Now I've got to go back after I've started typing this and say, "Who is that guy that fell in the well? Who is he?" Then I go back and put it in or find something, but I don't question it when the character says it. Likewise, when Loomis cut his chest, I didn't question it. I just wrote, "Loomis slashes his chest." I didn't say, "Well, I

know what I am going to do. I'll have him cut his chest and—" I'm writing a scene—in fact, the last scene of that play I had not written, and it's December 1, and I had to have this thing postmarked by midnight, and it's about three o'clock in the afternoon, and I still have this last part of the play that's still not written. So I took my tablet, and I went to a bar, and I sat down. It took me about a half hour from the time I got there and a half hour later I wrote the scene. I will always recall this scene because I was sweating so. Sweat was just pouring off me. When I came out of that scene, I was drenched. I was soaked with sweat. I said, "I got it!" And I went home, and I typed it up, and at seven o'clock or eight o'clock I'm up there getting it copied so I can get it in the mail by midnight.

Shannon: I'm interested in the idea of being led by the characters and listening to the characters as opposed to manipulating and creating them. How does that work? How do you allow that to happen?

Wilson: Well, I think the key word is what you just said: "allow." You have to allow it to happen. In other words, I trust the characters. I've learned that if I just write down what I hear that the characters say, I have a premise; everything that they say is true. I don't have to use everything that they say, however, to tell the story. But the more I know, the more I know about the characters. The more they talk, the more I learn about the characters. Then I have the right to censor that and take parts. I know it's true, but I don't want to use that part. I'm going to use this part. So I just write down whatever they say without thinking. I started *Two Trains* with the line, "When I left out of Jackson, I said I'm gonna buy me a V-8 Ford and drive by Mr. Henry Ford's house and honk the horn. If anybody'd come to the window I was gonna wave. Then I was going out and get me a thirty-aught six and come on back to Jackson and drive up to Mr. Stovall's house and honk the horn. Only this time I ain't waving." Now when I wrote this I had no idea, and the character did not have a name. I had no idea who he was. But I started, and then it's like "Who is Stovall?" Why does this guy want to get this car and go by Stovall's, etc., etc.? So I more or less ask the character, "Who is Stovall?" And he says, "Well, I had this old farm down there, etc., etc.," and he started to explain the whole story about Stovall. Then, he started talking about Stovall, and then somehow he ended up talking about this woman who left him after nine years, and she wouldn't even shake his hand. And now I have a woman character, and I have to decide whether I am going to go to her and get some dialogue or whether I want her to be a character. Then I decided that I didn't want her to be a character and that I would just use Risa as a character, and you could see through his relationship with Risa some possibility as to why his wife may have left. And I thought Risa has to carry all of the women's stories in the play. Risa is the only woman who has to carry all of them and somehow make sense of certain things you know. But I just wrote down whatever—at some point I named him Memphis. I have a couple of short stories with a character named Memphis, who was a farmer—a sharecropper, down in Alabama—that I'd used. And I liked that name. It's the name of an Egyptian god, Memphis. Sterling because he's a sterling man. I knew what his name was before I ever wrote a line of dialogue for him, which is unusual. Most of the time I don't know who they are. If I'm writing and I don't know the name, I just put a little dash and keep on going. And so Memphis, and there's this guy who's talking back to Memphis. I don't know who he is. I put a dash.

Holloway's name was originally Brownie, but I had used a Brownie in *Fences*. Troy talks about Brownie. Brownie's kind of an Uncle Tom character, so I didn't want people to think that this was the same Brownie. So I changed his name. I got his name from a blues song.

Shannon: Now Hambone and Gabriel—do they have any relationship? They seem to be similar.

Wilson: I think so. In one instance, there is something that I call a "spectacle character." It's part of that. They are both mentally deficient. One has a war wound, which I think is most important. They make me mad when I read the reviews and they would refer to Gabriel as an idiot or some other kind of description without making reference to the fact that this man had suffered this wound fighting for a country in which his brother could not play base-ball. That was the important thing about Gabriel. Gabriel is one of those self-sufficient characters. He gets up and goes to work every day. He goes out and collects those discarded fruit and vegetables, but he's taking care of himself. He doesn't want Troy to take care of him. He moves out of Troy's house and lives down there and pays his rent to the extent that he is able. Yeah, there is some correlation between them [Gabriel and Hambone]. But they are very different in the sense that, one—Hambone has a much more important part in *Two Trains*. He has an effect on everybody's life in the play. He starts off as this guy who says, "I want my ham!" But he emerges as most important because of his life and his death. Risa has this relationship with him. Sterling gives him help. Memphis is throwing him out. Memphis can see himself, "I'm going back to Jackson one of these days." Well, that's Hambone. "Man been 'round here saying the same thing for ten years." Well he's [Memphis] been around for ten years too. He has to come to see that. So Hambone's presence, first of all, and his death affect the whole play, and then Sterling can resurrect and redeem Hambone's life by taking the ham. This produces the man of action. Without Hambone, you don't have a Sterling. And also it's the demonstration of his willingness to shed blood in order to get the ham. So when he comes back inside, it's very important that there is blood on his face where he cut his face, where he cut his hands. So it's the willingness to bleed, Loomis's willingness to bleed, the willingness to shed blood.

Shannon: "I don't need anybody"—what was it?
Wilson: "I don't need anybody to bleed for me. I can bleed for myself." There's also Boy Willie's willingness to engage Sutter in battle. He doesn't like say, "Oh there's a ghost," and run the other way. He went after the ghost whose presence is made known to him through this force field. Only he goes toward it as opposed to run from it.

Shannon: Absolutely. Troy's personification of Death through wrestling—
Wilson: He's wrestling with Death. In fact, when Troy got shot when he was trying to rob this guy, he fell forward. He said, "When the guy shot me, I jumped at him with my knife." So here's a man who has pulled a knife on somebody who could pull a gun and shoot him. He takes that, but then he comes forward and ends up killing him. So there's always that willingness to shed blood.

Shannon: Are you moved to write plays in the future giving women more voice?
Wilson: I always say whatever the material dictates, that's what I will follow. However, in the play that I am working on now, which was originally an all-male play, I looked up one day, and this woman had come on stage and sat down in a chair. The guys in the play said, "What the hell is she doing here? I thought you told us that this was an all-male play. What's she doing?" Then they started shouting, "Get out of here!"

Shannon: This actually happened?

Wilson: No, this was in my head. They said, "Get on away from here. Man, what she doing?" I said, "Hold up a minute. Let's go find out." So I went over and I asked this woman what she was doing, and she said, "I want my own scene." She just sat there, and they're shouting at her. These are crude men who were working. At first when she came in, she said, "Mr. Wilson said that I could come in." That's when they came and got me. And I said, "You want your own scene?" She said, "Yes, I want my own scene." Okay, I close my tablet up, and I'm thinking about this. In the process of writing this all-male play, this woman emerges into the play. Now I've got to figure out what to do with her—not only that, but she wants her own scene.

Shannon: Could that perhaps be the voice of a critic or two suggesting—

Wilson: No, it was the voice of this woman saying, "How are you going to write this play about these guys and not include me in it? I'm a part of it. They didn't get to be who they are without me, etc., etc. You can't ignore me."

Shannon: So that is part of listening to the characters?

Wilson: Yeah. That was unconscious. How could I write a play without a woman in there? That's what I was trying to do. She said, "I got a part in this story. You gonna write a play about blacks in America in the forties and ain't going to have no women in it? How ridiculous can you get!" I said, "Well, you are right." So then I opened up my pad and said, "Okay, you got your own scene." This guy knocks on the door. He had a radio under one arm and a chicken under the other. She knew his name and invited him in, and I closed up my tablet. Now I've got to figure out how I'm going to use that. What's happening is that it is emerging as my man-woman play, which is something that I have, at some point, included in all of the plays, but I never really focused on black man–black woman relationships. It was a big thing, but that's just not something that I chose. Maybe it's just something that I had been wanting to write for a long time. But it's not that I am crazy; it's just me telling myself, "Okay, you're ready to do this now." I think that I have acquired a certain maturity. So I think that all of that is possible.

Shannon: I've noticed that Pittsburgh locales in two of your plays in particular—*Two Trains Running* and *Jitney!*—are about to be demolished.

What does the imminent wrecking ball suggest in these two works? What does the city mean to your play?

Wilson: I set them in Pittsburgh I guess because that is what I know best. I think that a lot of what was going on in Pittsburgh was going on in Detroit, Cleveland, or anywhere black Americans were. So they actually could be set anywhere there is a black community in various cities. There's some peculiar kinds of things in relation to Pittsburgh. And that's what I know best. I couldn't set them in Cleveland because I don't know Cleveland, but you could transfer them to Cleveland and they would play just as well.

Shannon: In previous interviews, you've noted the influence of the blues, Romare Bearden, Amiri Baraka, and Jorge Borges. What or who influences you most now?

Wilson: I think that they are the same. The blues I would count as my primary influence. I've been more and more influenced by art, whether it is Bearden or any artist. It's the idea of the artist. It's the visual artist and how they think and how they approach a particular subject—what they want to paint about. I'm not sure that a writer can use the same approach as a painter, for instance. Even though the painter's tools are different—he's working with form and shadow and mass and color and lines, I think that there are some corresponding things in the tools of the playwright. In some of my characterizations, I use color. So I became more and more fascinated with painters. So Bearden has become more of an influence from art.

Baraka less so. Mainly the ideas that Baraka espoused in the sixties as a black nationalist—ideas that I found value in then and still find value in. Baraka's influence is not so much upon the way that he writes or his writing style other than the ideas of the sixties that I came through and improved a lot using that influence. Jorge Luis Borges, the Argentine short story writer—I was just fascinated with the way he tells a story. I've been trying to write a play the way he writes a story. One of his techniques is that he tells you exactly what is going to happen. He'll say the gaucho so-and-so would end up with a bullet in his head on night of such and such. At the outset the leader of an outlaw gang with a bullet in his head would seem improbable. When you meet the guy, he's washing dishes, and you go, "This guy is going to be the leader of an outlaw gang?" You know that he's going to get killed, but how is this going to happen? And he proceeds to tell the story, and it seems like it's never going to happen. And you look up, without even knowing it, there he is. He's the leader of an outlaw gang.

Shannon: So he doesn't spoil the plot by telling it. He sort of initiates suspense.
Wilson: Yes. The suspense is how is this going to happen? You know that this guy is going to get shot in the head, and it's so masterfully done that you don't see it coming. Even if you stop and say, "Okay, how is he going to get shot?" Then, there it is. It just unfolds itself. It is the idea of the discovery as to how it happens. See if you write a play like that, the audience will be just intrigued with trying to—So it's more or less in the play that I'm doing now, which is a murder mystery in which somebody named Floyd Bannister gets killed. There are all kinds of possibilities. Any number of people may have killed Floyd Bannister in the play. And then if you have a scene with Floyd Bannister in it, you go, "Hey, Floyd, you're going to get killed!" You know that about him, so you then have to look at Floyd in whatever relations he is having with anybody in the play. He gets into an argument with someone and you say, "Could that be the guy who killed Floyd?" because you know this. So then it becomes intriguing just sitting there trying to figure it out. But what most intrigues the audience is that you know he is going to be killed and he doesn't.

Shannon: It sounds challenging to translate that to the stage.
Wilson: Oh, it is. I'm just not sure how to do it. I haven't been sure of how to do anything other than when I started *Joe Turner*. I started *Joe Turner* as a short story. On page twelve of the story, I said, "You've got to write another play. Maybe this is the play." I said, "I can't make this story into a play. How am I going to do that?" So I wasn't quite sure how to do it. But the fact that I don't know how to do it is what makes it challenging. I say to myself, "If I can do that it would be quite interesting." I'll try anything. If it doesn't work, tear it up and start on something else. Writing is free; it doesn't cost you anything. There is nowhere where it says that five hundred words cost twenty-five cents or a dollar. They're free.

Shannon: Do you have a lot of incomplete projects lying around?
Wilson: Oh yeah. I've got all kinds of stuff—a bunch of stories, some plays that I started and abandoned. But all of that is important. *Ma Rainey* I

started writing in 1976. I actually wrote it in 1981, but I started a play called *Ma Rainey's Black Bottom* in 1976 and abandoned it because I didn't know what I was doing. So I've got parts of plays and stuff that I'd written, and all of this stuff proves useful. I may go back to it. I may ultimately go back to *Fullerton Street* and say, "Okay, how can I approach this differently—the same story in a different way now with what I have learned about playwriting?" So I don't consider anything a waste of time.

Shannon: That was your forties play—*Fullerton Street*? You've since decided to write another forties play, *Moon Going Down*. How is that going?
Wilson: Well, that turned into this play with this woman. Instead of being about all of these guys in a turpentine camp, this woman—and I always say if your idea doesn't change, then you're not writing deep enough because you start off with an idea that turns out to be something entirely different once you get into the actual writing process. Your writing more or less dictates itself. It has its own requirements. And this woman suddenly appears. Now I'm going to have to deal with her. If she's in her scene in her apartment, then maybe this play doesn't take place in a turpentine camp.

Shannon: Would it be kind of awkward to put a woman in a turpentine camp?
Wilson: Well, it might be possible. I don't know if that is the correct setting though for what I want to say at the moment, so I may end up having to abandon the turpentine camp idea. Only it may not be a turpentine camp in the forties. It may be a penitentiary in the nineties in which there is the same kind of situation. So the idea can change as it grows and develops, and it very often does change.

Shannon: You've made several geographic relocations since Pittsburgh. What motivated your most recent move to Seattle? How has the move affected your writing?
Wilson: Well, I haven't really written anything since I've been in Seattle, although I can write anywhere. I don't think that will affect my writing. I moved to Seattle because I got divorced. Seattle is a nice town. I had been there a couple of times, and it was as far west as I could get and as far away from New York as I could get. And I didn't know anyone in Seattle. I still don't know anyone in Seattle. That's fine with me.

Shannon: So it wasn't an aesthetic move?
Wilson: No.

Shannon: How have two Pulitzer Prizes affected you?
Wilson: Neither one has affected me. What it does is change the way people look at you, but it doesn't change the way I look at myself. What did I do? I wrote some plays. I wrote a couple of plays. I've been writing twenty-six years, and I've got a whole bulk of writing.

Shannon: I think that also has a lot to do with the fact that you are not a one-shot playwright. Sometimes you may rest on your laurels and not push yourself to go beyond that.
Wilson: Yeah, here again I've been a writer for twenty-six years, and it is what I have chosen to do with my life. Even behind *Ma Rainey*, I didn't just suddenly become a writer and pick up a pen and say, "Oh, I'm going to write a play." I had been wrestling with ideas and forms of writing and trying to say all kinds of things many years before. It's just part of being a writer.

Shannon: Have you seen the sitcom *Roc*? As you know the whole cast of the Broadway production of *The Piano Lesson* may now be seen every Sunday evening prime time. What are your thoughts on this transplanted cast and about the show?
Wilson: I like the show. Here again, it's a sitcom, and I think you have to approach it as that, which is the lowest common denominator. This is, after all, TV, and it's a comedy. They're concerned about advertisers. That's where they make their money. They're concerned about the ratings. So we're not going to get world-class drama. I think they did a good job. The only criticism that I have—first of all, it's constructive criticism—is that there is always in the episodes I've seen a moment in the plays that I would call a "sharp moment" when the comedy is suspended for a moment.

Shannon: When they deal with serious issues?
Wilson: Sometime the whole show can deal with serious issues, but even within that—. There's a moment where—I think one moment was when the father was talking about working on the railroad and some of the mistreatment everybody got. So the fact that you have those kinds of emphases on things is important. The criticism that I have is in regard to Joey, the character of Roc's brother Joey, who, as old as he is, is living in his brother's

house. His brother has this thing about wanting him to move out anyway. The father I can see living there, but Joey I think should be trying to find a way to get out of the house. Joey, who's a musician, but we have no indication of this either. Here again, there isn't any interest in his music. We've never seen him engaged with anything. I think the first episode when he came home, they had a gig, but the band broke up or something. And I think he should constantly be trying to put the band back together, and there are all kinds of humorous things and reasons he can't and reasons why he's still there. And he and Roc argue about him being there and have these comments. Then it becomes funny that he can't get out of the house even trying. Something always goes wrong. I think at some point, some episode, something should be seen. Otherwise, he becomes lazy and shiftless like white people seem to think of Joey: "Well, as long as I live here rent free on my brother and eat his food, I'll do that."

Shannon: That comes through loud and clear, though—that he is a parasite.
Wilson: They play this thing with the women with him. Joey is always with some woman. He walks in the bar—. You know, there is a certain responsibility that you have. In other words if there is a woman sitting at the bar and you go over and talk with her, you walk over with a certain responsibility. You can't just walk over and think, "You don't mean anything. You're just another woman. There's one over there too, so there ain't no difference in y'all." And that's what you get from that kind of portrayal. All he has to do is see a woman, and he forgets about everything else. And I think that another white attitude that they have is the way whites view black men.

Shannon: The writers are basically white.
Wilson: No, not necessarily. That doesn't matter. If the writers are black, then they're writing what the white man wants them to write. Still there is always some white person who, having set themselves up as a custodian to your experience, will tell you how to do it. The actors go to auditions and have these people tell them, "You're not black enough. You're not buoyant. Can you do it a little more black?"

Shannon: Sounds like *Hollywood Shuffle.*
Wilson: As long as white people maintain those positions, they can say—. Quincy Jones is not producing the show as an example; the white guy is. See,

it's all filtered through his sensibilities, and they may get some things right, but I think on the whole—.

Shannon: It's troubling. It's not easy to watch sometimes. Some episodes are troubling.

Wilson: What I absolutely cannot watch is *In Living Color*. And this is done by black folks. "Here we are. We go'n clown. We go'n act up." I haven't watched any more than sixty seconds of it.

Shannon: What are your goals beyond the ten-play cycle? What impact do you envision the cycle will have in years to come?

Wilson: Well, I don't know what impact it's going to have. I certainly hope it has one. At least you'll have a dramatic—my idea of a dramatic history of black Americans.

Shannon: It certainly is the first time that it's been done.

Wilson: Okay, but here again I stumbled onto that, and I'm glad I did because it enables me to keep a focus. Otherwise I'd have to come up with some ideas to write the plays; only I just have to think of the decade and then go from there. I think I prefer starting like that.

Shannon: What do you think about the current status of black theatre?

Wilson: I think, one, it's not institutionalized. The difference between white theatre and black theatre is that there are hundreds and hundreds of institutions that support white theatre. You can walk into any university, and they have a theatre program that supports white theatre. You have two-hundred-and-some-odd regional theatres in the country with budgets in excess of a million dollars. Only it isn't black. So you really have a lot of institutional support for what I call white theatre and nothing for what I call black theatre. The National Black Theater Conference, however, that they had in Winston-Salem, North Carolina—I was talking with some other people who were pleasantly surprised to find out that everybody did not know everybody that was out there. So that was the first time, in a long while anyway, that everybody became aware of everybody else. Of course, at the conference they talked about the idea of networking.

But I think after becoming aware of each other, the next question is developing an agenda that will carry you forward. I think what I really see a drastic need for is a conference of writers, some serious kind of conference at which we tackle the problems of writing. I would just like to see all writers get together and hash out some ideas more or less. I think it's time for that.

Shannon: Black writers? All writers?

Wilson: Black writers. All writers are important, but I would never try telling anyone what you have to write. You can be a black writer and write whatever you want. I would never tell anyone what to write. You can only write what you feel to write anyway. I don't want anyone telling me what to write. And that was part of the thing in the sixties. People were talking about the black writer's responsibility. A black writer's responsibility is whatever he assumes that responsibility to be individually. So you can't say you're not doing right because you're not writing this kind of material even though you're black. You may not want to write it. You can't be forced to write it. If they assume that as a responsibility, then you have the basis to sit down and talk about what that responsibility should be—"Did you ever look at it this way?" But you can't force on anyone a responsibility for writing.

The fact is that we have not been writing long. We're relatively new to this. We don't have a large body of literature that has been developed by blacks because at one time it was a crime to teach blacks how to read and write. Europeans have been writing stuff down for hundreds and hundreds of years. Blacks, coming from an oral tradition, didn't see the necessity to write it down. We just didn't do that. So we're in America. We've been here since the early seventeenth century, and we know that there is a value to writing things down. But still it is something that is relatively new to us. I think that if writers get together, then we could—I'm not talking about coming up with any manifesto. But I think there are some questions of aesthetics and questions of exactly how writers can contribute to the development of the culture, not contribute to anyone's polemic, not contribute to anyone's idea about what we should and should not be doing, but to the thing that remains the basis of our culture. "This is our culture. How can we contribute? How can we develop it?"

Shannon: I see that you are doing just that in your work.

Wilson: I have always consciously been chasing the musicians. You see their expression has been so highly developed, and it has been one expression of African American life. It's like culture is in the music. And the writers are way behind the musicians I see. So I'm trying to close that gap. That is one of the things I like about Bearden's art is that I think he moved art closer to where the musicians were. But they've always been in the forefront. I think writers need to consciously be aware how our expressions as writers achieve the quality of the musician's expression.

Shannon: What are some of your current projects?

Wilson: Well, I'm writing this play. I want to put out a book of poetry, and at some point fairly soon, maybe after I write this next play, I want to write a novel, which I've got about sixty-some pages to. I want to do that except that in writing the novel there will be ideas from about ten different plays in there. Maybe I should just write the play.

Shannon: From poet to playwright to novelist? Do you see the next genre as more of a challenge?

Wilson: It's a challenge because you see years ago I thought the novel is this vast uncharted sea, and never honestly could understand how anyone could write a novel until I discovered that you didn't have to have the whole thing in your head when you sat down and wrote. And now I can see how you write a novel. It's the same as writing a play. You discover as you go along. When you write chapter 3, you don't know what's going to go on in chapter 7, but the material dictates; it has its own requirements. And then as you write you discover all kinds of stuff, and the next thing you know, you're on chapter 12 without planning anything. It's just there as the story unfolds. A novel is simply more words. It's an entirely different medium, so you have a chance to go inside your character's head if you want. You can do description. That's probably one of the most exciting things about it—the fact that you could describe something, and in the process of describing it, you can choose the language that describes it. You can mix up that language and maybe describe a very familiar thing in a fresh way.

Shannon: You seem to be very elaborate in your stage notes, so it seems that the novel would be your opportunity to get that kind of description into the text—make it part of the text as opposed to being aside from it.

Wilson: Also I have a very strong visual sense that I don't too often get a chance to demonstrate, except when I did the film script for *Fences*. It was fun because you're telling the story with your eye as opposed to your ear. So, yeah. I'm looking forward to it.

Shannon: My last question is what are the chances that you will come to visit us on the campus of Howard University? I'd love to introduce you to my students and to show you the campus.

Wilson: The chances are good in the sense, as I'm sure you are aware, of the position that Howard University occupies in the history of black America. I would be delighted to come. The question is finding a suitable time, but I would be delighted.

The Historical Perspective: An Interview with August Wilson

Richard Pettengill / 1993

From *August Wilson: A Casebook*, edited by Marilyn Elkins. New York: Garland, 2000, 235–54. Copyright © 2000. Reproduced by permission of Routledge/Taylor & Francis Books, Inc.

August Wilson visited Chicago for the opening of the Goodman Theatre's production of *Two Trains Running* on January 25, 1993. He came by the theatre for this conversation, which took place on the lunch counter of the *Two Trains* set.

Richard Pettengill: In *Two Trains Running* you chose to keep the major historical events of the period offstage.

August Wilson: The play does not speak to the so-called red lettered events of the sixties, because at the time all of that was going on—the assassination of Martin Luther King and Bobby Kennedy and all the anti-war administrations, etc.—people were still living their lives. You still had to go to work every day, you still had to pay your rent, you still had to put food on the table. And those events, while they may have in some way affected the character of society as a whole, didn't reach the average person who was concerned with just simply living. And so in *Two Trains* I was more concerned with those people and what they were doing and how they were dealing with it, than I was with writing a "sixties" play.

RP: Did the title come first?

AW: The title came first. The title came from a blues song called *Two Trains Running*, and actually that phrase is in several blues songs. It's most commonly followed by the line "two trains running, neither one going my way. One running by night, one run by day." There were two ideas in the play, or at least two ideas that have confronted black America since the Emancipation, the ideas of cultural assimilation and cultural separatism.

155

These were, in my mind, the two trains. I wanted to write a play about a character for whom neither of these trains were working. He had to build a new railroad in order to get to where he's going, because the trains are not going his way. That was the idea when I started out exploring.

RP: And how did you view the two trains when you had finished?
AW: In this play there are actually three ways you can change your life, but one of those ways, Prophet Samuel, is dead, so that one is gone. So there's Malcolm X, symbolized by the rally, although he never became as important a part of the play as I originally thought he might. The other way is Aunt Ester, who became more important than I thought she was originally going to be. So from my original idea—that there was a character for whom neither train worked—I ended up saying that you need both Malcolm X and Aunt Ester in order to change your life.

RP: How did the characters evolve as you wrote?
AW: The characters, as I write them, they grow, they change. West, the undertaker, was originally a much larger role than he is now, somehow a more important part of the play. I was fascinated with the idea of the personification of Death, and moved him in from some of my earlier work. In *Fences*, for example, Troy wrestles with Death. Here I wanted to actually bring Death on stage; here he is in person, this undertaker with these gloves on. But when I began to write the play and work with the characters, a lot of that became unimportant to the story. What happened was that it became largely about Memphis at one point, and then it was more about Sterling at another point. And gradually it became really about Hambone, because he is the one character that affects everyone else in the play. He's the one character who, when he dies, changes things. There are some big changes. Sterling pretty much stays the same: he comes in, he knows what he wants, he knows what he's about. But I did not know that Hambone was going to affect all the rest of the characters in quite the way he did.

RP: Where did Hambone come from?
AW: I just this moment remembered that Hambone was a character from a short story I wrote many years ago, a man who refused to accept less than what he felt he was due. That turned into the character of Hambone, and it was a matter of placing him somewhere in the play.

RP: And Holloway?

AW: Holloway became the character that knows everything. If you say, "How long Ruffin been dead?," he'd say "Oh she been dead twenty-three years. Died right after the war." He'd say "Where you going? I'm going to get some cigarettes. What kind you smoke? I smoke Kools." He'd say "You can't go down over there, you got to go down over there. He charge two cents more than. . . ." Whatever the situation is, any question anybody has, he's the character who knows the answer. Consequently, in order for him to know the answer, Holloway's got to ask a lot of questions: "When she die? How long they been married?" I discovered in the process of writing the play that whenever you get stuck and you don't know where you're going, you just ask that character a question. You trust him and he'll tell you the answer. So a lot of the things that came about, a lot of the exposition, a lot of the things I found out about the characters, I got from Holloway by simply asking him. Once I had that character in the play, it became easier to write the other parts.

RP: Is Aunt Ester related to Bynum in *Joe Turner*, in that she helps people to find their song?

AW: It's all basically the same theme. Aunt Ester says it most clearly: you've got to return to your past. If you drop the ball, you have to go back and pick it up. There's no need to continue to run to the end zone, because it's not going to be a touchdown. You got to have the ball. It's a matter of reclaiming the past, as opposed to discovering who you are. I think we know who we are, but it's a matter of reclaiming and saying—irrespective of recent political history—that we come from a long line of honorable people.

RP: Memphis is certainly focused on reclaiming the past.

AW: Absolutely. That's why we can crystallize more on that character. He became the one who was the least complete without doing that. Having played by the rules, so to speak, and in the end up still losing the game, he said "Let me make up some rules, I'm tired of all of you making up the rules all the time. I got some rules of my own."

RP: Memphis's name links him to the South. Was that conscious on your part?

AW: It was, yeah. Memphis, again, is a character from a short story I was writing a long time ago. There's Memphis and another character from the

story, a woman character, name of Selma. These are both cities. Then, of
course, I've got Toledo in *Ma Rainey's Black Bottom*. That's not a bad idea,
naming characters after cities. Troy too. So Memphis for me is a special
name. I always say that if I had a male child, I would name him Memphis.
It's also an Egyptian God. I like the name a lot, I might even rename myself
that. (Laughs)

RP: Memphis owns the restaurant, but who runs it?
AW: Risa, without question. At some point I realized that nobody in that
whole restaurant can do anything without Risa. (Laughs) They can't exist.
It's Risa this, Risa that. There's a point in the play where Sterling talks about
"if you get fired" and she says, "I ain't worried about getting fired." Memphis
wouldn't know what to do without her, so there's no question of that. One
of the early questions I had was: why did Memphis's wife leave him? Then
I thought, well, if you just hang around here for a minute and watch how
he deals with Risa, then it will come to you why his wife left him. At some
point I knew why she left.

RP: I'm interested in the question of Risa's scars. Some Africans scar
themselves to make themselves more beautiful.
AW: (Laughs) That came from the same place as Hambone wants his
ham. It's just something that popped in my head. Starting out I knew that
Memphis's wife had left him, but I didn't know why, so I decided that his
wife was not going to be a character in the play and that the only female
character in the play was Risa. So I thought, Risa has to carry the wife's story.
She has to carry the story for all of the women mentioned in this play.

One of the large ideas that men and women wrestle with is the question
of self-definition: women define themselves in terms other than the terms
men define them in. Men see Risa as someone to sleep with, in terms of sex,
in terms of her body. The scars on her legs became a rejection of that definition. I don't think I pushed it as far as I could have. The reason is very
simple: I didn't understand it as well as I would have liked to. I think I was
just on the edge of it. So I resolved that I would explore fully, or at least more
fully, in my next play, the whole idea of male/female relationships.

RP: There's clearly more to her self-scarring than the explanation she offers.
AW: The only thing I knew was that I did not want a moment in the play
where you say O.K., now she's going to tell you why she did this. I don't know

exactly why she did it, so I couldn't have written the moment if I had wanted it. I had a couple of things earlier on that defined her more, but for some reason I took them out. This may seem odd, but I liked her flat, or flatter, than the men in the play. I thought it might make her stand out more, or call attention to her. It might make you wonder who she is and how she functions in that world with all of those men. I didn't have the space and time within the play to fully develop her character. And as I looked at her, she became more interesting being not quite fully developed.

RP: Wolf is another significant character name.

AW: Wolf is very interesting. It's real subtle in the play, but I think that the one thing Wolf is lacking is a male/female relationship; he cannot trust anyone. Wolf likes his women in the daytime, because he doesn't want to close his eyes. And I thought, how sad. He becomes one of the most defined characters because of that aspect. All through the play, he makes constant reference to that. And in his whole relationship with Risa, he's so intensely jealous of Sterling. In a sense, he's incapable of things which Sterling can do. He's incapable of trusting or even of loving, and he knows this. So as opposed to being a womanizer, he's almost the opposite of what his name would imply.

RP: He depends on the notion that if he dies, all the women in Pittsburgh are going to cry.

AW: It's all a sham, though. The idea is no one will want to show up at his funeral, no one's going to cry. That's his tragedy, there's no woman that's going to cry when Wolf dies. Maybe Sterling, maybe Memphis might pause and say "You know, Wolf was all right with me." But there isn't any woman anywhere so far in his life that is going to cry. So he goes, "when I die, every woman in Pittsburgh gonna cry." That's just braggadocio stuff, whistling in the dark. He defines his character in a simple stroke with a line like that. It's very poignant for me; it's just like, man, he doesn't have anybody. And then he watches Sterling come in and get someone.

RP: How did Aunt Ester evolve as you worked on the play?

AW: As I was writing her, somehow she became 322 years old. I asked myself: Can I do that, can I write a character that is 322 years old? I said, yeah, I can. If only one person in this play believes that this woman is 322 years old, then that's how old she is. Now, any thinking person will stop and think it's impossible for us to live to be 322 years old. So, let's say that Aunt Ester is a very old woman who claims to be 322 years old, claims to be ageless, timeless. In actuality, she's probably only ninety-seven. But she's old, and she's still alive; it seems like she's been here forever. Beyond that, of course, she represents the entire 349 years that blacks have been in America. She represents our tradition, our philosophy, our folk wisdom, our hobbies, our culture, whatever you care to call it. All of that is alive, and you can tap into it if you know where to go, what to say.

I find it interesting that Bynum, in *Joe Turner's Come and Gone*, has to pass a couple of tests. When he meets the shiny man on the road, the man asks him does he have anything to eat because he was hungry. Bynum didn't say "go get your own food, I just got an orange for myself." He gave the man an orange, and the man said to come and go along the road a little ways with him. You have to do all these things in order to be shown the wisdom. Sterling knows he's got to go back to see Aunt Ester. He goes back, she's asleep, and so he goes back again. If he doesn't go back the third time, he's missed it; he never has the experience of going to see Aunt Ester, and he never gets whatever it is she has to give him. You have to work to earn that, it's not just there for you. All that is what I was trying to do there.

RP: West doesn't earn the experience.
AW: Oh no, West, of course not, he values money over everything. I don't know why it's that way, but somehow the more money you have, the wealthier you are, the more important money becomes for you. The man in the play who is most capable of throwing twenty dollars in the river doesn't want to do it. The man who has two dollars, Sterling, says if he had twenty dollars, he'd throw it. He didn't even have twenty dollars to throw, but if he had it, he would. And when he got it, he did.

RP: What do you think drives Memphis, as opposed to Holloway?
AW: Memphis is a little different than Holloway. Memphis's got something to say about everything and he generally finds something wrong in everything. "People ain't doing this right, they ain't doing that right, this one ain't doing the other thing right. That boy ain't got good sense. Risa ain't cooking things right. This ain't going right." All the way through. "West cheating the people here, telling the people this." You name it, anything that comes up, he jumps right on it: Black Power, Vietnam. "I don't want that Malcolm X."

RP: There's a kind of rivalry between him and Holloway, which we see when they each tell the story of Hambone and Lutz.

AW: Holloway's telling the wrong story. Memphis always tries to straighten the person up if they don't know the full story: "That ain't how it went." Also, it's so easy for us to say, "Here's the white man mistreating black folks again." But it's much more interesting, I think, if you can see how that happened. Memphis says, "Lutz told him if he painted his fence he'd give him a chicken. Told him if he do a good job he'd give him a ham. He think he did a good job and Lutz didn't." So then Hambone goes, "How you doing boss? Yeah, good job ain't it? Where's my ham?" And Lutz says, "Nahh, I don't think it's a good job, take a chicken." That becomes more plausible than someone just trying to cheat someone out of a ham. I mean, who would do that? So the differences in the story become important in that regard; then you can understand that it's really just a misunderstanding and they're both stubborn men. It's just, "I want my ham. Take a chicken." Which one of them is going to break down? And of course the longer that went, I'm sure, the firmer Lutz's resolve got. Memphis says, "Lutz ain't gonna give him no ham . . . cause he don't feel he owe him. I wouldn't give him one either." Memphis would do the same thing. If he does not owe you fifty cents, he's not going to give you fifty cents. If he owed you he would give you. He pays his bills, he pays Risa her due. There's not even a dispute about the three dollars, he takes her word. "I told you I put the three dollars back. . . . Well here . . . take this. . . ." But if he don't owe you, you not gonna get it. And that's the way Lutz is. Lutz don't owe him a ham. He ain't gonna pay what he feel he don't owe.

RP: Once Hambone dies, there's a sense of lost opportunity.

AW: Oh yeah, without question. Holloway's the one who lays out why Hambone might have more sense than you or me, but even though Hambone's having a hard time with people in life, most everybody lets down a little after his death. Once he's dead, he can't get his ham. Lutz can no longer suddenly break down and give him his ham. It's impossible, because he's no longer there. Suddenly they feel the loss, what his death means. Everyday he goes by without his ham, and the possibility always exists that he might one day get it. But when you remove that possibility, it becomes evident to everybody that he never got his ham. I think that's the sense they feel.

RP: Would you want to encourage audiences to keep open the idea of two trains when thinking about the play . . . different possibilities for interpreting that title?

AW: Oh yeah, sure, and they have to be aware of the choices that we as black Americans need to make. We've been debating an idea for maybe sixty or seventy years now, and I think it's time we have really intensive debates and make a decision to go down one of those roads or the other. What I have discovered is that the people ultimately will decide. You cannot force a solution. The people as a group will decide that this is the thing to do, just like most of us ended up in the North. We all originated in the Southern plantations, but somehow we live all over the United States . . . as far as Seattle, of all places, which is where I live. Somehow that was the right thing to do, to leave. So I think people ultimately will decide. It may be this generation who decides and moves collectively in one direction or another.

RP: You've said before that African Americans have made some incorrect choices, referring to their leaving the South. What should they do now?

AW: Well, I think we need to make an honest assessment, an analysis, of where exactly we as a people are. I think if we do that, we'll find out that we're in a worse position in American society in 1993 than we were in 1940. If you look at the black American communities in 1940, when we were operating under the idea of separate-but-equal, we had communities that were economically viable. You couldn't play in the white baseball league, so you started your own, you had a Negro baseball league. This Negro league had black owners as well as black players. And on Sunday, the people in the communities got together and went to the ball park. They paid their two dollars and they watched the ball game and they cheered. Mr. Smith sold his peanuts, and Mr. Johnson sold his chicken sandwiches. But then once you say, "OK, you guys can play in the white major leagues," you no longer have a Negro baseball league and you no longer have a Negro community. It's the same thing with businesses. When black women could not go into the department stores downtown and try on dresses, then they had a store in their own neighborhood that was black-owned. Once you say, "OK, you can go downtown now," then you no longer have a store in your neighborhood.

If we begin to make an honest assessment here, we will find out that we are in a pretty bad position. What we should do is to return to our ancestral homeland in the southern United States. If five million people were to move to, let's say, Alabama or Georgia, that's five million people that suddenly have to be fed. That means someone's going to have to own some supermarkets. That's five million people that need to be housed. Who owns the lumberyards? Just in the process of providing food, clothing and shelter, you create jobs for yourself. Then you begin an economic base. You build houses for five million people, then you take all that money and open you up a bank. Suddenly, we're talking about hundreds of millions of dollars here, just in lumber.

We do not have a relationship with banking capital, which is primarily the reason we are in the conditions that we are in. I walked down here today, in downtown Chicago. I thought I was in a city that was approximately 50 percent black, and yet everything I see is owned by whites. Every single thing. All these buildings are owned by whites. The post office is owned by whites. Every single thing, every business that you walk by, every building, every house. They own the river. There's nothing that you own. Truly you are an outsider. And it should not be that way. Maybe we could own a couple of things. Saks Fifth Avenue, that's ours. Lord and Taylor, that's ours too. You can't own them all, but in fact white people do. Suppose these five million people move down to Georgia. Then we could build a Saks Fifth Avenue or a Joe's Fifth Avenue or a Joe's Fourth Avenue which is black. Nike shoes? Why don't we own basketball shoes, why don't we own the basketball team, the basketballs? If five million people moved down South and you began to own at least something, the houses you live in, the supermarkets, food, shelter, and clothing, then you move from there, you begin to vote. You register to vote the first day you get there. You could get a couple of black senators. Then the Senate will, in turn, represent you. Let's say you elect a governor of the state of Georgia. If the state of Georgia is 70 percent black, then the resources of the state go to whoever lives in the state, be they white, black, or Chinese. The resources of that state are used to further the life of those people. So this 70 percent, we tax ourselves. Hey, we're raising taxes today. Sales tax 9 percent. Somehow you don't mind paying sales tax if you see that it's coming back to you in some form or fashion. You can cuss the governor out if you want to, but you'll pay your 9 percent. You'll see it show up; they don't just clean the streets in the white communities now. Now we can have street sweepers every week, matter of fact we can get together and vote on twice a week. If that was the situation here, the city of Chicago would be entirely different. All these buildings and all these things generate money and jobs, and none of it ever goes to the black folk that make up approximately 50 percent of the people that live here. Just imagine if 50 percent of that went to the Negro . . . overnight he would be in an entirely different position. The proof of this is if you look at the Saudi Arabians or the Arabs fifty, sixty, seventy, eighty years ago before the discovery of oil, and all of a sudden they were doing OK. They discovered the oil, you see. It's the same kind of situation.

I think we should all go back. We should all move tomorrow, while we still can before the government says we can't. We should move down there and register to vote, elect ourselves as representatives within the framework of the Constitution of the United States of America, and begin to provide do-for-self food, clothing, and shelter. I think if we did that, fifty years later we'd be in a much stronger position in society than we are today. If we continue to stay up here in the cities and go along the path that we're going along now, I'm not sure we're going to be here fifty years from now.

RP: Do you feel that there's an actual chance of this movement coming about?

AW: I think the people will discover that themselves. The people will say, "Why don't we go on back." It may already be happening as we sit here. Maybe we just need to spur them on a little bit. The fact is that we came up North around 1915 through 1940. It wasn't overnight. If we did it then we can go back now. Why not? This time the people going back are much different people. We're more educated people. We're more politically sophisticated people. I think if we go back, we'll have a lot of things to offer. When the Soviet Jews were migrating into Israel, they were welcomed with open arms by the Israelis because they were bringing skills, knowledge, and services to them. It strengthened their country. We have human resource and potential, and we waste it; we should begin to utilize it for ourselves. As Africans in America, we are the most educated Africans on the planet Earth. We have doctors, lawyers, hydraulic engineers . . . you name it, there are black people in the United States of America who do it, and the only difference is they work for white people as opposed to working for themselves. If you put all these skills together, then you're going to have doctors and people who know how to build houses and who know how to build machinery and construct factories and things of that sort.

RP: Do you see a movement in a place like Atlanta toward black empowerment?

AW: I think so. I think you will find that more in Atlanta than in some of the other places. If you could duplicate Atlanta in D.C.—or Chicago for that matter—it would be very interesting; Atlanta remains a kind of beacon of light in that regard. But if you triple the black population of Atlanta, then you have that much more potential; it doesn't have to be in Atlanta, it could be somewhere else. Let's have a bunch of Atlantas all over—why not! We're thirty-five million people.

RP: To return to your writing, what have you been working on since *Two Trains*?

AW: I'm writing a play called *Seven Guitars* which is set in the forties. It's a murder mystery of sorts about a guy named Floyd Barton. He used to be Floyd Bannister until someone told me there was a baseball player named Floyd Bannister, so I changed it to Floyd Barton. I hope there's not a football player named Floyd Barton. It's a murder mystery in the sense that by trying to find out who it is that killed Floyd Barton, we have to look at Floyd Barton's life, the social content of his life in Pittsburgh in 1948. The idea came, again, from a short story I wrote about a guy who was killed. By going through all the boxes of papers in his room, you discover who he was simply by looking at the contents of his life. So that's what I'm doing, and the play is a flashback within a flashback within a flashback. It's like a Chinese box where you suddenly discover it's a flashback, and when you discover where you are, that turns out to be a flashback too. So eventually we arrive at a different place. Beyond that, all the male characters in the play are blues musicians. It's about their relationship to society, to white society and to black society. Whereas in black society they are carriers of the culture, a very important part of everyday life, in white society they are vagrants, drunkards, they are constantly harassed by the police, they've no visible means of support, they're in and out of jail, etc. So there are two different values at work here. The play is about blues musicians, one of whom is Floyd Barton, who has been murdered. But it's really unimportant as to who killed him. It's more important to find out what's beyond that, about male/female relationships. We see Floyd Barton and his relationships with various women in these flashbacks.

RP: Two years ago you spoke of this play as a series of short vignettes. Did you abandon that idea?

AW: I abandoned that idea, but I haven't abandoned that idea. That now belongs to another play. This one, as I worked on it, began to change. I've always said that if it doesn't change, you're not writing deep enough. So it changes and becomes something else. The idea of those little five-minute set pieces, I think I'm going to return to them.

RP: You'd also mentioned working on a play called *Moon Going Down*.

AW: That's become less of a project, primarily because I don't know anything about turpentine camps. I don't know why I got the idea of doing that. I always thought it would be fun to do an all-male play at a turpentine camp. I may do it one day. But it would have to be after I found out what a turpentine camp was and exactly how turpentine was made.

RP: We have learned a great deal from you over the past decade, through the plays. I'm curious to know how you feel your own perspective has grown over this period. And how do you view your earlier work from this vantage point?

AW: My views change every day in the sense that there are a lot of things that influence you every day just in the process of living. You hopefully become wiser, you gain more insights. As you get older there are some things that you can see more clearly than you could five years ago and certainly more clearly than you could twenty years ago. I'm the kind of person who likes to look back—I benefit from the historical perspective.

I can see myself as a young man, when we were trying to alter the relationship of black Americans to the society in which we lived. One of the ways of doing that, of course, was to get some power, and also to alter our shared expectations of ourselves. But one of the things I realized as I was writing *Two Trains Running* was that we had isolated ourselves from the Sterlings of the world. We isolated ourselves from that energy. Somehow by trying to speak for the people we got way out in front of the people and left the people behind; we forgot to follow them where they were going. It was a romanticized vision; it was part of being young, part of youth. We were all twenty-three, twenty-five, all young men engaged in a society. What I would hope is that young men today are still involved in trying to alter their relationship to the society which now, more than ever, needs to be altered.

This is all to say that I enjoy the historical perspective. So therefore, after having written *Two Trains Running* and now working on *Seven Guitars*, I can look back and what becomes clear to me is how odd *Fences* is. It's the odd man out, so to speak. If you pull *Fences* out, a more natural progression of my work would have been from *Ma Rainey* to *Joe Turner* to *The Piano Lesson*. And yet *Fences* can also be the fulcrum, the centerpiece, the thing upon which everything turns. In other words, if you're fashioning a chain or something, I'm not sure that *Fences* should necessarily be the odd man out. Maybe we need another similar kind of play that would balance it or complement it.

RP: What was the particular challenge in your mind as you attempted *Fences*?
AW: Well, when I first went to the O'Neill with *Ma Rainey*, some of the playwrights and other people at the conference thought I was trying to write an autobiographical kind of *Ma Rainey*; they felt Ma Rainey should have been more involved in the play, but I said, no, no, I didn't want to do that. I wasn't trying to write a play where you had one big central character which all the things revolved around. I know how to do that, I said, and that isn't what I wanted to do. So I went home afterwards and I said to myself: now that you were telling all these people you know how to do that, do you really know how? And I said, yeah, I think I do, and I sat down and wrote *Fences*. The challenge was to write a play that had a central character which was in virtually every scene, and the whole play spun around him. You could almost call it *The Life of Troy Maxson* or just *Troy Maxson*, but that would have been a bit pretentious; it just didn't work for me. My challenge now would be to write another one, to find a character that is as representative of black America in the eighties as Troy was in the fifties. I don't know who that character would be, but having found that character, then I think the more you know about him, you just put him in every scene. Have the events of the play surround and involve him and put in all the stuff you're supposed to do, like his growth and changing fortune or whatever. I'm not sure of all the rules, but you just intuitively find your way through to the ending.

RP: It seems to me that there is less attention in *Fences* than in the other plays to questions of Africa, identity, heritage.
AW: Yes, I'd agree. But these Friday night after-work rituals that Troy engages in have a particularly African American bent to them, though it was less so

than the bones rising out of the ocean in *Joe Turner*, or the ghost in *Piano Lesson*, or Aunt Ester.

RP: Looking back on *Ma Rainey*, what comes to mind?
AW: I think *Ma Rainey*, the more I think about it, is probably my boldest play, structure-wise. *Joe Turner* is my favorite, but *Ma Rainey* starts to nudge out some of the others, coming in second place. Maybe it was all fresh to me then.

RP: Lloyd Richards has said that when you started out with *Ma Rainey*, it was two plays.
AW: Well, I started the play in '76, but at that time I didn't know how to write the male characters. Then by '81 I felt I could, so I started working with them and my tendency was to leave Ma out. I told my friend Claude Purdy that I'm planning on dropping Ma and having the play be about the four guys in the band. But he said no, don't do that, keep Ma in there. So the challenge from that point became how to blend the earlier parts of the play that I wrote in '76 with the parts with the four guys in the band room. There was this one moment, which for me was a crystallized moment (the audience probably didn't notice it) when Ma goes into the band room. She entered that space, and for me that was the moment that wedded those two plays together. Up until that point, as long as she stays in the recording studio, it was two different plays. But when she walks in that band room it was just like inserting the key in the lock, and the play was joined from that point on.

RP: Why is *Joe Turner* your favorite?
AW: I think because it is a large play in terms of the issues and things it deals with: large issues like the question of identity and spiritual isolation and spiritual discovery and redemption. The bones rising out of that ocean—when I wrote that I thought, okay that's it, if I die tomorrow I'll be satisfied and fulfilled as an artist that I wrote that scene. I think you can go a lifetime and not arrive at that scene which for me crystallized everything, because it was a symbolic resurrection of those Africans who were lost, tossed overboard during the Middle Passage, and whose bones right now still rest at the bottom of the Atlantic Ocean. It was like resurrecting them and marching them up on the ground and walking them around in Chicago right now. I'm not sure that anything I've written since then has crystallized as clearly

what I wanted to say. With Loomis in that one scene, the defining moment, I found a way to crystallize that by having him slashing his chest. He was willing to bleed to redeem himself, because redemption does not come outside yourself. "You want blood? Blood make you clean? You clean with blood?" That one moment in which he becomes luminous, there's certainly not a moment like it in any of the other plays. So I think for all those reasons it's my favorite.

RP: The movement toward finding an ending to *Piano Lesson* was a long one, wasn't it?

AW: That's because I was stubborn, I think, and hopefully I learned something there. I didn't want to say what happened to the piano, because I didn't think it was important. But the audience, as I discovered, wanted to know, and they felt it was very unfair to sit there for three hours and not find out what happened to the piano. I always knew what happened: it was just a question of keeping the lights on for another two minutes at the end. Then we could see Boy Willie come down and say that he was leaving because Berniece had found the one perfect use for the piano: to exorcise Sutter's ghost. Then there was no way Boy Willie could take that piano. Up until that moment it was his piano, he had every right to take it until Berniece found a use for it. I always knew that, but I just didn't tell the audience. I'm wondering about that now as I'm getting into *Seven Guitars*, with the question of who killed Floyd Barton. I said earlier that it's really unimportant who killed Floyd, but I don't think I can set up this play and then tell the audience well, you know, you really don't want to know who killed him. I may have to figure out who did it and tell the audience.

So that was the problem with the ending of *Piano Lesson*, and also there was another problem: you have an ending that is supernatural in that here's a man wrestling with a ghost. In film you might be able to show that a little better. At one point we had pictures lining up in the backdrop which were the ghosts of the yellow dog. I think we should have stuck with that idea, but with like two thousand pictures, so that it becomes every man. When Berniece is calling out the names of her ancestors, Papaboy Charles and Mama Ola, I always wanted people in the audience to toss out their grandmother's names, somebody *they* were calling on. I could just see this thing building, with more and more people shouting out things. Berniece's playing the piano, Boy Willie's wrestling with the ghost, she's calling, "Mama

Ola, Papaboy Charles," and somebody in the audience is saying "I love
Betty Smith." I thought if you could actually do something like that it would
be great. Anyway, I was being stubborn and resisting the idea of saying
what happened.

RP: Looking back at *Piano Lesson*, having finished it, what do you feel you
achieved in that play?
AW: I don't know if we achieved anything beyond raising questions: What
should we do with our legacy? What would you do if this was your piano?
What is our future? Why do we stay up here and let Boy Willie go back
down and get some land, something under his feet?

   Boy Willie empowers himself. He has a very good clear plan, the best
plan of anyone I know that was presented in 1936 about his future. He
understood that if you had a piece of land, everything else fall right up into
place. You can stand up right next to the white man and talk about the
weather, the price of cotton, anything else you want to talk about,
economics, politics, whatever it is. Then you can stand and look around.
Land is the basis of independence. People all over the world fight about
what? They fight about land. Here's a man who says, "Just give me a little
piece of land and I'll be satisfied, I'll build me a future with it. I can always
get me another piano. With that cash in my pocket I'll get me six pianos;
if that piano can help me get some land, let me get my land." It's just a
question. Maybe he was right, maybe he was wrong, but I think the play
stated the question clearly.

RP: Back to *Two Trains*, Lloyd has mentioned that finding the end was not
the problem, it was finding the middle.
AW: I had the ending before I had anything else. After having wrestled with
The Piano Lesson ending, I thought, well, I've got an ending here; Sterling
taking a ham and bringing it to West. Then it was a matter of working
backwards. I knew how it was going to begin, with Sterling coming in. What
I wanted to do was set up this situation, this environment, and show you
what that was like, and then have this new force come into that environment—something new to which everything in that environment had to
adjust. So I had that and I had the ending, but how you got from there to
there I wasn't quite sure. I didn't know what was going to happen with
Sterling and Risa. I didn't know what his and Memphis's relationship was

going to be. I didn't know if they were going to end up killing one another or what. I just knew this man was coming—he'd just gotten out of the penitentiary—into this environment, and he was going to cause everyone to respond to him. And the upshot of it is he's going to end up taking this ham and giving it to the undertaker. What his relationship with the undertaker was, I didn't know, I just knew it was the undertaker. I'm not even sure I knew how Sterling related to the play. So I think that's what Lloyd means— the middle was a question of finding all of that. In the first draft it was not clear, and I had to go clarify some of the steps to be taken to get to him bringing the ham. But I always knew that Hambone would die, and that Sterling would get the ham. Those are the things I knew. And even after we started rehearsal, it was a matter of how do we clarify this, and how do we get there? What happens after he hits the numbers? Does he get paid? Does he go up and confront them? How is this reported? Those kinds of things were on the page, but they still had to be clarified. The parts that obscured things just had to be cut, and it became cleaner and clearer. So that was the thing about finding the middle. But listen, I'd love to find the middle any day as opposed to trying to find the end. Give me a beginning and an end, and I'll find the middle; it's a much more enjoyable process.

Men, Women, and Culture:
A Conversation with
August Wilson

Nathan L. Grant / 1993

From *American Drama*, 5 (Spring 1996), 100–22. Reprinted by permission.

In a very short time August Wilson has left an indelible mark on the American stage. The recipient of many awards for his work in theater, including two Pulitzer Prizes, one for *Fences* (1986) and another for *The Piano Lesson* (1990), Wilson continues his weave of the African American experience through a larger and sometimes hostile American culture with his newest play, *Seven Guitars*. I caught up with Wilson in Seattle's Capital Hill district; politics, theater, and of course, coffee, were the order of the day. The date was April 26, 1993; he was in the middle of writing *Seven Guitars* and the characters had just begun to speak to him. What follows is a colloquy about African American culture, American sexual politics, and how these and other issues move through his stagecraft.

Grant: In *Fences*, Troy Maxson lives desperately on one side of a time line—the difference between segregated and integrated baseball. Are there other time lines that black folk have to reconcile?
Wilson: It's the line of slavery, slavery and emancipation. We're all living on a side of this time line, all black folk in America.

Grant: What makes Troy heroic? He's an ex-con, ex-baseball player, now a garbage collector; he exploits his brother and cheats on his wife—what is redeeming about him as an African American man?
Wilson: I think that, for me, this may be nothing more than his willingness to wrestle with his life, his willingness to engage no matter what the circumstances of his life. He hasn't given up despite the twists and turns it's given him. I find that both noble and heroic.

Grant: Troy was "young and anxious to be a man" when he met Rose. Is there something specific about time or anxiety that speeds black men along?
Wilson: No, I don't think so. I think that when you're grown, you're grown. You feel the need to exert your manhood; I don't care if it's at fifteen or twenty-seven. When it happens, it happens. Some people are forced; I mean, for instance, the conditions under which Troy grew up and the conditions under which he lived. He was forced at fourteen to become a man, to take care of himself and do all the things that normally your father would do. So in that sense, it may have been necessary for blacks to grow up a little bit quicker.

Grant: But both the young Cory and the young Troy seem to step into manhood when their fathers have fallen. How do you visualize that for the stage?
Wilson: I'm not sure, other than to say that you got that from the play. [Laughter] I think that's kind of interesting—I never looked at that, but I think that when all humans, when your back is to the wall and you're forced to do something, then you find out what your measure is. So if you don't have a father, then you're forced to become a man without that guidance, and you simply do it.

Grant: I guess what was behind that question was whether that is what black men need to be men—do they need to have an Oedipal moment of truth with Dad as a demon to be conquered or to be found wanting?
Wilson: I'm not sure. I guess both Troy in this story and—the thing there for me would be the fact that all these many years later the cycles come into play, from Troy and his father, to Troy and his son, and possibly, Cory to *his* son. I don't know exactly why that is.

Grant: One could say that different elements of black masculinity come across in the Pulitzer Prize winners. Troy is rageful and defiant, like a Stagolee; Boy Willie, more of a trickster figure. Is that part of the particular success of these plays—their atavistic recreations or recolorings of black masculinity?
Wilson: I hadn't thought of that either, actually. But first of all, I think all of the plays have been successful in the sense that they are, finally, honest. It may be a question more of timing than anything else in terms of those plays being Pulitzer Prize winners. Although it's interesting that they both have that aspect . . . no, I don't think so; *Joe Turner* would be right in there with Loomis.

Grant: But Loomis doesn't realize himself really until the end, whereas Boy Willie—

Wilson: Oh, yes, I see what you're saying. I hadn't thought of that either. It's just been important to me that they be vivid male characters.

Grant: Since you set your plays in the past, does this cast light on the present in some way? Is the present thus its own proscription against what black men *shouldn't* be?

Wilson: In many ways, I think it is. I've said in the past that given the benefit of historical perspective we're able to see someone like Boy Willie with his plans in 1936 going down a particular road, and you want to say, no, that's not going to happen that way. We know that now because these are the 1990s, so if you look at where are we in relation to where we're going to be—in other words, if this is 1936, can't we do some projection into the future as we can into the past to see where it is that we need to go. I think that the one question that blacks have been asking since the Emancipation Proclamation is whether we should continue to develop our own cultural values separately or integrate into American society and adopt its values. We're trying to figure out how we're going to play this game, how we're going to fit into American society. And there are some who say, let's just integrate, and others who say that the values of their grandparents and rituals of social intercourse they developed and passed on are valuable and not worth giving up for someone else's idea of how to live in the world. If you look at the situation in 1993, and if you can look backward, there should be some clues to what we should be doing for the future.

Grant: Given what you say, then, what about Boy Willie? *The Piano Lesson* is set in 1936, that's two years before Scottsboro—he wants to sell off a part of his history even though he doesn't know that Scottsboro is going to be the issue that it is.

Wilson: First, I feel compelled immediately to correct something and that's that he doesn't want to sell off part of his history. Quite the contrary. Boy Willie, not his sister, is the one who embraces his history. He's not afraid of the piano. She can't bring herself to touch it. He doesn't need this piece of wood to remind him of who he is, to remind him of who his daddy was, to remind him of his daddy's heroics—he doesn't need any of that. But he does need some land. He does need to build a future.

Grant: So where are we in terms of Boy Willie's values? Isn't it considered anti-African to want to sell off one's values for land? I'm thinking—
Wilson: No, he's not selling off his values. He's embracing them. Land is the basis of independence. If he gets some land, he could be for the first time able to get the very land that his grandfather had farmed as a slave. He has, in fact, come full circle. That's much more important than a piece of wood. Even though his grandfather made all those beautiful carvings on the piano, it's the only thing he has to make a future with. So he sees how he can take that piano, sell it—and get some money to buy some land to become independent. That's not anti-African; that's *pro*-African. The ancestors applaud that.

Grant: How is it, then, that the play ends up where it does, with Boy Willie deciding that he *won't* sell off the piano, since its historical value actually frees them from Sutter's ghost?
Wilson: It's not its historical value that frees them from Sutter's ghost. It's the *use* of it that frees them. You see, the play's about Berniece, it's not about Boy Willie. Berniece is the only character in the play who goes through any changes. She is forced to confront *her* unwillingness to embrace her past, her unwillingness to tell her daughter—she feels the piano's a *burden* to her daughter. "Maretha can go on and have opportunities that I didn't have," she says. You mean you're not going to tell her who her granddaddy was?

Grant: But then don't you miss every opportunity—doesn't Boy Willie miss every opportunity to tell Maretha who her granddaddy was if he sells off the piano?
Wilson: No. He could tell her, "Hey, you know, we used to have a piano sitting right over there." [Laughter] "And it had these carvings on it. Lemme tell you about that piano." You see, the fact is this: *Berniece* is not telling her. Boy Willie tells her about the piano; there's a scene, in fact, in which he tells Maretha what happened with the piano. Berniece has to learn to embrace her ancestors. When she goes over to the piano and breaks her self-imposed taboo, plays the piano, calls the ancestors on the piano, Papa Boy Charles, her mother and father and grandfather, the Ghost of the Yellow Dog, and what-have-you, all the gods come and chase Sutter's ghost out of the house. She has liberated herself, and she will never be the same, the house will never be the same, Maretha will never be the same. No one's life will ever be the same from that moment on. Boy Willie says, "Oh, wow! You've found a use for the

piano," which is what he says earlier, that he would relinquish his claim if she would use it, if she were using it even for something as simple as giving out lessons to help her make her rent. His complaint is that she's not using it; she's just letting it sit there. Once she'd found the perfect use for the piano, he couldn't take it. That's why he relinquishes his claim, and that's why he admonishes her at the end—"You and Maretha better keep playing that piano; cause ain't no tellin', me and Sutter both liable to come back."

Grant: That's interesting because in that connection there are also the issues of Christianity and your uses of it. There's one scene in which Boy Willie rejects the whole notion of Christianity in a very powerful gesture. This kind of portrayal, I think, has been misunderstood by audiences, or rather what appears to be an indictment of Christianity has been misunderstood. Is that accurate?
Wilson: It's not an indictment of it. The Christian church is one of the reasons that we're still here. It's one of the institutions that has in fact enabled our survival. That does not mean it's perfect—

Grant: But by "here," do you mean being in existence—
Wilson: In 1993, in the world.

Grant: —or in the condition that we're in as African Americans?
Wilson: First, our condition can always be improved. If you're not here, then you're in a museum somewhere. [Laughter] The condition needs improvement. But spiritually, the Christian church has been important for us; and in some instances it has also failed us. I think we need to face that. One, it's not anti- . . . you mentioned something about Boy Willie and being anti-Christian—

Grant: In other words, Avery's [the preacher who woos Berniece] remedy does not work, and he winds up leaving the house—
Wilson: Okay, but before we get to that, though, for Boy Willie, it's simply a question of believing "the whole Bible or half the Bible." He's saying you can't go with anything halfway. The Bible says, "An eye for an eye, a tooth for a tooth, a life for a life." You can't pass up that part and pretend it isn't there. The failure of Avery to exorcise the ghost of the white man from black folks' lives may be the failure of Christianity to—I always find it very interesting

that it is in the name of the same God to whom blacks pray that blacks have
been lynched and abused. All too often, Jesus has listened to the Klan. So
salvation comes first from the self. Then you can thank Jesus for giving you
the strength to save yourself. But black folk are always looking for something
to come from outside of themselves in order to effect their salvation or
change their condition in the world. If you wait for somebody else to do it, it
won't get done. I don't care if it is God. God's busy. [Laughter]

Grant: And so that's how we come to Herald Loomis in *Joe Turner's Come
and Gone*—
Wilson: Right. He says, "I don't need anybody to bleed for me; I can bleed for
myself."

Grant: Right. His spirituality seems trapped in him until he lets it go. What's
at work there, and what's in the symbolism of the cutting of his chest?
Wilson: The cutting of the chest is simply the shedding of blood. Let's look at
Loomis. Here's a man who's thirty-one years old in 1911, which means he's
born in 1880. By the time you're a little boy, seven years old, the first thing
you discover is your daddy with the mule out there working the land. This is
who you are. You're not sent to school, you don't learn anything about reading or writing, whatever you learn you learn from your daddy. There's a place
called Africa? Did people tell you that? Does his father even know that, when
he's out there working the land in the 1880s? You don't know how big the
country is, you don't know anything about the United States, anything about
Europe, anything about Africa. You don't know anything about who you are.
Some man comes along, grabs you, makes you work and just keeps you
working. You notice all these black folk working there, and you say to him,
"Hey, why'd you do this?" You don't even know about slavery! You don't even
know that hundreds of years before, your great-granddaddy and his daddy
were slaves. Oh, you might have heard little rumors about it, someone might
have told you something like that, but basically you don't know anything
about the world.

Loomis just doesn't know who he is. So when he sees these bones rise up
out of the water and take on flesh and they're black just like him, he is in
effect witnessing himself being born. He understands then that his existence
is the manifest act of the Creator. Therefore he has to be filled with God's
majesty. Since he is of God, then he must be filled with His majesty. So that's

when he says, "Jesus? No, no! I don't need nobody to bleed for me. I can bleed for myself." I've got everything I need for my life contained here [Wilson points to his heart]. Self-definition is self-determination. It's a very important thing. You must define yourself.

Grant: Describe the song that Bynum says we all have and must follow. Was the migration period a period in which we could have lost that song?
Wilson: No, I don't think we could have lost it even then. Identity means understanding your political history as well as your social history. It means understanding that you come from a long line of honorable people who were slaves. The conditions of your life, the political circumstances of your life having been subdued, if you will, through slavery, your having been forced into slavery—from that I think there are some people who feel a sense of shame. But that was honorable—the purveyors of slavery were dishonorable—but there's a long line of honorable people, and so you can hold your head up and stand up even though your past history includes slavery. I think that Bynum is simply saying that understanding and knowing who you are and also having that political understanding, that political awareness, as well as the social awareness as an African, is in essence your song. You in fact need that, and you must not ever let anyone take that away from you.

That answers the question of whether we should want to adopt the cultural values of someone else. I think that our cultural contributions to American society are becoming so significant that this American culture is largely our culture at the same time. In other words, there's a European culture, there's an African culture, then there's American culture. And American culture is significantly influenced by African culture. So if you decide to become an American, you're not giving up that much.

Grant: You're really describing what Du Bois said about black twoness—"two warring ideals in one dark body," the best of the African, the best of the American—in the black.
Wilson: We have to define what an American is. America is still in the process of becoming. At the moment it's largely European with very significant African influences, but I'm not going to make any mistake in thinking that the African influences are not powerful. The whole concept of Black Power as it appeared in the sixties was a very valid concept. I think there are

different ways, as a result, of empowering yourself. To return to the South, the ancestral homeland, is for me a way of empowering yourself.

Grant: Why don't we see black women in your plays being as angry and as expressive as Levee [in *Ma Rainey's Black Bottom*]—with the possible exception of Ma, of course.

Wilson: That's a good question. It probably has to do with the fact that I'm a man. I do create some black women characters and try to be honest in their creation, but it's very hard to put myself in their space. I don't know . . . It's just very hard to do. For instance, Risa in *Two Trains Running*—I felt that it was right in having her refuse to be defined by her genitals, and I felt this was a blow for self-definition by having her define herself as other than a body by cutting her legs. But I couldn't go beyond that into making some heavier interior psychology of it. Not that I didn't want to, I guess, but I don't know it. I thought I was right on, though, in having her do that without my fully knowing why.

Grant: You anticipate a question I was going to ask about Risa's self-mutilation. Its purpose does seem to be that of a barrier; it's more effective than closing the legs. Can the argument be made that a similar scarification endured by any of the male characters would be devastating to them—that they might not recover from that?

Wilson: I don't know; all of the male protagonists . . . well, not all of them, have scars. Loomis has his scar, a self-inflicted scar; Troy was shot—

Grant: But they're enlarged by those scars—or am I misreading? I feel that the women in your plays are by contrast diminished by their scars.

Wilson: No. I think Risa's scars function the same way as all the rest of the scars. Particularly the same as Loomis's scar, in that those are self-inflicted wounds. But they're liberating at the same time. Loomis's cutting his chest means his severing his bonds. You know, there's so much that gets read into this, the symbolism of accepting responsibility, demonstrating that he can bleed for himself. In a similar way I think Risa's scarring in a sense defines her. It puts her above those women who accept the definition that men impose upon them. So I think it makes her larger as opposed to diminishing her. It certainly doesn't make her less.

Grant: What about Berniece? Crawley's death is her scar. She carries that with her and releases it for a moment when she embraces Lymon.

Wilson: You have to go through Berniece to get to Risa. Risa is 1968; Berniece is 1936. Here's a woman who's still largely defined by men. Her function and presence in the world is in relation to them, basically in the service of them. But I very pointedly have her uncle Doaker taking care of himself. It's not an accident that he irons his clothes and cooks for himself. Someone else with a woman in the house would have her do all the "woman things." But it was very important to me that Berniece not do these things and that Doaker be self-sufficient. She still exists in relation to him, although she is trying desperately to define herself. Avery broaches to her the matter of her living by herself, and she tells him, "What's the matter? You mean I can't be a woman without a man?"

But it's true. Nobody's ever going to look at him and say, "Reverend Brown ain't married." But they'll see her and whisper. That's just the price of being a woman in 1936.

Grant: But the same kinds of questions get asked of Risa.

Wilson: They talk about it. Nobody asks her.

Grant: How is that different, though, over thirty years? They talk about her the same way that—

Wilson: They talk about her, but she is not talking about herself in those terms. By truly closing up, she's rejecting that talk, in essence. I think what Berniece was trying to do in 1936, even in her dialogue with Avery, was trying to define herself outside of any relationship with men, which is I think what Risa is doing. Berniece has said, I've got a lot of woman left. Avery says, well, where is it? Risa, for six years, has closed up, but she's trying to define herself—she doesn't need a man in order to be complete, in order to be whole.

Grant: Does Berniece marry Avery?

Wilson: *That* I'm not sure about. I think I can go into why I think she doesn't. And I think she doesn't because the kinds of men she has known in her life, starting with her father—and her uncles and her brother and her husband—were all different kinds of men from Avery, men who have not been so readily accommodating. So I think for that reason she doesn't see him as someone who has the warrior spirit. He wouldn't be what she has known men to be. Though I think that's her initial attraction to Avery, that he's different. With any one of the other men, you got to take a moment, you've got to bind their wounds, send 'em back into battle, or go to their funerals.

Grant: Does Risa lose a sense of that self-definition when she falls in love with Sterling? There's something undefined about their relationship. He could wind up in jail, or dead—he's just that kind of character. He could wind up hurting her in some way.

Wilson: I don't think he's going to hurt her. But he might go to jail. That's why she's attracted to him; again, he's that Crawley-kind of character to which she's attracted. But he's the only one who ever accepts Risa for being Risa, even though he approaches her by saying, "Mm, with hips like that there, bein' nice and healthy like you"—but he still recognizes something in her and accepts her beyond that. That is the thing which I think opened her up to him. This is his willingness to embrace Hambone [the play's shell-shocked veteran] with the same spirit in which he embraces her and all these other qualities. He demonstrates for her his personality, and she goes for it—more so than her demonstrating her personality and having him go for it. She's who she is, having cut her legs for whatever reason, but he doesn't even care why she cut them. He does say that she shouldn't have done that, but that's as far as it goes for him.

Grant: How do African American men and women really come together in your plays? In what you've just described, it seems to be with pain. By contrast, there's this one instance in *Piano Lesson* where Wining Boy is reminiscing about Cleotha in such gentle terms that throughout the audience there's the sense that something tender is happening there. I'm wondering why this doesn't happen more often at the center of your plays—why there doesn't seem to be this kind of tenderness between black men and women.

Wilson: I don't know. I guess the relationship between black men and women in *Ma Rainey's Black Bottom* is one between Levee and Ma, a relationship of conflict, competition. You also have the relationship of Dussie Mae and Levee, which is sexual, a man and a woman out for what they can get, but that's not what the play's about. There's Rose in *Fences*—

Grant: She's tender, but Troy is not.

Wilson: Okay, but there may be some moments of tenderness between them . . . Well, I'm not sure. What I'm saying is that none of these relationships are at the center of the plays. They're an addendum to the play, they're not what the play is about.

Grant: Is there a risk of conflict by putting harmonious characters together at the center of the play?
Wilson: No, there's no risk of conflict. For all the characters, whether they exist in harmony or not, the major conflicts are really conflicts with the presence of white society. The culture is in conflict with white society. Generally that's the largest conflict in the play, and within that you have the characters in conflict—sometimes with one another. In a sense, though, there's always harmony within the lives of the characters. For instance, as much as Berniece and Boy Willie battle, as much as they appear disharmonious, Berniece is forced to play the piano to save Boy Willie and to support him in his struggle with Sutter. When she does that, they become one. When the conflict within the society at large—white society—comes in, then these people unite on the basis of their commonality of culture. So to make the black characters harmonious does not distort the potential for conflict because here again, it's coming from somewhere else.

I don't know why that is. Here again, the man-woman relationship has not yet been the focus of the play, where I think impressions about whether it's necessary for them to be harmonious or what exactly would be their conflicts would then be explored in that context. One of the things I'm exploring in my next play, *Seven Guitars*, is a largely man-woman theme. I realize that I've largely written around that. There've been a few scenes, but they haven't been really front-and-center of the play.

Grant: So then why have you been characterized as being sexist in your plays?
Wilson: Oh, that characterization would be wrong. I don't know that anyone's made it. I would say the opposite—I mean, I see myself characterized by honest treatment of women in the plays. Some people, particularly black actresses, want you to go further. I have to tell them, you have to write that part. I'm just doing the best I can. I'm trying to be honest, and I am sensitive to the situation. You also have to be historically correct in the sense that, women in 1936—I'm sorry—were not liberated. They were not the same as women are in 1993. Originally I had Berniece in *Piano Lesson* utter some very feminist ideas. These were not ideas that were even in the world, that she would have even been aware of in 1936. I had to take that away from her.

Grant: Do you see yourself as a writer in the mold of Charles Chesnutt, who twisted the black linguistic mode to foreground African American culture? In other words, whereas black speech was thought to be substandard, Chesnutt gave us a new projection of that speech and with it an expression of cultural power.

Wilson: I thought that way myself early in my career. The reason that I couldn't write dialogue when I was writing plays back in 1968 is because I didn't value and respect the speech patterns. I thought that in order to make art out of it you had to change it. I was always trying to mold it into some European sensibility of what the language should be. There's a quotation by Sekou Toure: "Language describes the idea of the one who speaks it." This idea really changed my life. I then began to see that there's a thought process behind language that is itself a cultural process. Once I discovered that, it was just a matter of letting people speak as they spoke, speak as who they are.

I remember that I once had some problems with some producers of *Fences* because of repetition. For instance, Troy says to Rose, what're you cookin' there? I got some chicken. I'm cookin' up some chicken with collard greens. You already said that, the producers said. Why are you repeating that? But that's the way black folks say it. The language is the language of the people, and you can't deny them that. To deny them that is, here again, denying them their humanity, trying to make them into somebody else. And so, I salute Charles Chesnutt and, yes, his Conjure Woman tales.

Grant: Is this why African American speech is so important to the characters in your plays?

Wilson: It's important to them because that's who they are; this is the way they speak. We can say exactly the same things as others, but we say them differently because we're a different people. And there's other cultural things at work. So when a black production of *Death of a Salesman* is done, something's wrong. Black folks don't speak like that, first of all. The language is different. They wouldn't say, wouldn't even do the things Willy Loman does. A black man as a salesman might be lynched! It's not a job you could easily do. Say you're selling a few envelopes at a store. Knock at the door, walk into that store, and the man at the door says, yeah, boy, go 'round to the back. It's ludicrous to try to do that kind of work. Blacks speak differently, think differently; they respond to stimuli differently.

Grant: When you talk about cultural difference I think mostly of *Piano Lesson* where that difference seems to abound. Where, for instance, is the story of the Ghost of the Yellow Dog from?

Wilson: The Ghost of the Yellow Dog was actually a short story I wrote many years before. It was my attempt to portray those benevolent and vengeful gods of the African pantheon. If you mess with me, the Ghost of the Yellow Dog will get you. You mess with any black folk, the Ghost of the Yellow Dog's gonna get you. [Laughter]

One of the parts of the play I like is when Wining Boy talks about going down to stand on the spot. Originally in the story, you'd stick out your hand at that spot and the god would give you five. But he stood on the spot and called out the names of the ghosts, and they talked to him. The important thing that people are missing here is that you have to *know* the names of the ghosts, or you have to know the names of the gods, which is what Toledo tells Levee [in *Ma Rainey*]. Knowing the names of the ghosts allows you to tap into your ancestral energies, or spirit, or however you want to put it. So that was an attempt to create the gods for African Americans, and it had to do with the railroads. It had to do with these similar things that are so much a part of our experience here: where the Southern Railroad crossed the Yellow Dog, and Bessie Smith of course has her "Yellow Dog Blues," and the line is, "I'm going where the Southern crossed the Yellow Dog." There's that blues element, and these are important icons of black American life. So I thought right there of that point in the railroad. I believe that if you go down to Mississippi where those two railroads cross one another, or I think if you're just standing anywhere on that land, you'll find it's just—Wining Boy says—there's a lot of things you've gotta find out on your own. [Laughter] It just filled me up in a strange sort of way to be standing there on that spot, and I would like myself to go down there. Some of the people associated with the theater in New York happened to be down there, at that spot where the Yellow Dog crosses the Southern—where it makes a square—and they brought back from that square a bolt, a piece of metal, from the railroad. It came from a sacred spot—at least it's sacred to me—maybe not to anyone else. [Laughter]

The reason that the horseshoe was considered good luck is not because of its shape—it's because it was metal. You could put that over your door, and the god Ogun, the god of iron, would protect your house. The most common piece of metal in those days was a horseshoe. That's how all that came about.

Grant: What can be, and what should be learned by the white theatergoer?
Wilson: The fact that black Americans have their own culture. While we all do the same things, we all do them differently. We decorate our houses differently, bury our dead differently. Sometimes the differences aren't all that great, but if you ever went to a black funeral and then to a white funeral, you'll definitely know that there are two distinct, separate cultures at work. Neither is better than the other one. They're just two different ways of approaching life. Some whites are surprised to find that blacks have their own approach to life, that they have their own ways of viewing things. Blacks who are offended by this difference are those who have adopted the white approach to life.

Grant: Would Berniece be offended? Why does she say to Maretha that she shouldn't "show her color"?
Wilson: She says that because she's embarrassed. "Showing your color" means being black. She's telling her to go down there and act as white as you can. Pretend you're not black. Go and obey those people down there! There are these white people down there who are going to show these kids how to live. Here's the way you do this; here's the way you do that. The irony of this whole thing. White social workers would come into housing projects and "teach" black women how to clean their houses. And yet what do black women do? They clean white folks' houses. Something ain't right here, as Herald Loomis said. So this is another example of Berniece's not being able to embrace her past, not being able to embrace her culture until she goes over and plays the piano. She's denying all that because she wants her kid to become a school-teacher or something, maybe. Again, it's giving up too much for that little entree into the society. You have to trade a part of yourself. That's too much of a trade-off.

  Now if you were going to ask what I thought you were going to ask, whether people are embarrassed by the use of the word nigger in the play, which is used a lot, that's another situation.

Grant: What are your thoughts on that?
Wilson: That's part of the language. I've heard people say that all my life, and I hear people say it now in an attempt to be authentic, to tell it like it is. We're all sensitive, both black and white, to that word, and we're more sensitive if we're sitting next to a white person in a theater. We're doubly sensitized to it because, oh my God, they've heard it too. [Laughter]

What's happened is that I've really become aware of its use to the point that I can't write it anymore. Every time I write it I ask, can I do without this? And most of the time, maybe 90 percent of the time, I say yeah, and then I scratch it off. So I probably won't be using it as much in future plays as I have in the past. I think *Two Trains Running* was the play in which it was used the most, and that was interesting because it was set in 1969.

Grant: I didn't count them.
Wilson: [Laughter] Well, in *Two Trains*, it's a lot.

Grant: Seems that there'd be a lot in *Piano Lesson* as well.
Wilson: No, not quite that many. But hey, I don't count 'em either! [Laughter]

Grant: Would you say that the social content of black theater is necessarily identical with its dramatic context?
Wilson: No, not necessarily. It's all in the structure of the play. For instance, in my plays, character takes precedence over plot. It's not to say there's no plot. People have said there's no plot in *Two Trains Running*. There is a plot. It's very clear. It's not a plot as you're accustomed to seeing; it's not a plot as you would want it laid out. As I look at most plays, there's very little dialogue. They just say a few words here and there. Here, the plot comes out of all this dialogue. People take the time to talk. There's a lot of talk in the play and the plot comes from there, so it comes from the characters first. But there's a sharp sense of the dramatic at work in all the plays, even if it's not readily recognizable, because, after all, this is made out of black culture.

Grant: What holds *Two Trains* together? Could it be the linkage between the discussions of Malcolm X on the one hand and Aunt Ester on the other?
Wilson: It's Hambone who holds it together.

Grant: And so how does that work?
Wilson: The crucial question of the play is: could you stand in front of Lutz's market every morning for nine and a half years? Should you accept partial payment for what you know is due you—or should you get the whole thing? Half the Bible versus the whole Bible, right? In Hambone's case, are you willing to take a chicken when you should have a ham? Is something better than

nothing? Not always. As he points out in the play, it's better to take nothing than to take the chicken. It's going to constantly remind you that you should have the ham. It is Hambone's position—which is the same position that Memphis [the owner of the restaurant where the action takes place] takes with respect to his property. Sterling, too. I try to have each of the characters in the play confront in some manner this question of whether something is always better than nothing. That's what holds it all together—it's not Aunt Ester, it's not Malcolm X—those are little extraneous things about which one might ask, what are the lives of these people made of? And here's some of the things their lives are made of.

Grant: So this question would characterize all of the plays, wouldn't it?
Wilson: I think this question is part of the thing in all of the plays, yes.

Grant: Is that a question that you as a playwright, or social critic/playwright are always trying to ask?
Wilson: Or answer. I don't think anyone should be forced to make those accommodations and take less than what they're due for whatever reason. If you're owed your ham, then you should get your ham. It's as simple as that.

Grant: Why does Hambone die not getting the ham?
Wilson: Because he didn't take it. That's how you get your ham in American society. If you're standing around waiting for someone to give it to you and they don't give it to you—well, look at American society. There's some nice land out there, someone says. Who's got it? another says. Indians, another says. Well, let's take it. It's the same with the ham. That's the premise for life in American society. It's the American way.

August Wilson:
Bard of the Blues

Carol Rosen / 1996

From *Theater Week*, 9 (May 27, 1996), 18, 20, 22, 24–28, 30–32, 34–35.

Seven Guitars is August Wilson's latest play in his epic cycle chronicling every decade of twentieth-century black experience on the borderline of the American dream. The current New York production makes Wilson second only to Neil Simon as the only living American playwright to have seen at least six of his plays produced on Broadway. And in the tradition of Eugene O'Neill, whose tragic vision prevailed in all of his Broadway plays, August Wilson also views America as a land populated by "possessors dispossessed." Wilson's heroes, like O'Neill's lost souls, find their ambitions and hopes thwarted, and they seek salvation in dilapidated domestic or social settings ripe with symbolic potential. Also recalling O'Neill's poetic outsiders, Wilson's characters speak a stylized version of colloquial language, their vernacular angling towards poetry. But August Wilson has an agenda quite unlike those of his white, Euro-centered counterparts in the American theater: his goal is to create a direct and spiritual theater language analogous to the musical language of the blues.

Like many other playwrights, Wilson claims to hear compelling voices. Unlike many other playwrights, however, he seems to mean this literally, presenting himself in otherwise subdued, even hushed tones as a medium by means of which the restless spirits of his people seek expression. So Wilson is not only the artist as historian, the artist as mythmaker; he is also the artist as shaman. In the course of our conversation, carried out primarily in his own hesitant and thoughtful hum of a voice, Wilson suddenly demonstrates this mystical power, speaking briefly in the harsh, uncompromising voice of a convict in a prison yard, a man with a deep scar and with a razor stashed in his mouth, a character in his next play, to be set in the 1980s.

Wilson shapes his plays exclusively out of the stories, folklore, dreams, songs, and prayers of black characters who come to him in search of an author, and they haunt him, demanding to be heard, seen, and revivified onstage. Wilson finds the Black English dialect spoken by many of his characters—with its urban, working-class rhythms, slang, and patois—to be a poetic and subversive language. Through these characters and their distinctive voices, Wilson has found his mission and his gift. It is to depict the life-affirming aspects of the daily negotiations, the survival mechanisms, and the plans gone awry in every generation of heroic lives systematically devalued by the dominant culture.

August Wilson agreed to talk at his favorite Broadway diner, a homey place in which a symphony of clattering silverware and dishes sounds like a rehearsal for *Stomp*. This is where Wilson usually holds court, and indeed, prominently displayed on the wall is a framed *New York Times* photo of him enjoying his lunch there. Wilson appeared in his signature cap and trenchcoat (but he seems to have quit smoking), looking more professorial than revolutionary. When asked, he graciously agreed to move our talk to a quieter space, because although he speaks eloquently and poetically about his own work and about cultural and social issues, he sounds for all the world like a high speed version of Marlon Brando.

Theater Week: What is the special nature of your relationship with your director, Lloyd Richards?
August Wilson: For many years, Lloyd was a producer of these plays as well at the Yale Repertory Theatre. And the play needs a director. Lloyd directed *Ma Rainey's Black Bottom*. He also produced *Fences*. I guess he hired himself as a director when we did *Fences*. It's made the plays have a seamlessness in that there are the same two artistic sensibilities at work.

TW: Have you tried working with any other directors on any of the plays in the cycle?
AW: I haven't, no, because I haven't had the opportunity.

TW: You live in Seattle, and yet you have not worked at the Seattle Rep with Dan Sullivan.
AW: I live in Seattle. And I haven't worked with Dan Sullivan. I've had my plays produced at the Rep, but if I worked with someone other than

Lloyd, Daniel would not be my choice of director. He's a very good director, but I think I'd want to find a black director.

TW: What else is there about Lloyd Richards's direction that makes him so well suited to your plays?
AW: I would say the fact that he's black and we share that sensibility and the culture. I don't know much else beyond that.

TW: *Seven Guitars* is set in 1948. Is this play the only missing piece in the cycle as you conceived it?
AW: Well, *Seven Guitars* is one of the missing pieces. . . .

Okay, let's back up a minute. 1911 is *Joe Turner*. 1927 is *Ma Rainey's Black Bottom*. 1936 is *The Piano Lesson*. 1948 is *Seven Guitars*. 1957 is *Fences* and 1969 is *Two Trains Running*. And I have a seventies play, *Jitney!*, included as part of my cycle.

TW: If you continue to track history by dramatizing decades, will you next depict contemporary life, the period of your own adulthood?
AW: The sixties was actually my adulthood. I came into manhood in the early sixties. *Two Trains Running* was that period of time. In 1969, I was twenty-four years old.

So what's left is the eighties and nineties when you deal with my adulthood as a middle-aged man as opposed to as a young man.

Seven Guitars is the forties and it fills in that gap there. Then I have the two ends to work on. So next I'm working on the eighties and then I'll do the early 1900s, the first decade of the twentieth century, and be done with that part of it. I'll never stop working, but I'll be done with that part.

TW: You said once that *Fences* began for you with an image of a middle-aged man holding a baby. Do you always start with an image?
AW: Sometimes it's with an idea. Sometimes it's with a line of dialogue. Sometimes it's just a burning passion to say something, even if you don't know what it is you want to say. [Laughs]

This play started with an image of seven men with guitars on stage. Someone named Floyd—it was Bannister at the time—but someone named Floyd Barton had been killed, and these men were in a lineup and they were responding to this unheard and unseen voice, this disembodied voice. "No, sir," "Well, I know Floyd for however many years," etc.

I thought by doing that, I would go on to do two things. I wanted to expose—sort of look behind—the songs, to the interior psyche of the individuals who create the songs so you see how the blues are created and where in essence they come from.

I was interested in showing the relationship between those men and white society, and between those men and black society, where from one viewpoint, they're seen as drunkards and vagrants and things of that sort, and then from the other, they're seen as carriers of the tradition, a very valuable and integral part of the community and the culture.

So I began to work at putting these scenes together. This all happened in my mind, of course, but one of the guys came to me and said, "What the hell she doin' here? Tell her to get the hell out of here. You say this an all-man play."

I looked over and there was this woman sitting on the stage. "Tell her to get the hell . . . ." I said, "No, I'll take care of it, man." So I went over, and I said, "Excuse me, what are you doing here?" She said, "I want my own space." I said, "You want your own scene?" She said, "No, I want my own space."

I didn't know what she meant by that. So I said, "I don't know how I'm going to deal with this." I closed my tablet and I walked away. A couple of months later, I sat down one day and I opened my tablet. I said, "Okay, you've got your own space." There was a knock at the door and a woman answered the door. There was a man standing there with a radio and a chicken and he had come courting. That turned out to be Vera. And the man ended up being Floyd. It was various other men at different times.

And then I let Vera in and then these other two women walked in behind her. [Laughs] So I ended up with four men and three women.

TW: So now the play has seven characters, but only one guitar. Why do numbers crop up so often in the dialogue, even in the title? Does the number seven have special significance?

AW: I don't have the men with seven guitars on stage anymore.

At one point, as I was writing the play, there was something called "The Numbers Section." In everything in that particular section, I tried to deal with numbers, various dates and any way that you could get a number—how long the records were, two minutes, thirty-seven seconds, whatever—I dealt with numbers.

I didn't consciously do that. Of course, there's seven birds over there, and seven is a mystical number and involved a lot in superstition and things of that sort, and it's a winning number on the dice, things of that sort. Hedley says, "Inside each man is seven generations," but he says, "The seventh son of the seventh son is a big man, but I am not the seventh son. I'm just a poor black man who has grown up without knowing the joys of a woman."

TW: Do you think of the seven characters as guitars themselves?
AW: Absolutely. Yes, that's why there are seven characters. As it turned out, they are the seven guitars. They each have their individual voices and their individual characters. And if they're the guitars, then I guess I'm the orchestra. I'm not sure. [Laughs]

TW: Could you be the guy in the pawn shop?!
AW: That I'm not. I am *not* the guy in the pawn shop! However you want to cut it.

TW: This production of *Seven Guitars* has traveled across America. How has the play taken shape in the course of its journey?
AW: We had a much longer journey with *Piano Lesson*. This has been relatively short. We started it last January at the Goodman Theater and we went from there. In September, we mounted the show at the Huntington Theatre in Boston. And then we went to ACT in San Francisco and then down to the Ahmanson and then to New York. That's a much shorter journey than most of my plays have taken.

I don't think it's changed its shape, but I think it's changed considerably since Chicago. I rewrote and added scenes, for instance. That was a big change. I didn't add any characters, but I tried to define them better and I added a couple of scenes that I thought would help to do that. And I continued working on it since then.

TW: I've heard that the first scene of the play was originally part of the final scene.
AW: No, no. It functions as a bookend; it functions as a flashback. We begin the play the day of the burial of Floyd Barton as the characters have come back from the cemetery. And then we flash back—I hate that word, but we do, we flash back—to Floyd's life. Then at the end of the play, we come back to them in the yard after they've come back from the funeral.

TW: Why don't the characters identify the killer? Are they protecting him?
AW: He's not being protected. No one knows he's done it, first of all.
Canewell suspects it. He says, "What did he give you?" and having seen
Floyd in the yard with the money, he has it sort of figured out, but they don't
know that he did it. *He* [the killer] doesn't know he did it.

TW: The audience suspects he is going to do it, the minute he shows up with
a machete.
AW: I did not know he was going to do it the minute he showed up with a
machete. Maybe the audience does.
    It took me a long while to figure out who was going to do it. [Laughs]
I started out knowing that Floyd Barton was murdered and I had no
idea.

TW: Your choice of the killer makes the death of Floyd all the more
wrenching. As in *Fences* and *The Piano Lesson,* you create a no-win situation,
evoking a sense of loss and bewilderment because no resolution is possible.
If the police killed him it would all be so cut and dried.
AW: It's tragic. It wouldn't be tragic if the police killed him. Hedley—yes, it's
very interesting that their paths cross. Of course, Floyd has to assume the
responsibility for his own death, his own murder. Had he not been standing
in the yard with the money, then Hedley never could have assumed that he
was Buddy Bolden, etc. Had he not robbed the place, then had the money,
he wouldn't have been standing there. So whatever events conspired to have
him standing in that yard at that precise time, he has to himself bear the
responsibility for that.
    It was difficult to kill him that way. . . . Once I knew that someone was
going to kill Floyd Barton, I toyed with the idea of having it be someone
outside the play. But that didn't work. And once it was going to be someone
inside the play, I liked my characters and I didn't want to make any of
them murderers. [Laughs] So I came up with a way to have that happen
without Hedley being the murderer per se.
    You see, if Buddy Bolden is bringing some money from Hedley's father,
he represents his father's forgiveness. Also, Hedley is going to use the money
to buy a plantation, not to get rich, but so the white man doesn't tell him
what to do anymore, to become independent, land being the basis of
independence.

In a way, the play says that anyone who is standing in the way of a black man's independence needs to be dealt with. So it's very necessary that Hedley decides that Floyd, as Buddy Bolden, is the messenger, the courier who would like to keep the money, who will not give him his money so he can buy his plantation. It means it's a betrayal of Hedley's father.

Of course, the tragedy is he's not Buddy Bolden, that he is Floyd Barton. It's a mistake. It's an honorable mistake, but it is a mistake.

TW: Would you consider Floyd to be your first tragic hero?
AW: No, not the first hero. Boy Willie [in *The Piano Lesson*] is very heroic. Troy [in *Fences*] is a very heroic man. Sterling [in *Two Trains Running*] is very heroic; Levee [in *Ma Rainey's Black Bottom*]—even though he kills, for all his misguided transferred aggression and misguided heroics—he still has that warrior spirit.

TW: These other characters you mention are compromised heroes, but Floyd has a strong sense of his own place in the world, of his special value to the community as an artist. He is going somewhere.
AW: Yes, yes. His death is a most unfortunate occurrence. One of the things that is interesting if Floyd goes out and gets the instrument of his hero, Muddy Waters, and Hedley goes out and gets the machete, which is the instrument of his hero, Toussaint L'Ouverture.

They both feel compelled to get these things. And Hedley is warning Floyd. He loves him; it's like his son and he would do nothing to harm this man. He's rooting for him and looking out for him, telling him, "Watch your back; they're after you." The last thing he would do would be to harm Floyd. And they don't know, but it's just fated that their paths were just crossing.

TW: Somewhat like Gabriel in *Fences,* Hedley is a loose-cannon character who inhabits a realm other than that of your more realistic characters. His actions take on a symbolic valence. He does not behave according to laws of logic, but he functions as an instrument of death.
AW: They have their own interior logic. For instance, Hedley refuses to go to the sanitarium. Now, if my father died from lack of proper medical care, then all of the sudden you want to give me—"I don't know, it's a trap."

See, so it's also where he's been, the truth that he has accumulated in his life. It's no different than when I get a letter from AT&T saying they want me to join a Reach Out America plan, that they can save me some money on my long-distance calls. I look at that with great suspicion and go, "Wait a minute, this is not right. You guys rarely try to save anybody any money. You know you're out to maximize your profits. What do you mean, you're going to save me some money?"

It's the same thing. "Come on, we want you to go into the sanitarium." And you go, "I don't know, it's a trap." Every encounter he's had with white society has been a trap of some sort. So why wouldn't he assume that? So the logic is not the common logic, but he has his own interior life and his own interior logic that is rooted in *this* world. He doesn't go around saying he's a prophet or a Messiah or anything. He talks about Marcus Garvey, he talks about how he wants to be the father of the Messiah.

TW: In the script there was a moment when the characters all take turns speculating about what each one would do if he or she were God.
AW: That's no longer in.

There was a bunch of stuff—I took a lot of stuff out. Otherwise, it would be a four-and-a-half-hour play. I had to try to find those moments that best served the material. This [section] was an addendum to the story, to the actual events of the play. Particularly with my plays, it's sometimes necessary, because it illuminates the characters and illuminates their logic and their thoughts and the world that they live in. You have to make choices. Sometimes it's difficult.

TW: That passage shows how cynical the characters are about the possibility of being saved by some outside force.
AW: Oh, you're never saved by any outside force. It all comes from within you.

TW: Some of your stage directions, particularly at climactic moments, seem very difficult to realize in performance. In *Fences,* for example, Gabriel is described as letting out an "atavistic cry" and dancing with such abandon that he "opens the gates of Heaven." In the movie industry, such a description is termed "hyping the script"—when the writer eloquently calls upon the actors and the director to deliver the impossible.
AW: It's a great theatrical moment. Make of it what you want. It's a challenge to the actors. I think people take that moment and do something really stunning with it. Other people don't rise to the occasion or the challenge.

What do you do? I almost wrote a moment like that for Hedley in *Seven Guitars*. He had realized that this is Floyd.

TW: *Fences* was going to be adapted for the screen. It has not yet been turned into a film, has it?
AW: So far, no.

TW: Are you still expecting it to become a film?
AW: I am, yes.

TW: What is holding up the project?
AW: The problem was: a black director. They have since agreed to hire a black director. We may do that; we may make the film with John Singleton. You know Hollywood.

TW: Do you consider your plays autobiographical?
AW: They are not autobiographical. All the characters are entirely invented. They're not based on anyone that I know or anyone I know about. None of the events of the play is based on my life or anyone's life that I know. These are just things I make up. In the sense that all of the characters all come out of me, they are probably all me, the different aspects of my personality. But it's not my life, and it's not anyone who I know.

TW: Are there things in your life that you would not write about?
AW: No, I can't think of anything. But there's nothing in my life I *would* write about. I don't have any secrets, but I don't think it's that important. . . . You make art out of your life and you have one life and you have small art. I'm not interested in that.

I'm interested in something larger than that. I have a four-hundred-year autobiography, if you will. Since 1619, the early seventeenth century, my ancestors have been here in this country and I claim all of that. I can write about that experience and any part of it.

TW: Would you consider yourself a political playwright?
AW: Absolutely. All art is politics. I'm one of those warrior spirits. The battle since the first African set foot on the continent of North America has been a battle for the affirmation of the value and worth of one's being in the face

of this society that says you're worthless, etc. In that sense, everyone's history
has its own political dictates, and so I attempt to follow them.

I think that as blacks, we need to alter the relationship that we have to the
society. In the sixties, the catchword was Black Power. And equally important,
perhaps more so, we need to alter the shared expectation that we have of each
other as blacks. My art hopefully contributes to that.

TW: You are describing the potential effect of your plays on both white and
black audiences. Do you write for any particular audience?

AW: No. I write for an audience of one, which is the self. I write basically and
selfishly for myself as the artist. [It's] the same as Picasso when he painted a
picture, and he put red here and he put blue there. He's not painting for
anyone; he's doing the expression to this thing that beats in here [he thumps
on his chest], and whatever artistic tenets that he may follow, whatever he's
trying to accomplish in his art, that's what you do.

I do place black Americans at the center of the universe, in the world.
As Africans prior to coming over here, they existed, and they were the center.
Everything revolved around them in their world view. Over here, all of that
has been taken and stripped away. So I say, "Let's look at it. The world is right
here in this back yard." There is no idea that cannot be contained by black
life. We have the entire world here.

TW: Your plays show the heroic side of characters whose lives have been
devalued by the dominant white society.

AW: Absolutely. You get a different perspective. The people always knew they
had a value. They had fallen into a political circumstance in which they were
enslaved, but they always knew that there was a value to them, even if their
captors and their enslavers did not see that or recognize that. The people
always knew and they continued to pray to their gods.

Someone else looking over here would look at them and say, "They're very
strange people. They don't have no language, they don't have no custom,
they run around half-naked, this, that, the other." But it all depends on where
you're standing. If I'm standing over here, I can understand how you could
see that. But the people knew themselves.

TW: There is a line in *The Piano Lesson* that describes the difference between
blacks and whites in America. It goes, "A black man can't fix nothing with the

law." And in *Seven Guitars*, Red Carter says, "I have more money than the law allows."

AW: I took that line out too. [Laughs] I was talking about that the other day: "I have more money than the law allows. I must have. The police arrested me for having too much money. They put me in jail. They said if I had that much money, I must have stole it." This is so true, you see.

TW: Yes, it's important for the play, too, because, in a way, Floyd dies for having too much money. Having money is dangerous for him.

AW: That's very interesting. I may put that back, now that you mention it. A black man walking down the street and he has like $5,000: "You're going to jail, I swear, where did you get this money from?" A white man walking down the street, police stop him and he has $5,000, "Okay, you're on your way to the bank. We know it's your money." They don't assume you stole it. It's an entirely different world.

TW: Some of the prefaces to your plays include what might be called "odes" to the blues. In the preface to *Ma Rainey*, for example, you celebrate the "braggadocio and rough poignancy" of music which serves as a source of "instruction and reconnection." You write of this music as armor, "girding" listeners for battle. How are your plays like the blues?

AW: I don't know anything about music. I don't play an instrument. I've never studied music. I know that contained in the blues is an entire philosophical system; contained in there is the cultural response of black America to the world in which they found themselves.

This response is the thing that enables your survival. It teaches you certain ideas and attitudes that enable you to still be here in the year 1996 and hopefully in the year 2096, although there are no guarantees.

I think it [the blues] is the best literature that the blacks have. It's certainly at the bedrock of everything I do, because it's the world and the people. The music comes out of black life as created by black people.

TW: In *Seven Guitars*, one of the characters literally sings the blues. Many of the monologues have the potential to become blues lyrics.

AW: "My feet ain't on backwards." Actually, we use that in the song—they do sing one song, half a song—they are rehearsing a song in the yard, "Going Back to Chicago." It comes out of the events of the play, Floyd going back to

Chicago, trying to take Vera with him. He takes the line that Vera tells him, "My feet ain't on backwards." Anyway, it has the call and response, the—whatever—that you find in the music.

It's not surprising, because the music is made up of black life, and the plays are likewise made out of the same thing the blues are made out of. So they are blues. I am the blues. Willie Dixon said, "I am the blues." I love that saying.

I met Willie Dixon once. He said, "We ought to get together." I said, "We're already together. We're already together." [Laughs]

TW: The action of your plays often revolves around the pursuit of a relic: an object freighted with symbolic, even magical power. Does anything function this way in *Seven Guitars*?
AW: That plantation. The land being the basis of independence, the land meaning that. So that the white man doesn't tell you what to do anymore. I think Hedley in particular is tired of living under oppression; he's tired of living where someone is in a position of authority over him and telling him what to do. So then the money represents a means to acquire that. Money, in that sense, is a magical something.

TW: Which artists would you cite as having influenced your work?
AW: Luis Borges, the Argentinian writer. Bearden, the painter, collagist. Amiri Baraka, [formerly] LeRoi Jones, with his ideas of black nationalism in the sixties. What I call my four Bs—Bearden, Baraka, Borges, blues. Those are the major influences in my life.

TW: How have you been influenced by Baraka's work?
AW: The ideas of black power, black nationalism . . . He had four revolutionary plays that are very beautiful in that book, *Four Revolutionary Black Plays*—

TW: Alice Childress wrote a play called *Trouble in Mind,* in which an actress in rehearsal bitterly catalogues all the stereotypes of black women she has portrayed onstage. Your female characters certainly get their moments to shine: the women's monologues from your plays are frequently heard at auditions. Do you consider yourself a feminist playwright?
AW: No, I don't think of myself that way. I sit down and try to create honest characters, and I try to look at women as defined by themselves, and not necessarily defined in relation to men.

But that's a feminist statement right there: you look at women. The definition of woman [means]: as outside of any relationship to a man, because society has told them that they are defined only in relation to men. I think that women have proven otherwise.

I have some very feminist ideas in Berniece, in one of the earlier drafts [of *The Piano Lesson*]. But these were ideas that she would not have come to in 1936, so I had to take them out of the play. I had to put her where she belongs, and put her as close to having that kind of feminist consciousness as I could comfortably do without someone saying, "These are 1970 ideas."

TW: Are the women seen as magical in *Seven Guitars?*
AW: That's just the natural magical properties of women. Nothing unusual about that. [Laughs]

TW: In *Seven Guitars,* Ruby is repeatedly characterized by her aunt as someone with "a little fast behind." Then Ruby turns out to be an angel.
AW: Any time I do a workshop, I always say, "Whatever you say characterizes you, and it *may* characterize someone else. Those characterizations are all suspect, until proven otherwise."

Her aunt says, "Oh, Ruby . . . this and that," but she may not necessarily be that way. Just because someone says it, it doesn't have to be true.

Ruby is a very confused—Here is a woman who is a Virgin Mary. She's pregnant, she's driven out of wherever she is, she comes into another situation, and here are all these men. Hedley goes, "Listen, I understand you got a bad start in life."

You see, I took some of this stuff out of the play.

TW: You didn't take out her dream, where she sees herself as an angel, did you?
AW: Yes. She saw the halo on her head. Everyone had a dream at one point. I took all the dreams out. There was the dream of the bicycle, looking in the mirror, the halo.

TW: But you say "Ruby is the Virgin Mary" as if it were obvious. Without her dream, it's not so obvious.
AW: I was working on that. What Hedley offered her was, he would restore her virginity and she'd become the mother of the messiah and then, after she did that, he said, "The Bible said, 'I want to make all things new, wipe the

slate clean.'" That's when she turns up in a red dress, having the virgin in red, having been remade, so to speak, even though she is pregnant.

TW: So keeping the dreams in the play would make sense.
AW: It also makes for a *long* evening. [Laughs]

It was a long play, and parts of it began to get lost. And I was working on this halo and I was working on all this kind of stuff. And the audience wonders what the hell is going on? I began to take some of those things away to make it clearer, to keep what I saw as the more important parts, to keep it clear and focused on what the play is saying with Floyd and Hedley's story.

TW: The action of your plays often unfolds in unconventional ways. In *Seven Guitars,* for example, the first scene is the aftermath of the action.
AW: *Fences* was my only play that I would consider more conventional. The others have been ensemble pieces with their own rules, their own definition, my own way of executing Aristotle's *Poetics*. My interpretation of all that.

TW: All of your characters seem to believe in ghosts. Do you believe in ghosts?
AW: I've never seen a ghost, but I think enough people have seen them, that I believe all those people who say they have seen them.

TW: Do you consider your plays to be religious in any sense?
AW: I'm a religious person, although I don't practice a particular religion. Life is religion. Religion is certainly a large part of culture. And here again, working with the culture, you have religion. It's not necessarily Christianity, it's not necessarily an African religion, it's just religion, those things that religion is composed of, [including] mythology.

TW: Joe Louis is important to *Seven Guitars*, not just as a historical marker, but as a symbol—almost a myth—of hope.
AW: Yes. Well, Joe Louis was important to black America. Every time Joe Louis would go out there and fight, what he represented was [a response to] the condition of black America, all those lynchings, the effects of all the segregation. If only through America's mind, it was a way of engaging that, and doing battle with that. And Joe Louis always emerged victorious, and that gave the people something they needed to get out of bed in the morning.

And they would carry that victory for a long while, maybe until the next Joe Louis victory. Then they had to go down there and say, "Yessir, boss, I do dis here," and they went out on their jobs and did whatever. But they could do it easier the next day.

Someone should write what Joe Louis really meant to black America.

TW: In each of your plays, the era is illuminated by characters' reactions to events of historical significance occurring offstage. Have you begun work on your 1980s period play?

AW: I don't know what's going to happen in the 1980s. I have an idea that I'm working on. The new play is set in 1984. I don't know the events of the play. The guy has a scar on his face. I generally start with a line of dialogue.

[Wilson begins speaking in the voice of the character.] We were sitting out in the yard, the big yard [of the penitentiary] and he said to me, "Where'd you get that scar from?" He didn't say, "*How* you get that scar?" He said, "Where you get it from?"—like you walk down the street and get one. "Where you get that scar from?" Like maybe he thought it was his or he should have it. I kind of laughed, spit out my razor blade in my hand, and hit him across the face with it and said, "Now you got one, too." He didn't say nuthin' to me for the next five years. I guess he figured he said too much, huh?

[Wilson stops speaking in the convict's voice.] I thought, whoa, who's this guy, a ruthless character.

The only thing I know about the play is that his father killed a man. His surrogate father killed a man. He killed a man, and he has a seventeen-year-old son who's getting ready to kill a man. And the whole purpose of the play may be to stop the seventeen-year-old son from doing it. I'm not sure. That's really all I know about it at this juncture.

TW: You welcome these voices that come to you.

AW: Yes, I do. I know there's a story about the scar. I'm scared to ask him though.

This guy I'm scared of. I want to find out some more about him, but I have to tread lightly. I'm not going to ask him how he got his scar. I've never written a character like that. I hope he comes back to me when I sit down to write this voice.

I've got to find some others, too. But when you become engaged in that process, you have to open yourself up and be willing to accept whatever it is and be welcoming to it. Actually, you're calling up this thing from deep down inside . . . this landscape of the self . . . you have to be willing to face whatever you uncover.

TW: Is there a procedure by which you do that?

AW: You set it up so it happens. It's not easy, so what you have to do is, you have to assemble all your strength and all your courage and get all that together, and it's going to be a battle. It's going to be painful. It's going to be a war. You say, "Okay, I'm ready to do this now." But [laughs] you put it off until you're ready, until you're spiritually strong. Then you say, "Okay," and then you turn on the typewriter or take your tablet, and say, "I'm off on this journey now, and I don't know where the hell it's going, but I've got to do this."

In *Joe Turner,* Bynum says [of his calling], "I don't do it lightly. . . . It costs me a piece of myself every time I do it." And sometimes I feel like that: It costs you a piece of yourself. You just have to be willing to pay that price: to get this guy to talk with me, and to try to understand someone who would kill another human being, try to understand someone who so casually would slice him—what, where, how, who, why?

TW: Is there any accounting for how or why all those characters and stories are inside you?

AW: I open myself up to it. It has something to do with my own personal spirituality, I guess, my own personal trek, my own personal odyssey through American society over the past soon to be fifty-one years. And it has to do with my embrace of the stimuli that are all around us, my embrace of the world of the blues, my continual mining of that, discovering gems in there that people just overlook in my estimation.

And it's the joy also. Working as an artist is a joyful process. I don't create my art out of pain and suffering. I create it out of the zestful, joyous part of life. Pain and suffering are parts of death, which is a part of life. But the joyful part is the ground on which I stand.

An Interview with August Wilson

Bonnie Lyons / 1997

From *Contemporary Literature*, 40 (Spring 1999), 1–21. © 1999. Reprinted by permission of the University of Wisconsin Press.

August Wilson was born in 1945 in Pittsburgh to a black mother and a white father, a German baker who abandoned the family. He was raised by his mother on The Hill, a black ghetto of Pittsburgh, quit school at fifteen, and then split his days between the streets and the public library, where he particularly explored the section marked "Negro." His discovery in 1965 of Bessie Smith and the blues gave him a world that contained his imagination. His interest in black cultural nationalism in the 1960s led to his co-founding Black Horizons Theatre, a community theater aimed at raising black consciousness in Pittsburgh in 1968. His work with community theater was hampered by some of the usual problems, including unpaid actors having to rehearse after working all day, and in 1971 he began to concentrate on writing poetry and short fiction.

After unsuccessfully submitting several scripts to the Eugene O'Neill Theater Center, home of the National Playwrights Conference, Wilson submitted *Ma Rainey's Black Bottom*, and in the summer of 1982, Lloyd Richards, the director of the O'Neill, invited Wilson to attend. Since that time Wilson's career has been linked with Richards, whom Wilson has called his "guide, mentor, and provocateur." All of Wilson's plays have moved from the O'Neill, to Yale (where Richards is the dean and artistic director of the Yale Repertory Theatre), to Broadway under Lloyd Richards's guiding hand.

August Wilson is the most ambitious and one of the most esteemed American playwrights of our time. His extraordinary life project is to complete a ten-play cycle chronicling the black experience in America, one play for every decade of the century. So far he has completed *Joe Turner's Come and Gone* (1988) for the 1910s, *Ma Rainey's Black Bottom* (1985) for the 1920s, *The Piano Lesson* (1990) for the 1930s, *Seven Guitars* (1996) for the

1940s, *Fences* (1986) for the 1950s, and *Two Trains Running* (1992) for the 1960s. As he discusses in the following interview, he is currently working on the play for the 1980s. While his plays are scorching indictments of racism and often include disclosures of past traumatic racial incidents which have scarred the characters, his work also celebrates the joy of music, food, stories, humor, and love. Wilson's most obvious strengths as a playwright are his ability to create vivid, fully realized characters and to provide them with rich, graphic, metaphorical language.

This interview took place in February 1997 in Merchants Cafe in Pioneer Square in downtown Seattle, near August Wilson's office. Dressed in a white dress shirt and tie coupled with a casual jacket and a cap, Wilson was soft-spoken and somewhat restrained at first. He became more and more animated as he spoke about his passion for black life in America and for his plays. Wilson is well aware that he created his characters, but he spoke of them with such knowledge and affection that I was reminded of the famous story of Balzac calling for his characters on his deathbed.

Q: Elsewhere you've talked about writing as a way of effecting social change and said that all your plays are political, but that you try not to make them didactic or polemical. Can you talk a little about how plays can effect social change without being polemical or didactic?
A: I don't write primarily to effect social change. I believe writing can do that, but that's not why I write. I work as an artist. However, all art is political in the sense that it serves the politics of someone. Here in America whites have a particular view of blacks, and I think my plays offer them a different and new way to look at black Americans. For instance, in *Fences* they see a garbage-man, a person they really don't look at, although they may see a garbageman every day. By looking at Troy's life, white people find out that the content of this black garbageman's life is very similar to their own, that he is affected by the same things—love, honor, beauty, betrayal, duty. Recognizing that these things are as much a part of his life as of theirs can be revolutionary and can affect how they think about and deal with black people in their lives.

Q: How would that same play, *Fences*, affect a black audience?
A: Blacks see the content of their lives being elevated into art. They don't always know that is possible, and it's important to know that.

Q: You've talked about how important black music was for your development. Was there any black literature that showed you that black lives can be
the subject of great art?

A: *Invisible Man.* When I was fourteen I discovered the Negro section of the
library. I read *Invisible Man*, Langston Hughes, and all the thirty or forty
books in the section, including the sociology. I remember reading a book that
talked about the "Negro's power of hard work" and how much that phrase
affected me. At the time I used to cut the lawn for a blind man named
Mr. Douglas, who was the father of the Olympic track star. After I read that,
I didn't so much cut his lawn as plow it, to show the Negro power of hard
work. Looking back, I see that I had never seen those words together: "Negro
power." Later of course in the sixties that became "black power." Forty years
ago we had few black writers compared to today. There have been forty years
of education and many more college graduates. And it's important to remember that blacks don't have a long history of writing. We come from an oral tradition. At one point in America it was a crime to teach blacks to read and
write. So it's only in the past 150 years that we've been writing in this country.

Q: Elsewhere you've said that the primary opposition in your plays is
between blacks who deny their African roots and those who don't. Would
you still describe your work that way?

A: Today I would say that the conflict in black America is between the middle
class and the so-called underclass, and that conflict goes back to those who
deny themselves and those who aren't willing to. America offers blacks a contract that says, "If you leave all that African stuff over there and adopt the values of the dominant culture, you can participate." For the most part, black
Americans have rejected that sort of con job. Many blacks in the ghettos say,
"If I got to give up who I am, if I can't be like me, then I don't want it." The
ones who accept go on to become part of the growing black middle class and
in some areas even acquire some power and participation in society, but
when they finally arrive where they arrive, they are no longer the same people. They are clothed in different manners and ways of life, different thoughts
and ideas. They've acculturated and adopted white values.

Q: Can you conceive of an authentically black middle-class person? Aren't
you one?

A: I would say that, yes. I went to the home of a black chiropractor whose
wife was also a professional in L.A., and I was surprised how black he was,

but it's not common. European immigrants faced a similar situation when they arrived in this country in the early 1900s. Margaret Mead writes about the anxiety to become Americans, giving up their own languages, being ashamed of their Old World parents. But for blacks there is a bigger problem, because even though the recent white immigrants had different ethnicities, they were all Europeans.

Q: You're self-educated. How do you feel about schools and self-education?
A: The schools are horrible and don't teach anybody anything. From about the fifth grade on, I was always butting heads with my teachers. I would ask them questions and they would say, "Shut up. Sit down," because they didn't know the answers. So I'd go to the library to find out. When I quit school at fourteen, I didn't want my mother to know, so I'd get up and go to the library and stay there until three o'clock. My mother taught me to read when I was four years old, and in the library for the first time in my life I felt free. I could read whole books on subjects that interested me. I'd read about the Civil War or theology. By the time I left the library, I thought, "Okay, I'm ready. I know a lot of stuff." It always amazed me that libraries were free. Now of course you can learn everything at home on the Internet. But the way education is structured in schools, you have to take all kinds of required courses before you can get to the subject that interests you. In 1987 I gave a lecture at the Carnegie Library in Pittsburgh and was able to return a book, *The Collected Poems of Paul Dunbar*, that I had checked out of the library in 1959. For thirty years I kept that book, taking it with me every time I moved—which was often whenever the rent was due. Actually the library let me keep the book.

Q: Elsewhere you've talked about Athol Fugard's plays as an important influence on your work. Are you in sympathy with black South African playwrights who consider the situation of black South Africans their legitimate material, not his?
A: I am in sympathy with them, even though I admire Athol Fugard's work. He wrote those plays out of his magnificent spirit that made him want to fight this racial battle at a time when black playwrights in South Africa had no outlets for their work. Those people were voiceless. That was good. But ultimately, ideally, I think he should write about the white experience in South Africa and more about himself, from his own focus.

Q: When you look at your work as a whole, what patterns do you see?
A: *Fences* is the odd man out because it's about one individual and everything focuses around him. The others are ensemble plays. I think I need to write another one like *Fences* to balance it out.

Q: Do you think you might write a play with a woman at the center?
A: It's possible, but it would be a bit more difficult for me. But right now in the play I am working on, the character I call my spectacle character, like Gabriel in *Fences* or Hambone in *Two Trains Running*, is a woman for the first time. And that character is generally a big character, so I'm working on that.

Q: Elsewhere you've said that you start plays with an idea. Can you talk about what kind of idea? Is it a social or historical idea?
A: Let's take the play I'm working on now. In it I'm interested in examining family structure, to see if it broke down and when and why that occurred. The play is set in 1985, but it means going back twenty years to see how we got to where we were in 1985. In this play a number of characters have killed other men. Through the characters and events of the play I want to explore the family and to expose the culprit. That's important.

Q: From your description it sounds like your new play will be about violence as well as the breakdown of the family. Are they related?
A: When I look at the situation of black America in 1985 I want to see where these kids got these guns. I personally think I can trace it all back to Bernard Goetz in his paranoia shooting those four black kids on the subway, two of them in the back. He was seen as heroic. And shortly after that, young blacks were shot in Teaneck, New Jersey, and chased down streets in New York and beaten with baseball bats and shot. I think the black kids said, "Wait a minute, we're under attack here." And they went out and got guns. They armed themselves because they were under assault. Now, unfortunately, they are using the guns on each other. But Goetz is where it began.

Q: In the past you've said that the situation for blacks in America is worse now than it was forty years ago. Do you still think so?
A: Without question, yes.

Q: What would make it better? Let's say you had great political power, what would you do?

A: I would make an announcement that slavery is morally reprehensible and will never occur again. The Emancipation Proclamation was a military move, not a moral admission, so this needs to be a policy statement. Then having said that I would tell blacks they are free to participate in American society as Africans, that they don't have to give up their heritage. We have black doctors, lawyers, hydraulic engineers, artists, and they all work for someone else. None of them work for themselves. Every manhole cover, mailbox, building, or street is owned by white people in virtually every city in America. The only area in black life where I see people participating as Africans is in the area of rap music. They aren't censored, they say what they want to say, they do what they want to do, they set up their own record companies. Why are all the most influential black scholars at Harvard and not at Howard? We need to make Howard University as desirable a university as Harvard. I also find it interesting that none of the historically black colleges have a black studies program. And at the graduation at black colleges they don't sing gospel.

Q: How were things better in the forties?

A: We used to have our own black baseball league, for example. Everything was black-owned. On a Sunday black families would go over to the field, and some would sell peanuts or chicken sandwiches and so on. We were more self-sufficient. When blacks were finally allowed to play in the white leagues, the loss for the black community was great. Similarly in the forties black women were not allowed to go downtown and try on dresses in the department stores. So we had our own dress stores in the neighborhood and the doctors and dentists and teachers and business owners all lived in the same neighborhood, and we had a thriving community. Then the doctors and dentists started moving out, and the whole community began to fall down. So now we're in a situation in which the basketball league is 99 percent black, but it's owned by whites. If all the money made from black sports and black music were in black hands, if it were spent in our neighborhoods, things would be very different.

Q: Elsewhere you've said you want your audience to see your characters as Africans, not just black folks in America. Can you talk about that?

A: I'm talking about black Americans having uniquely African ways of participating in the world, of doing things, different ways of socializing. I have no fascination with Africa itself. I've never been to Africa and have no desire to go. I've been invited several times and turned down the invitations because I don't like to travel. When my daughter went to college, she called me all excited that she was studying about Timbuktu. I told her, "You study your grandma and her grandmother before you go back to Timbuktu." People don't want to do that because soon you wind up with slavery, and that's a condition people want to run away from. It's much easier to go back to the glory days of Timbuktu, but to do that is falsely romantic. It doesn't get you anywhere. I remember when I first went with a friend to a Passover seder and heard them say, "When we were slaves in the land of Egypt." I met a kid in 1987 in New York who thought slavery ended in 1960. This is God's honest truth. He was seventeen years old and he thought slavery ended in 1960. That's our fault. Like the Jews, we need to celebrate our emancipation; it would give us a way of identifying and expressing a sense of unity.

Q: Do you see anything anomalous about your wanting blacks to see themselves as Africans but your not having any desire even to visit Africa?
A: I'm simply saying blacks should hold on to what they are. You don't have to go to Africa to be an African. I live and breathe that. Even in the sixties, with all the romantic involvement with Africa, I never wore a dashiki to participate in the Black Power movement. Africa is right here in the southern part of the United States, which is our ancestral homeland. I don't need to make that leap across the ocean. When the first African died on the continent of North America, that was the beginning of my history.

Q: Speaking of your history, I remember reading that you said the first word you typed was your own name. Do you have any interest in autobiography?
A: Not about me as an individual. I don't like to read biographies or autobiographies myself. And if your material is autobiographical, sooner or later you're going to run out of material. I take the entire black experience in America, from the first black in 1619 until now, and claim that as my material. That's my story, my life story, and that's a lot to write about. But in truth, whatever subject you take, you as a writer are going to come up with something that is based on who you are, so even in choosing the black experience I am writing it from my own perspective.

Q: Do you have any particular fondness for one of your characters more than the others?

A: No, but *Joe Turner* is my favorite play. I like all my characters, and I always say I'd like to put them all in the same play—Troy and Boy Willie and Loomis and Sterling and Floyd. I once wrote this short story called "The Best Blues Singer in the World," and it went like this: "The streets that Balboa walked was his own private ocean, and Balboa was drowning." End of story. That says it all. Nothing else to say. Since then, I've been rewriting that same story over and over again. All of my plays are rewriting that same story. I'm not sure what it means, other than life is hard.

Q: At various points you've said that the only institution in the black community that you affirm is the church, but at other times you have affirmed Amiri Baraka's comment that when a person looks in the mirror he should see an image of his God, and that black Americans don't because Jesus was white. Could you talk about your attitude toward Christianity?

A: The Christianity that blacks have embraced, they have transformed with aspects of African religion, African style, and certainly African celebration. The church is the only stable organization in the black community, and the community is organized around the church. If you want to disseminate information in the black community, the way to do it is through the church. But as a whole, the Christian churches have been the source of organizations like the Christian Knights of the Ku Klux Klan, and even today the church sanctions inequities. When I grew up in Pittsburgh, blacks couldn't go to our black church for confession; we had to go to a white church for that.

Q: Could you talk about your relationship with Lloyd Richards?

A: Because he has directed all my plays, the plays are all the product of the same two artistic sensibilities. They become seamless, like one play.

Q: Has your relationship with him changed over the years?

A: Not really. What Lloyd will sometimes do is tell me to see if I can cut something, but he won't ever tell me what to cut.

Q: Have you ever moved a scene from one play to another?

A: Part of Loomis's big speech in *Joe Turner*—"My enemies all around me picking flesh from my bones. I'm choking on my own blood and all you got to give me is salvation"—those words were originally Troy Maxson's. Both men are questioning God, wondering why suffering occurs when God is here and God loves us all. Troy is telling God, "I did everything You asked, I walked through the valley, whatever You asked me to do I did. So where is my given? Where is what You owe me? I ain't done nothing. I ain't asking for nobody else's. I'm asking for mine." In their different ways Maxson and Loomis are asking the same theological questions. And I've got other stuff that was cut from various plays, including this wonderful little scene with a black cat. That scene was originally part of *Seven Guitars*, in fact we played it in Chicago before it got cut. It's going to turn up again someplace. I just love it, this black cat.

Q: Elsewhere you've praised a willingness to bleed and shed blood. Speaking of blood and scars, is Risa's act of scarring her own legs positive in the same way Loomis's act of slashing his own chest is at the end of *Joe Turner*? Are they symbolically similar acts?
A: Loomis is not only illustrating his willingness to bleed but saying that if salvation requires bloodshed, he doesn't need Christ to bleed for him on the cross. He's saying something like, "Christ can do some stuff I can't, but if it's about bleeding, yeah, I can bleed for myself." Risa's act is an attempt to define herself in language different from what society uses for women. So I think both are positive. Actually, for a while I was concerned because all my protagonists seem to have scars. People often tell me that I must have a scar, but I don't have a scar anywhere. But I think it's symbolic of being marked. It's a willingness to do battle. It doesn't matter if you win or lose, it's just the willingness like Boy Willie grappling with the ghost in *The Piano Lesson*.

Q: You've said that you try not to create characters who are victims. Yet aren't all these scars a sign that they have been victimized? Is the issue how they deal with their victimization, how they respond to it?
A: We're all victims of white America's paranoia. My characters don't respond as victims. No matter what society does to them, they are engaged with life, wrestling with it, trying to make sense out of it. Nobody is sitting around saying, "Woe is me."

Q: You've never focused a whole play on a relationship between a black woman and a black man. Why?

A: First of all, it's difficult. You have to write the woman's part. I think *Seven Guitars* comes close. When I was writing that play, I tried to work on that aspect. Some of the scenes between Floyd and Vera never made it into the final version. Other developments took over. But I'm exploring that relationship in the play I'm working on now.

Q: So for a male playwright, it's easier to create male characters than female characters?

A: It's certainly easier for me. That's one part of it; the other part is that I may be afraid of writing a soap opera. The man-woman relationship is certainly an important part of life, but I think you need to place it inside something else, something broader. In the play I'm working on, there is an emphasis on the male-female relationship and also the mother-son relationship, which I'm developing in depth for the first time, with the woman as the spectacle character.

Q: Could you talk a bit about what you mean by a spectacle character? Is this character a spectacle for the other characters?

A: No, they're fully integrated into the other characters' lives, but they are a spectacle for the audience. I think that's my interpretation of Aristotle's spectacle in the *Poetics*.

Q: Do you think you define plot the same way Aristotle did?

A: For me plot grows out of characterization, so there are no plot points. The play doesn't flow from plot point to plot point. I guess it's easy to plot that way, since every TV drama moves along those lines. It becomes very mechanical. Some people call my plays plotless; that's simply because they haven't been able to recognize the plot in them. In my plays you don't say, "Here is a point here, hold on to this because we're going to need it." I think you need to hold on to everything. In my plays things happen gradually, and you come to see why things are in the play. For example, in *Seven Guitars* you hear four men talking, and you may think the play is not going anywhere. But it is. All that stuff, every single thing they talk about, connects and is important to your understanding of the drama.

Q: It may seem a strange connection, but are your plays more like Chekhov's than most playwrights', both in their being ensemble plays and in their seeming plotlessness?

A: I think you're right. I didn't know Chekhov's work, so there is no question of influence, but when I saw *Uncle Vanya*, I thought, "He's cool. I like this play. Yes, it's just people sitting around talking, and the drama is made out of the talk, but there are things going on, a lot of stuff is happening." It was good that I saw *Vanya* since I had thought I was doing something unique.

Q: Do you think there's any correlation between how much a play changes as you work on it and the quality of the final version?

A: No. *Joe Turner,* my favorite of my plays, didn't change much. The title changed—it was originally named after one of Romare Bearden's paintings. And originally there was supposed to be a real competition between Seth and Selig over this store that becomes available. That would have been interesting sociologically because Selig was white but Seth had a more secure financial position. But as I worked on the play, I realized that that competition was too much sociology, that what I was trying to do was something else. I wanted to keep the focus on Loomis and Martha. I start with an idea, but as I work, things expand and change. The fun process of writing is figuring out where you're going and how to get there. That's where the real creativity is. I'm just beginning to discover that confidence is one of the most important things that an artist needs. If you don't have that confidence, you simply can't do the work.

Q: Has it been the extraordinary acclaim that your plays have received that has enabled you to become more confident?

A: I'm not sure that's how you gain confidence, through having your work endorsed. You have to know yourself and what you're capable of. It's a matter of exploring inside yourself, of having the courage to face your demons and your confidence that you can, that you'll survive the encounter. All of these things are what makes the art. If you take the easy way out and avoid going deep inside yourself, you get art that is less than it can be. Robert Duncan talks about surety as a line of poetry burned in the hand. Surety enables you to say, "I can get these words to say what I want them to say." I worked for many years as a poet before I acquired that surety.

Q: Does having grappled long and hard once with your inner demons give
you more courage to grapple again?
A: The grappling strengthens your spirit and emboldens you for your next
journey. You tell yourself, "Oh yeah, I was here before. Get away, you
demon—I'll step on you!" Each time you go inside and you find new
demons. You're just exploring yourself; it's like walking down the landscape
of the self. The process is about making art, and what you choose to write
about is totally different from autobiography.

Q: In the past you've mentioned the importance of listening to your characters and trusting them. Can you talk about that a bit?
A: You listen to them, but you never lose consciousness that they are your cre-
ations. When I first started writing plays I couldn't write good dialogue because
I didn't respect how black people talked. I thought that in order to make art out
of it I had to change it, make it into something different. Once I learned to value
and respect my characters, I could really hear them. How you talk is how you
think; the language describes the one who speaks it. When I have characters,
I just let them start talking. The important thing is not to censor them, to trust
them to just talk. What they are talking about may not seem to have anything to
do with what you as a writer were writing about, but it does. Just let them talk
and it will connect, because you as the artist will make it connect. Let's say one
guy goes, "Always seemed like I had a halo around my head." Another guy says,
"Yeah, I remember the time you come and asked me did you have a halo, talking
about did you have a halo." And the first guy says, "You see I went to everybody,
I went and asked my mama. She said, 'You ain't got no halo but you still my
angel child.'" You might think, "What are these guys doing standing on the corner talking about having a halo?" You find out that this is a really interesting
conversation, that they are saying what they think of themselves. The more my
characters talk, the more I find out about them. And the more I find out about
them, the more material I have. So I encourage them, I tell them, "Tell me some
more." I just write it down, and it starts to make connections. When I was writing *The Piano Lesson*, Boy Willie just announced that Sutter fell in the well. That
was news to me. I had no idea who Sutter was or why he fell in the well.

Q: And yet how central that development turns out to be.
A: At first Sutter was a black man; later that changed. You have to let your
characters talk for a while, trust them to do it and have the confidence that
later you can shape the material.

Q: What other surprises have your characters had for you?

A: When Loomis cuts himself in *Joe Turner*. Of course everything was pointing toward that, he couldn't have done anything but cut himself, but I didn't see it yet. That particular scene took me about twenty-five minutes to write. I was home working on the play. It was December 1, and to get the play in before the O'Neill deadline I had to put the play in the mail by midnight. I also had to have copies made, and there was three feet of snow on the ground. I went into this bar-restaurant on Grand Avenue in St. Paul, and I had no idea what Martha and Loomis were going to say to each other when they finally got together. Then I just wrote it in one shot. I simply sat down and wrote it. I don't think I changed a word of it. I just wrote to the end of the play and Loomis cut himself. That was the first time that kind of experience happened to me. I was there at the house of God, I was there. When I looked up, I was drenched; my clothes were sticking to me. I looked at my watch and saw that it was twenty-five minutes since I had started. And I had my play, I knew that I had the end of it. Up until that hour I had no idea what was going to happen.

Q: Do you still write mostly in bars and restaurants?

A: I write at home now more than I've done before. I started writing poetry when I was twenty years old, and you cannot sit at home as a twenty-year-old poet. You don't know anything about life. At that time many of my friends were painters, and I'd go visit them. I'd hear them complaining about needing money to buy paint supplies. And I realized how lucky I was because my tools were simple. I saw that I could borrow a pencil or paper, that I could write on napkins or paper bags. I'd walk around with a pen or pencil and paper, and I discovered poems everywhere. I was always prepared to write, and I just continued to do that over the years. Once when I was writing on a napkin, a waitress asked, "Do you write on napkins because it doesn't count?" I had never realized that if I'm writing on a napkin I'm not really writing. I'm telling myself, "This is just a napkin, for God's sake." It frees me up. If I pull out my tablet, I'm saying, "Now I'm writing," and I become much more conscious. She saw it; I didn't recognize it, but she did. That's why I do things like write on napkins. Then I go home and there's another kind of work. Taking the stuff out of notebooks from bars and restaurants, typing it, rewriting. Sometimes I'll copy out one line of dialogue and it will expand into two pages before I go on to the next line.

Q: Has your process changed much over the years?

A: My writing process is more or less the same. But I haven't been able to find a place in Seattle where I'm comfortable writing. I went to this one place, and there must have been around fourteen people sitting around writing. And I thought, "I've found the place where writers come." I sat there and I waited but nothing came. I thought, these other people are taking all the writing stuff in the air, they're taking it all away. Afterwards I made this joke about how my muse got into an argument with someone else's muse and had been put out of the restaurant, but I didn't know it, so I was sitting there waiting with nothing happening.

Q: *Fences* is organized around Troy Maxson, and *Seven Guitars* is a murder mystery told mostly in flashback. Is *The Piano Lesson* a kind of debate between Berniece and Boy Willie?

A: That play sets up the question of whether you can develop a sense of self-worth by denying the past. Everyone sees the play differently than I do. Because Boy Willie wants to sell the piano, they think he is trying to deny the past. But Berniece cannot even touch the piano—she's the one who is denying everything, she's the one trying to run away from the past. He is saying, "I don't need a piece of wood to tell me who I am, to remind me of my past. If the wood can give me a future, if selling the piano will enable me to buy the land where we were slaves, then I've come full circle." That's what he is trying to explain to her. If she had a use for the piano like giving music lessons to help pay the rent, then he would be willing to relinquish it to her and say he's got to get the land a different way. So it's when Berniece breaks her self-imposed taboo against touching the piano, when she calls on her ancestors, that something radical changes. The ghost Boy Willie was wrestling with upstairs gets off of Boy Willie, and Boy Willie knows something important has happened. When Berniece calls on her ancestors, she's calling on the ancestors inside herself, not something outside herself—just like Loomis recognizing he can bleed for himself. And when I was writing the play, I thought, if we do this right, people in the audience would call out the names of their ancestors—"Sadie Smith, Cousin James, I want you to help me." It would take a lot of trust because that name is sacred to the person, but through that the audience would feel like a community. I can see it happening with a black audience, because black people do that in church all the time. The audience calling out names sacred to them would disrupt the play, but the performance would have another kind of intensity.

Q: In your cycle of plays, you'll have one play per decade of this century, but in your introductory note to *Seven Guitars* you say, "Despite my interest in history, I've always been more concerned with culture." Could you talk a little about history versus culture?

A: I'm more interested in the historical context than in actual history, so for example I changed the actual historical date of a Joe Louis boxing match because it suited my dramatic purposes. I always come back to the quote from James Baldwin about the black tradition, which he defined as "That field of manners and rituals of intercourse that will sustain a man once he's left his father's house." The primary focus of my work is looking at black culture as it changes and grows in evolving historical contexts.

Q: Bynum in *Joe Turner* and Aunt Ester in *Two Trains Running* are similar characters in reclaiming and holding on to the past. Does the fact that Bynum is a character in a play set in the early years of this century and Aunt Ester is ancient suggest a fear that these kinds of people and certain folk connections are in danger of disappearing?

A: Aunt Ester suggests that your experience is alive, that there is a repository of wisdom and experience a person can tap into.

Q: How about all the characters' talk about her great age and illness?

A: But she doesn't die. She's sick, anybody who is 322 years old is gonna get sick once in a while, but she ain't gonna die. Hambone dies, Malcolm dies, but she doesn't die.

Q: You've talked about your fear of theater becoming an elitist form because of the cost of tickets. Do you have any idea what people who are committed to theater could do to avoid that, or is that coming toward us inevitably?

A: I think it's the nature of the beast. Lights, sets, costumes, actors' salaries, rehearsals—there are enormous costs. But we could have more than one kind of theater; we need more theater on street corners, theater in the schools. Theater should be a natural part of everyone's ordinary life, or else it will become like opera where tickets cost seventy-five dollars. In other parts of the world, in places like Haiti, there is art all over, paintings on walls, on trash cans, in hallways. We need to have theater that is everywhere, like that art.

Q: In addition to plays, you've written poetry, and now you're also writing a novel. Can you talk about the differences between those forms, and whether material comes to you in one form or another?

A: For me, poetry is distilled language. Somewhere I read poetry defined as enlarging the sayable. I like that definition, and I think poetry is the highest form of literature. Writing a novel is like setting out on this vast, uncharted ocean. I never knew how anyone could do it. But now I see that like any kind of writing, you start with the first word and finish the first page. Then you've got a page and you go on to the next. I realized that writing a novel is like writing a play in that you don't have to know where you're going. You just go and you find out as you go along. You plot your way, whether with a compass or by the stars. I've had this idea for a novel for many years now. I've got about sixty pages; in the past month I've written another ten pages, because the novel is there and it wants to be born. But I can't write the novel, because I've got to finish three plays to complete my cycle. I've got to stay on track. I need to write plays faster; I can't take three or four years to write one. For me the big difference in writing a novel is that a narrator can take an audience to places you can't on a stage.

Q: How about the internal life? Some people think that a novel can explore a character's inner life in a way a play can't.

A: No, I think a play can do that through dialogue—the talk replaces that analysis. What I can do in a novel is take you down this dusty road and have you taste the dust. Suddenly it gets dark and two million crows come flying across, going south. They black out the sun. I can't do that on stage. But in a novel I can make you see those crows and have that mean something.

Q: Playwrights have taken quite varying positions about the importance of production. Edward Albee has taken an extreme position, saying, "A first-rate play exists completely on the page and is never improved by production; it is only proved by production." Do you agree?

A: I agree with that, because the play is there on the page; it provides a road map or a blueprint. I don't write for a production; I write for the page, just like a poem. A play, like a poem, exists on the page even if no one ever reads it aloud. But I don't want to underestimate what a good production with actors embodying the characters offers. But depending on the imagination of the reader, he may get more by reading the play than by seeing a weak production.

Q: What have the productions of your plays not directed by Lloyd Richards been like?
A: I like when directors try different things even though they don't always work. I don't want to see a production that's a damn near duplicate of the original. One production of *Ma Rainey* had a spiritual dancer in it. I personally didn't think it worked, but I didn't mind them trying it out. What I objected to was their listing the spiritual dancer under the list of characters as if that dancer was part of my script. Another production had Hambone after he died come back dressed in a white suit looking in the window of the restaurant. The audience loved seeing this homeless person in an elegant white suit. I wouldn't have done that if I were directing the play, but it worked for the audience.

Q: Have you ever been drawn to directing your own plays?
A: I started my career in the theater as a director, but I've never wanted to direct my own plays. I've always wanted to see what someone else brings to them. Likewise I make very few set notes or costume notes, because I don't want to take away the job of the set designer or costume designer. They should get to do the work they were trained to do.

Q: One playwright has said that drama is made up of sound and silence. Do you see drama that way?
A: No doubt drama is made up of sound and silence, but I see conflict at the center. What you do is set up a character who has certain beliefs and you establish a situation where those beliefs are challenged and that character is forced to examine those beliefs and perhaps change them. That's the kind of dramatic situation which engages an audience.

Q: Then is the conflict primarily internal rather than external, between characters?
A: Internal, right, where the character has to reexamine his whole body of beliefs. The play has to shake the very foundation of his whole system of beliefs and force him to make a choice. Then I think you as a playwright have accomplished something, because that process also forces the audience to go

through the same inner struggle. When I teach my workshops I tell my students that if a guy announces, "I'm going to kill Joe," and there's a knock on the door, the audience is going to want to know if that's Joe and why this guy wants to kill him and whether we would also want to kill him if we were in the same situation. The audience is engaged in the questions.

Q: Tell me about your teaching.
A: I don't really teach; I just on occasion offer little workshops. I've done three-day workshops at a Tucson writers' conference three years in a row. The students all show up with plays or scenes they want to read. I tell them that after the third day if they still want them read, we will read them. But because of all they've learned in those days, they always say, "Give mine back to me, don't read that."

Q: What kind of techniques do you use?
A: After we talk about what a play is, I ask them to invent a painting and then describe it. That word-painting becomes the set description, but they don't know it. You have to trick them.

Q: And does the trick free them up?
A: Oh, absolutely, absolutely. Because they are not conscious of what they are doing. If you tell them to write a description of a set, they get too conscious and can't do it. One guy described a train station in his word-painting and said, "There's a woman wearing a white dress over there and some guys sitting in another part of the station." Then I started asking questions. "Is she coming or going?" "Going." "Where is she going?" "To visit her grandmother." And simply by asking these questions we find out who this person is. Then we'll find out about these guys over in the other part of the station. All of a sudden the student yells, "I can write a play about this!" You've caught him totally by surprise. Until we fleshed out the painting, he didn't even know who the woman was. I ask the students what the people in their paintings say and how they talk, and gradually they see that characters characterize themselves through their speech. They begin to build character portraits.

Q: This word-painting technique sounds a lot like your writing on a napkin.
A: Yes, I think it's about changing their approach. I tell them anybody can write a play, just like anybody can drive a car. All of us can learn the rules of

the road, make the turns, switch on the lights. But there is Mario Andretti out there. I can't make them all into Mario Andretti; obviously. I've never taken a playwriting class or read any books on it. Everything I know comes from my own writing. Those students, many of whom came back all three years, really did become better playwrights; a couple of them even had productions of their plays produced. Then I quit going. After I finish these three plays, I think I'd like to teach and write that novel. But first I've got to finish those three plays. That's first.

August Wilson on Playwriting: An Interview

Elisabeth J. Heard / 1999

From *African American Review*, 35 (Spring 2001), 93–102. Reprinted by permission of Elisabeth J. Heard.

How does August Wilson view his plays and the process by which he creates them? Where does he start when writing a new play? Is August Wilson writing with a particular audience in mind? Joan Herrington, in "*I Ain't Sorry for Nothin' I Done*": *August Wilson's Process of Playwriting*, attributes Wilson's success in playwriting to his influences, which he himself refers to as the "*four 'B's'* "—the blues, the playwright Amiri Baraka, the painter Romare Bearden, and the short story writer Jorge Luis Borges. She also discusses what she calls Wilson's "new methodology of playwriting," which entails revising the plays during the rehearsal process. Wilson first used this revision strategy with *The Piano Lesson* (1995) and decided to employ it again for the 1996 version of his play *Jitney*, originally written in 1979. Wilson's return to *Jitney* and the evolution of a significantly different version has sparked an interest by critics in Wilson's playwriting methods.

After seeing the Goodman Theatre's production of *Jitney*, which ran in the summer of 1999, I wanted to know more about Wilson's playwriting methods and how he came to revise a play that he originally wrote twenty years earlier. Wilson very kindly agreed to an interview, and during our conversation he provided details on how he creates his plays. He discussed the process of how he works, how he views his revision strategy, and his relationship with actors, directors, and set designers. Wilson also revealed that, during the writing process, he sees himself as focusing on creating a piece of art, not as trying to create a text primarily designed to entertain an audience.

A lot of our conversation concerned playwriting. All audiences see is the polished, final product, but below Wilson offers important insights into the steps he takes toward creating that product.

Heard: How do you begin writing a play? Where do you start—with the situation, characters, settings, etc.?

Wilson: Well, I generally start with a line of dialogue. Someone says something and they're talking to someone else. I don't all the time know who's talking or who they are talking to, but you take the line of dialogue and it starts from there. The next thing you know you've got four pages of dialogue, and after a while you say, "Well, let me name this guy; let's give him a name. Who's talking?" And in the process of him talking you find out things about him. So the more the characters talk the more you know about them. It generally starts there. And then I say, "Okay, so where are they?" and then I'll come up with a setting or something. Once you get the set and one or two characters, then it begins to take on a life of its own. Other characters walk in, and I'm not sure how it happens from there, but it's a process. I don't, for instance, start at the beginning of the play and say, "Here's what's going to happen," and go from beginning to end. Very often I don't know what the ending is or what the events of the play are going to be, but I trust that these characters will tell me or that the story will develop naturally out of the dialogue of the characters.

Wilson has used this method to write seven plays, which have earned him two Pulitzers, a Tony, and six New York Drama Critics' Circle Awards. His long-term goal is to write a series of plays chronicling the African American experience in the twentieth century, and he plans to write one play for each decade. So far he has explored the 1910s (Joe Turner's Come and Gone), *the 1920s* (Ma Rainey's Black Bottom), *the 1930s* (The Piano Lesson), *the 1940s* (Seven Guitars), *the 1950s* (Fences), *the 1960s* (Two Trains Running), *and the 1970s* (Jitney). *Wilson's most recent project is* King Hedley II, *which is set in the 1980s and was produced at the Pittsburgh Public Theatre in the fall of 1999. Since Wilson starts his plays in the middle of the action with a line of dialogue, I was interested in knowing if he chooses the decade before his characters begin talking.*

Heard: Do you even start with the decade?

Wilson: Oh yeah, I start with the decade. I know some things when I start. I know, let's say, that the play is going to be a 1970s or a 1930s play, and it's going to be about a piano, but that's it. I slowly discover who the characters are as I go along. In *The Piano Lesson,* for instance, the question I had was, "Can you acquire a sense of self-worth by denying your past?" So I said,

"Okay, let me invent this situation and place characters on stage who ask that question. They don't necessarily have to answer it, but let's pose the question." So I know I want to do that, but *how* I'm going to do that I very often don't know. I do know some things before I start.

Even having decided on a decade, Wilson has a huge number of possible topics from which to choose. The 1920s was the age of blues and jazz (Ma Rainey), but it was also the age of prohibition. The 1960s left African Americans wondering about their place in society (Two Trains), but it was also a decade of war, assassinations of national figures, and the rise of the women's movement.

Heard: How do you choose the themes you're going to investigate for each decade? There are so many different things that can be chosen for each individual decade.
Wilson: I consider what I know about a particular decade and sort of go from there. I think if I knew other things then I'd write other things. The old adage is, "You write what you know," and even though you're writing about the 1930s, that's not what you're *really* writing about. You're only writing about love, honor, duty, betrayal. Those are the things which the play is made out of, and you're using 1936 Pittsburgh and that milieu to tell the story and to address those themes.

These themes are at the heart of all of Wilson's plays. Jitney *focuses on the value of family, friends, and community, especially when they are faced with an outside force which threatens to destroy all that the characters have worked hard to create.* Jitney *is the only play which was actually written in the decade in which it takes place, and given its uniquely immediate perspective I wanted to know how Wilson decided upon that particular setting for the 1970s.*

Heard: It's interesting that you chose the subject of *Jitney* for your seventies play. If you had to do it over again, would you still choose this subject?
Wilson: It is not so much *Jitney*, it's the period of urban renewal that was part of the early seventies and the late seventies. It is just a setting, if you will, an opportunity to use this group of men to expose the culture, to get at some of the ways that this particular community of people solved its problems, abused itself, and all those kinds of things. If I were to do it today I might come up with a different setting, but it would be the same community and

concern their struggles to remain whole in the face of all these things that threaten to tear them apart.

Wilson twice submitted his original manuscript of Jitney *to the National Playwrights' Conference of the Eugene O'Neill Theater Center, but both times it was rejected. The play was not professionally produced until 1982, when it was staged at Pittsburgh's Allegheny Repertory Theatre. While it received positive reviews, the play had some flaws. "The first draft of* Jitney *(1979)," writes critic Joan Herrington, "exhibits the insecurities of an inexperienced writer— repetition, glaring emotional signposts for the audience, inconsistent dialogue, and an obscure central conflict." The acts were also very uneven (the first act ran more than an hour, whereas the second was only twenty-six minutes long). Since* Jitney, *Wilson has written six very polished, successful plays, and I wanted to know what contributed to his evolution as a playwright.*

Heard: What contributed early in your career to your sense of what worked on stage and what didn't? Was it through your own success or failure? Through reading other playwrights or seeing other plays?

Wilson: I still don't know what works until it works, until I see it working. It wasn't through seeing other playwrights or reading other plays because I haven't done much of either of those. Again, you have an intuitive sense that this is dramatic or a nice shape to a scene; you intuitively know how to tell a good story (because all a play is is a story), where the highlights are, what information to withhold, and how to reveal things. This comes from an innate sense of storytelling. Here again you don't always know what works, but if you have an opportunity to workshop a play, see a production of a play, and sit with the audience in a play, you certainly can tell the parts that don't work. And then you say, "Show me the parts that do and I'll make the parts that don't . . . I'll make them like that." This is the general idea.

Wilson says that when he reread Jitney! *in 1996, the first time he had returned to the play in eleven years, he was surprised at how "short" the play was. Over the years, Wilson has become known for writing plays which often last more than three hours. Part of* Jitney!'s *brevity was due to the fact that it lacked the rich monologues which have become one of Wilson's signature traits. These monologues give Wilson's characters depth, and often the audience learns a lot about a character through a few simple lines. Through these monologues,*

*Wilson is able to create characters the audience can identify with. They become
people we know—the neighbor down the street, the store clerk, the town
drunk. My interest in his character development sparked my next question.*

Heard: What level of internal development of a character do you believe is
necessary to bring a character to life for your audience?
Wilson: I think that things like that [i.e., a few, simple lines], all of those
kinds of things contribute to the life of the characters; they don't have to be
big things, they can be little things, moments, like Doub in *Jitney* saying,
"Well, I won't worry, I got my railroad pension." That tells you an immeasurable
amount about the guy. He used to work at the railroad, and he worked long
enough that he has a pension from the railroad. The line used to read,
"I got my pension, and I'm not worried about it." Well, that doesn't tell you as
much. It tells you he has a pension, he worked somewhere. But once you say
"railroad," then you as the audience are able to connect him to every railroad
worker you know, and that makes him come alive more because now it is a
specific kind of thing. The man worked twenty-seven years on the railroad.
And he has two sons "like I tell my boys" (well, we don't know how many he
has), but that line didn't used to be in there. And by simply having him say,
"like I tell my boys," we immediately connect him to a family, connect him to
the railroad. He says, "I don't have nobody but myself," which implies that his
wife is dead, his kids are out of the house, and he worked twenty-seven years
on the railroad, and he's driving jitneys. So with just three or four lines of
dialogue we know a tremendous amount about this character. He has the
tendency to come more to life.

Heard: Was the absence of those lines a result of your being a beginning
playwright?
Wilson: I'm not sure that it was because it was my first play. I do the same
thing in the play I'm writing now. I think that it's part of the process and
the discovery that the playwright makes, and it doesn't have anything to do
with whether it's your first play or you're now more mature and you don't
make those mistakes. It would be nice, of course, if you hit it the first time as
you wrote. You may write the railroad pension the first time and you may
not, but if I look at the work I did yesterday, I would still see that there are
ways to improve it. Somewhere down the line in some rehearsal I may say,
"Oh, I see, why don't I just say the railroad there?" Those are not necessarily

things that were missing because I was a beginning playwright. It's just a part of the process of developing a play.

In 1996, Edward Gilbert, the artistic director of the Pittsburgh Public Theater, asked Wilson to revisit Jitney!, *which motivated Wilson to revise the play. Besides the fact that the play was too short and the scenes were uneven, Wilson also felt as though some of the relationships among the characters needed to be revised, especially the scenes between Becker, the hardworking owner of the jitney station, and Booster, his thirty-nine-year-old son who has just been released from prison after serving a twenty-year sentence for killing a white woman.*

Heard: What gave you the inspiration to keep revising the Becker and Booster part?

Wilson: I went back to the play in 1996 and decided to do some work on it, and the aspect of the play which needed the most work was the Booster-Becker thing—clarifying what their relationship was and how it had been affected by this misguided act on the part of the son, and how it affected the father and also the son. The two scenes that they have were originally one scene between the two of them, which I later made into two scenes, went back to one scene, and then to one and a half scenes. So it was the Booster-Becker thing that had the most revisions. That and the Rena-Youngblood scenes were the parts that I rewrote. The other parts are pretty much as they were written in 1979.

The revision of Jitney *has sparked an interest among critics in Wilson's revision strategies. Herrington states, "The changes Wilson made to* Jitney *reflected a new methodology of playwriting—specifically of rewriting—which he had developed while working on* Seven Guitars *at the Goodman Theatre in Chicago in 1995." This "new methodology" involved not rewriting the play before the rehearsal. Instead, Wilson waited until the rehearsal process began and then made daily changes to the script. If he felt that a scene needed to be changed or that a monologue should be added, Wilson would go home, do the rewrite, and bring the changes to rehearsal the next day. I asked Wilson about this revision strategy.*

Heard: I read that you experimented with a new revision strategy for this play. Will you continue to use this strategy with future plays?

Wilson: You are talking about writing in the moment?

Heard: Yes, getting feedback from the actors and directors, writing new parts, and bringing them the next day.

Wilson: That's a good way to work. I don't know if it is necessarily a new way to work because generally I'd do the whole rewrite, come to rehearsal, and continue to work on it. But one time when I did *Seven Guitars*, I didn't do a rewrite. I did the rewrite during the rehearsal process, and it seemed to work as well if not better than the other way. I guess I'm not consciously aware that I made a change, but I'll certainly continue doing what I'm doing, working the way I'm working, and I enjoy the rehearsal process and working through there. So I will continue that.

In the past I would rewrite the whole thing and bring it in, and, of course, there were certain revisions that were made in the rehearsal process. But the bulk of the work had been done, so I would sort of lay back off of it (if that's a way of saying it) because I already did the rewrite, and now I was just patching up various things. With *Seven Guitars* I didn't do the rewrite prior to rehearsal. I came into rehearsal knowing that the play had to be rewritten. And I did my rewrite there in rehearsal, which didn't allow me to lay back off the material and do patchwork. I had to get in there and do the actual work, which seemed to work better in the sense that I wasn't writing in a vacuum. I had the actors there, so you could press and then you could see a response, or you could do something and see an immediate response. If you're at home doing the rewrite, you can't get that response—you're sort of working in a vacuum, so to speak.

Heard: Were there other benefits from writing in the moment and getting the immediate feedback?

Wilson: I think so. It is a different kind of work, so you write different things. I think that if I'm at home sitting doing the rewrite, I'm going to write something different than if I'm there in the rehearsal room doing it. It's kind of hard to explain, but if you're tossed into the fire at any particular moment, then you are going to write something different than you will in another particular moment. And that is from day to day. Here at this moment on Tuesday at this rehearsal I'll come up with this, and I'm going to rewrite that; I'm going to rewrite it tonight. If I rewrite it next week I'm going to write something different. So you have to choose what is the right moment to do it because you sort of only get to do it once. I found more immediacy in the rehearsal process. I certainly wrote different things—I don't know if I wrote better things—and I enjoyed it.

Since this revision strategy depends upon the input of the actors, Wilson likes to have a major influence on the choice of actors. He is at all auditions and decides, with the director, who is right for the roles. I wanted to know if there was a correlation between having this much input and accepting the comments and suggestions actors may have during rehearsal.

Heard: Does choosing your actors give you confidence in what the actor says, or in the suggestions that he or she may have in order to help mold and craft the play to its final production?

Wilson: Not necessarily. Sometimes you can choose wrong. Sometimes you can get into rehearsal and say, "Wow, this isn't what I thought it was going to be." Some actors work well in rehearsal, show you different things; other actors will do the same thing all the way through. They're looking to you for something. You have actors and you watch them search, and then their search gives you ideas about the characters because they show you different aspects of them. And you say, "Oh, yeah, I see how he's playing that. He's playing this character this way, so I'll help him by writing for the character which he is portraying," while another actor will give you something different. So here again it is crucially important who those particular actors are and what they show you from day to day in the rehearsal room. They can help you develop the character that way. So you don't always choose right. Then again, you don't always get who you want, either. So it is six-in-one, half-a-dozen-in-the-other. I've been fortunate to get some good actors, and we've had a good rehearsal process, and they enjoy the work also. And if you have actors who don't mind if you bring in a new monologue from day to day, etc., they just roll with the punches. That's good when you have actors who are willing to do more and work harder.

Wilson is also known for choosing African American directors to direct his plays, and often uses the same director for several productions. Some of the directors he works with frequently are Lloyd Richards, Walter Dallas, and Marion McClinton; choosing the right director is very important to Wilson. I wanted to know how he envisioned the role of the director and what relationship he wants both with the director and between the director and the text.

Heard: I know that you play an important part in choosing the directors for your plays. Do you choose directors because you want them to carry out your vision, or do you choose those who will add something and go beyond the text?

Wilson: The director works as an interpretive artist, but he's still an artist, so you also have to give him room to create and to put his vision of the play or his translation or interpretation of the material on the stage. So you look for a director who has an overall sense of a play, and if you have a body of work, then an overall sense of your work, so that he or she knows what your requirements are. For instance, there are some lines that can be played rather broadly, but if you know my work, you know that all my characters maintain their dignity, and there should be no buffoonery on stage; so I look for directors who keep the actors reined in, and make a clear interpretation where all the actors maintain their dignity. Basically you look for someone who understands your work and who's part of it, whose sensibilities are similar to yours, whose feelings about the material are similar to yours.

Wilson's plays employ only one set, and he depends heavily on setting to create atmosphere. Consequently, the choice of scene designer is also very important to him.

Heard: Your plays are staged using only one set, which you describe in detail in the printed versions of the scripts. How important is it to you that set designers adhere to your vision of the set?

Wilson: I welcome designers who create the environment with a minimum of guidance. There are certain things that I require; they are relatively simple. I mean, for instance, if the play is set in a jitney station, I don't want the designer to put it in a backyard. But within the confines of that, I think that the designer is free to create his or her vision of the concept of what that space is like. These people have gone to school and have studied this, and they create the environment. I think that as a playwright, if I detail that environment, then I'm taking away something from them. I'm taking away their creativity and their ability to have input themselves, not just to follow what the playwright has written. So I do a minimum set description and let the designers create within that.

Heard: Even though the sets never change or move, there is still a sense of progression and movement within the plays. How do you maintain that forward movement in a play where the sets themselves stand still?

Wilson: The set is not the play, it's the environment for the play, so if you have motion in the play, so to speak, then the play will move. You try to structure a sense of progression into the play. You get a sense that you are moving toward a conclusion or a purpose for having these events in the play happen. Each of the events must connect to something, and ideally will propel you to the next event, and from that you get the sense of movement, even though, as you say, the set remains the same or is static. But the overall arc of the play or the motion of the play is set in that environment. I'm looking out the window here at these buildings in Seattle, and it stays the same, but there are all kinds of things that happen down there on that street. The set is the environment for the actors, but it has to be the right environment for this particular action for the play to take place in.

For Jitney's *set, the designers created the inside of a slightly run down jitney station. With the use of a scrim, the audience can see the street outside the station, which is lined with cars. Inside the station, the key prop is a telephone which rings constantly throughout the play and influences the comings and goings of the jitney station. I was curious about the extent to which the dependence on the phone was intentional.*

Heard: The telephone is an important prop in *Jitney* and plays an especially key role at the end. How do you see the phone functioning throughout the play?

Wilson: Yeah, it's intentional, but actually what it is is a wonderful device for a beginning playwright, because you can use the phone to get your characters on and off stage. So when I'm writing and following a particular track in the play and I get stuck, well, I'll have the phone ring, and then you get something new. The phone rings and Fielding takes a trip, and then you look up and there are different characters on stage and they begin to talk about something different. So the phone was, for me as a playwright, a device to get people on and off stage, particularly when I got stuck and didn't know where I was going. It becomes almost like another character; it takes on a life of its own, and it is there, and you can use it to comment on the action by deciding to have it ring. It's also the presence of the community, because there is always somebody at the end of that phone who needs to go somewhere—to the doctor's, to the grocery store, to the bus station—so it also serves to keep the community as a presence in the play.

As Wilson stated earlier, Jitney *is not just about a group of men who work at a jitney station. Wilson is exploring universal themes of family, community, responsibility, and integrity. How did he envision these themes coming across to and affecting an audience?*

Heard: What do you hope is the effect of *Jitney* on the audience? When the audience leaves the theatre, what issues would you like them to be thinking about? How would you like them to feel?

Wilson: I hope they have a good time at the play. I don't write with any particular message in mind, but I think you see these people struggling through their relationships and understanding how they each have disappointed one another. Then the son, at the end of the play, stepping into the father's shoes, seizing up the father's cause, his banner, becoming all the things that Becker would have liked for him (after betraying his best hopes for him), seeing some value in Becker's life and the way he has conducted it, and deciding to conduct his life in the same way—there is something about that, I think, that the audience can carry away. The idea of forgiveness, also, I think is large in there.

In this answer, Wilson seemed to be suggesting that he does not focus his thoughts on an audience when writing his plays. I wanted him to expand on this.

Heard: So you don't write for any particular audience?

Wilson: No, I write for the play, if you will. I write to create a work of art that exists on its own terms and is true to itself. I don't have any particular audience in mind, other than the fact that the play is an artwork which is written with the audience factor sort of built in so that, craft-wise, when you do your exposition, the exposition is for the purpose of the audience knowing certain aspects of the play at certain times, and knowing what happened prior to the events of the play and things of that sort, but I don't write for a particular audience.

Wilson's statement that he does not write for a particular audience may seem odd coming from a writer who has publicly stated his belief in the need to establish a separate African American theatre. Wilson's widely publicized 1996 speech at the eleventh biennial Theatre Communications Group National Conference at Princeton University called for an autonomous black theatre in which black artists can be free to express themselves: "We do not need colorblind casting; we need some theatres to develop our playwrights. . . . Without theatres we cannot develop our talents. If we cannot develop our talents, then everyone suffers: our writers; the theatre; the audience." How plays are written and where and how they are produced are, of course, somewhat different issues. However, Wilson's insistence that he considers his plays works of art and that he does not write with any particular audience (white or African American) in mind is surely significant.

Wilson does acknowledge the important role the audience plays in the final product, and he also realizes that the composition of the audience affects the play as well. An audience of mostly African Americans gives off a different energy than a predominantly white audience, and these differences change the experience of the play for both the actors and the spectators.

Wilson: One of the things that makes theatre so exciting, and for me what makes it such a wonderful art form, is that the audience participates (it is a live event) and influences what happens on stage. The communication between the actors and audience is different with each and every audience. If you do the play seven hundred times, you are going to have seven hundred different groups of people sitting out there, and so each audience has its own nature, its own thing, and they respond differently, and that's what makes it thrilling. You have a play, you have a large number of African Americans in the audience, and it is going to be a different response. And as a part of that the actors feed off of that audience, and they give a different performance, and that is what makes theatre. If it is on film or tape, the performance is set, and the audience doesn't have any influence over it. You go to the movies and you watch the movie, and that's it. You can't influence what is happening on the screen. But you can influence what is happening in the theatre, and that's what makes it thrilling.

Interview with August Wilson

Herb Boyd / 2000

From *The Black World Today,* April 26, 2000
(http://www.tbwt.com/views/specialrpt/special%20report-3 4-26-00.asp).
Reprinted by permission of Herb Boyd.

When August Wilson began his career as a playwright, it gradually dawned on him the goal of chronicling a century of African American history in a series of plays. With the rewriting of *Jitney*, his first full-length play completed in 1978, and its recent opening at the Second Stage off-Broadway, Wilson is two plays short of his mission.

A few weeks ago at the Edison Hotel—Wilson's favorite residence in New York City—the author sat for an interview and recalled his remarkable career that has earned him a slew of prestigious awards, including two Pulitzer Prizes, a Tony Award and six New York Drama Critics' Circle Awards.

Each of Wilson's plays depicts a decade in the twentieth century odyssey of African Americans, beginning in the order in which they were written— except for *Jitney* (1970s)—with *Ma Rainey's Black Bottom* (1920s), *Fences* (1950s), *Joe Turner's Come and Gone* (1910s), *The Piano Lesson* (1930s), *Two Trains Running* (1960s), *Seven Guitars* (1940s) and *King Hedley II* (1980s). Wilson, fifty-five and a native of Pittsburgh, the venue for most of his plays, relates in the interview that he is currently working on a play to capture the black experience at the turn of twentieth century and then to complete the cycle, one that will focus on the first decade of the new millennium.

"With completion of my latest play, *King Hedley II*, I have only the 'bookends,' the first and the last decades of the twentieth century, remaining," Wilson wrote toward the end of an essay recently published in the *New York Times*. "As I approach the cycle's end, I find myself a different person than when I started. The experience of writing the plays has altered me in ways I cannot yet fully articulate.

"As with any journey," he continued, "the only real question is: 'Is the port worthy of the cruise?' The answer is a resounding 'Yes.' I often remark that I am a struggling playwright. I'm struggling to get the next play on the page. Eight down and counting. The struggle continues."

The interview was conducted, transcribed and edited by Herb Boyd.

Herb Boyd: Perhaps a good place to start is with *Jitney!*, your first full-length play completed in 1978. Back in Detroit where I come from, we only used the word jitney—as opposed to taxis or cabs—when referring to the cars and drivers waiting outside supermarkets for fares. It means a little more to you and to the natives of Pittsburgh, right?
August Wilson: Since the 1940s, all my life, that's how you got around in the black community in Pittsburgh was with jitneys. They were a natural fact of life. These were unlicensed vehicles, only marginally legal. At one time they tried to organize the jitney drivers into a cab company called Our Cab Company, but for various reasons it didn't last very long.

HB: Why did you decide to focus on the jitney drivers for your first play?
AW: There were a lot of jitney stations in Pittsburgh, located in storefronts with a pay phone. It was a perfect place for a play because you had a set and a community of players who work together and have created something out of nothing, having no jobs. They are generally older men who had jobs working in the steel mills and on the railroad. If they were lucky enough to have a pension, there was a need to supplement with additional income, so they drove jitneys. And I think they do it because they enjoy the company of each other; they have something to do and it's a place to belong. They are a microcosm of the community at large.

HB: But in the vortex of the play there is a father/son relationship.
AW: That's right. It's about a young man, who in the midst of trying to right an injustice, spends twenty years in prison and his father never visited him. The reason he did not visit him is because he does not sanction the actions of his kid. He's a murderer and we find in the course of the play, shortly after he was sentenced to the electric chair, his mother died. So the father blames him for her death. She died of grief. This is the play's central theme, though there are several others.

HB: Your most recent play, *King Hedley II,* is also centered on the family but it's about the disintegration of the extended family.
AW: After you look at the eighties and the family structure and the so-called breakdown that occurred with grandmothers raising the kids, husband in

jail . . . add to this devastation adverse public policies, a welfare system that said a man was not allowed in the house, all of these factors led to the disintegration of the family. So in view of these calamities black folks found a way to band together and strengthen the family. If a kid's father is in jail, it didn't mean he didn't get parenting. He gets parenting by the community. So a community under assault begins to take care of itself. It's not so much a breakdown of the family in the play, but a break with the tradition of the extended family. It's the connection with the grandparents that is broken that causes many of the problems in the community.

HB: Many of us have an example of this in our families.
AW: I remember my daughter calling me from college and telling me that she had joined some Black Action Society and they were studying about Timbuktu. I told her that was nice but asked why didn't she start with her grandmother and then work your way back to Timbuktu. It didn't make any sense to me for her to know all about Timbuktu and know nothing about her grandmother. In this way, I felt she'd have a better sense of who she was and her current situation.

HB: In writing your plays you've pretty much followed the advice you gave to your daughter, don't you think?
AW: In order to understand who you are, you have to understand your immediate ancestors. You've got to make this connection with your recent past in order to understand the present and then to plot the future. I think it is important that my daughter understand that her grandmother could not go downtown and try on a dress. Many of us take for granted that we can try dresses on now, but we can't forget what was part of our past. Our parents and grandparents bore the brunt of those indignities and shielded us from them. We have to do something with that and not squander our inheritance. Back in the forties in Pittsburgh when we went to a store we couldn't get a paper bag; we had to carry our purchases out in our hands. I didn't find this out until I was older. My mother was smart. She knew if she had told me this, I would have come home one day with two thousand bags that I'd stole from somewhere and then ask her what else she needed.

HB: Thus far in your mission to capture the black experience decade by decade in your plays, you're about two from completing the cycle.
AW: I haven't done the nineties or the zero years, which I'm working on now.

HB: In capturing a decade, does it involve extensive research?

AW: The only research I do is to listen to the music. There's a lot of history of our people in the music. When I was writing *Ma Rainey's Black Bottom*, I didn't want to know anything about Ma Rainey. I figured what I needed to know I'd get out of her music. Listening to her singing gave me a good sense of who she was. When I wrote it, I gave her a nephew whom she promised her sister she'd take care of. I said, "Oh, my God, I hope she has a sister," 'cause she's got one now. And as it turned out, I was dead on the money because Ma adopted six or seven kids. I just sensed from her music that she had this nurturing kind of a thing and gave her a nephew. When I did *Joe Turner's Come and Gone*, I certainly did not think about anything that happened in 1911, but I had a sense that they didn't have cars but had horses. And I envisioned people coming into the cities, and there were boarding houses and people setting down roots. I believe if you do research, you're limited by it. . . . It's like putting on a straitjacket.

HB: How much of your personal history ends up in your plays?

AW: As I mentioned earlier about my uncle and his truck. I remember one time he was driving down a hill and singing Chuck Berry's tune "Maybelline," and the brakes went out. He started pumping the brakes and then he turned off on some side street and they finally caught. In *The Piano Lesson*, there is a scene where they talk about the brakes and how you have to pump them before they catch. So sometimes little things like that are remembered and get into the plays. As for my autobiography that you asked about earlier, well, the plays are my autobiography, decade by decade.

HB: August, several years ago you were quite outspoken about the racial aspects of the theater, debating various opponents about the necessity of black theater, directors, playwrights and other self-determination efforts. Have things changed enough to please you nowadays?

AW: No, they have not. The situation in America hasn't changed, so that hasn't changed either. One of things we've done is to concretize our efforts and we've set up the African Grove Theater at Dartmouth, and we realize that to bring about substantive change it has to be done step by step. We've gained expertise in other various fields of endeavor . . . so we have lawyers on our board. The idea is to bring this expertise to bear on the theater. Unless you have a strong board with vital connections to funding, you're not going to get very far developing black theater. In our research we discovered that some of the black theaters failed because of poor management skills, so we made it our business to go and get the skills. And at Dartmouth we've developed a theater training program . . . it's a beginning and in the near future we will have a convention but before this happens we need to organize some forty thousand black performing artists . . . perhaps ten years from now we can look up and find that black theater is something different than it is now.

HB: Around the country today at several regional black theaters there appears to be a concern to revive the old plays, rather than producing new ones. *Dutchman, For Colored Girls* . . . and other plays are being staged. How do you feel about this?

AW: You have to preserve. Look, right down the street you have *Uncle Vanya* and *Death of a Salesman*, which was written in 1949 . . . they make sure that every generation has an opportunity to see that play. We have to do the same thing. We have to make a decision which of our body of work we need to preserve. There is the gifted writer, Ed Bullins, but black theaters don't do his work. Kids growing up today need to see his plays. At the same time we need to develop new writers, and you have to give them an opportunity to learn by doing. It's not an either/or situation, but a combination of both. One of the newer playwrights I'm excited about is Marion McClinton, who is the director of *Jitney*. I can recall when I came into theater and how important director Lloyd Richards was to me. He taught me a lot of things about theater. He let me know that I was the writer and he was the director, and it was clear separation of responsibilities. But, of course, in the end you have to work together and we did that quite successfully. Among the things he taught me is how to watch a scene, and how a writer and director can see it differently. And then there is the subtle way that a difference of view is resolved. Lloyd was a great teacher.

HB: For your next play on the 1900s, have you decided on a theme or a thread that runs through it?

AW: In *Two Trains Running*, there's an offstage character named Aunt Ester. She's 349 years old during this play. In *King Hedley II*, she's also an offstage character but by now she's 366 years old when she dies in this play. Aunt Ester obviously represents our history all the way back to 1619 and that's the connection that if we don't value it, you lose it. So, to make the new connection, I will bring Aunt Ester back, but on stage this time in 1904. As usual, I started listening to my music . . . then I wrote her name down: Aunt Ester. I said "Okay," and then I have her say: "There's a lot of things I don't talk about . . . I don't talk about the water . . ." and then she begins to talk about the water. And then she says: "I don't talk about Geechee Dan. . . ." After getting these first lines down, I knew I was on my way. I had Aunt Ester, Geechee Dan and the water; that's all I needed.

A Conversation with
August Wilson

Sandra G. Shannon and Dana A. Williams / 2003

From *August Wilson and Black Aesthetics*, edited by Dana A. Williams and Sandra G. Shannon. New York: Palgrave Macmillan, 2004, 187–95. Copyright © Sandra Shannon and Dana Williams. Reprinted with permission of Palgrave Macmillan.

This interview with August Wilson (AW) was conducted by coeditors Dana A. Williams (DW) and Sandra G. Shannon (SS) on Friday, September 26, 2003 at the Edison Hotel in New York City.

DW: We interpret *black aesthetics* broadly in our collection. Can you speak a little about your interpretation of *black aesthetics*?

AW: I interpret *black aesthetics* as broadly as you do. As you know, you can write entire books on just the word *aesthetic*. I would say that the black aesthetic is black thought that is organized into conventions, and what those conventions are would be based on your ideas about the world. Translating that into art, its dimensions would be the aesthetic expression of those ideas. Now exactly what that aesthetic is we are still trying to find out, especially as it relates to black theater, which is still in its infancy. When you look at European theater, Europeans have been developing their aesthetic over thousands of years. So, we've been at this for a relatively short time. And we're still in the process of developing our conventions. So when you talk about conventions of black theater and a black aesthetic, you have to say that they are still in the process of being developed.

SS: Your aesthetic, based on the plays that you've written and the poetry as well, is informed by the blues, Africa, some aspects of cultural nationalism . . . a combination of those things. Are there any other things that inform your aesthetic?

AW: I think you would have to add to that Aristotle's *Poetics*. Here again, the art form that I work in is a European art form. So that would have to be included. But if you go to the Greeks or to the white American theater they will have Aristotle's *Poetics*, but they don't have the black nationalism, or the blues, or those other things that make black aesthetics unique. But this black aesthetic is still based on a European art form until it's defined otherwise, until some other form or method of what theater is and some new conventions are developed by black Americans. And I think that if you look at literature you'll see that black Americans are in a very unique position. They may be the only ones who are in a position to develop an American literature. And that includes theater. When the Europeans came to America to settle here, they brought with them European conventions. And so the literature that was created on this continent was not American but European with European conventions. The African, who came to America stripped of his culture and his language, didn't have any conventional baggage. And that's what allowed the blues and jazz to be developed; those conventions had to be developed. And so I think if you're going to have an *American* literature, an *American* theater, then it has to include and probably be led by African Americans. So when you see black theater, some of it is not based on Aristotle, and I think that is good.

SS: Black theater is writing against these conventions?
AW: Well, I don't know that it's so much against it. But we're in the process of developing different ideas about what theater is and in the process of developing those ideas. And here again, this is all very new. And in order to do theater you have to have the tools, and the tools are theaters. So the more theaters you have the more you are able to develop the tools. I think there is in the process of being developed a black theater that is not based on Aristotle's *Poetics* and European conventions.

DW: Sybil Roberts's *A Lovesong for Mumia*, which we've included in this collection, is among those plays that are not based on European conventions. *A Lovesong for Mumia* is very ritualistic and is birthed out of the concept of theater activism. In her essay detailing the development of the play, Roberts comments that there already is a constituency in black theater that is exactly what you call for—theater for the people and by the people—in "The Ground" speech. In addition to calling attention to this cadre of writers, what do you see as the most significant advance of the speech and the subsequent conference at Dartmouth?

AW: The African Grove Institute for the Arts (AGIA) came out of that. But the concrete results of black gains—I don't see any, none. I think it's been the opposite. These are not always the things by which we measure. But the important thing is we started with one black LORT theater, and we don't have any now. Jimandi Productions in Atlanta—a city that is something like 73 percent black—cannot support a black theater. They closed. It's not there anymore. I'm willing to bet that if you go back and look, after the speech there was less money given to black theaters than before. And there are reasons for that. And I think it's because in certain ways there's not a value for black theater. As long as the club doesn't close, we're doing all right. We just had the Black Roots Festival here in New York. It was myself and Derek Walcott, and we had a conversation. And the turnout was not a very large crowd. But if Teddy Pendergrass, Ice Cube, or 50 Cent were here, or if they had said, "We're going to have some music afterwards. Wynton Marsalis is going to come done and play his trumpet," then it would have been a larger crowd. But a conversation with two playwrights. . . .

DW: How do we change that? How do we promote both music-as-culture *and* theater?
AW: I think one has been more valuable to us, which is why we readily embrace the music. We understand the music as the thing that has enabled us to survive. So, we know what that is. But then this other thing? What is that, which I think is crucially important? I think when we look back in history, we'll see that in rap, it's the words *and* the music. That's very similar to the blues, where you have words to provide you with the information and music to give you the emotion. It's an emotional response to the information, and when you put those two things together, it's one of the unique things about the blues. The entire philosophical system is contained in the blues, and the emotional reference is provided in the music. So when Derek [Walcott] talked about Bob Marley and "No Woman No Cry," he pointed to the line "In the government yard in Trenchtown." Just that one line, and I thought, "Oh man, that's the line that gets me too." But the line without the music doesn't matter. It's the music that provides the emotional reference to the line that just grabs at you. If you heard the music without the line, it doesn't mean anything. It's the combination. And that may be the very thing that rap provides. So the whole future of theater may be based on some conventions of theater that rappers are developing now. It's like back in '65 when we used to

have poetry readings and jazz concerts. The jazz musicians would tell us we could read while they set up. People would come in and see us reading, and they'd walk right out until the music started. So, you can't compete with music if all you have is words.

DW: Well, now, most poetry readings have poets read with music behind them like in the sixties.

AW: That's what Baraka tried to do. He put out a couple of albums, but he got confused. They were trying to put jazz to poetry, but it was the beat, not the jazz. And the rappers sell the beat. And what I've found about rap is it's where we're going. I was talking to some kids at a school, and they were talking while I was talking until I said, "Anybody rap?" And that got their attention. So, I said, "Everybody come on up." And one kid comes up and says, "I'm the beat man." And I asked, "What does that mean?" And he says, I keep the beat. He was a big guy, and he said, "Most of us big guys keep the beat." And we played around. But the teacher got mad because rap is playground activity, and I had brought it in the school and legitimized it. And I was thinking, "You can use this to teach these kids how to read."

SS: You're on play number ten. How does ten fit into the aesthetic you've already created?

AW: Well, it's cut out of the same cloth. It's a summation, if you will. It tells where we are at the end of the century as we prepare to go on to the next century. It looks at what this one hundred years have meant and how we have fared. So, I think to do that I'm going to make use of some of the offspring of some of the characters from *Gem of the Ocean*, which is the first play. But so far, the play is tentatively titled *Radio Golf*. The structure of the play is relatively simply. Aunt Ester dies [in *King Hedley*] in 1985; her house at 1839 Wylie is abandoned, and they want to tear her house down. It's surrounded by empty lots, and they want to tear the house down and build a little shopping mall. And there's a question of who owns the house. And then the city battles to tear it down.

SS: After the tenth play, are you going to start experimenting with different forms?

AW: Well, I have some ideas about plays that did not fit in the cycle. And I want to explore those ideas. One thing I know I'm going to do is to participate in this playwright series at Signature Theater [in New York] in '05 to '06 I think. I'm having a series at the Signature Theater. They select a playwright every year, and they do three or four of the artist's plays. They have done a series on Adrienne Kennedy, Lanford Wilson, and Arthur Miller. They are going to do three or four of my plays in their season, one of which is going to be *Seven Guitars Too*, which is another way of telling the story of *Seven Guitars*. It's a five-minute-vignette kind of thing. Originally when I started *Seven Guitars*, I started doing it like that. But I realized it wasn't cut out of the same cloth as the rest. So, I want to go back to that. And it's very much different from what I do now. I think I'll do the one-man show ["How I Learned What I Learned"] again. I may have stumbled onto something because I only did two years of my life in the first show. So, I can foresee "How I Learned What I Learned . . . Reloaded" [laughter].

SS: Fiction?
AW: Oh yes. I have an idea for a novel. I've got about forty-two pages or something. When I actually sit down and write it, I'll just do it. But I'm tuning up my fiction muscle by writing and publishing a collection of stories before I tackle the novel just to limber up a little bit.

SS: I saw a comment from you about Suzan-Lori Parks that you tip your hat to her. Could you talk about her work?
AW: She's a very good playwright. She has a very unique use of language, which attracts me. Her work is unlike mine, but it's like mine since she's dealing with the black thematic thing. But I just love her language and how she writes. So many playwrights write small. And small things don't interest me. I like big things. And she tackles big things.

SS: Are there any other playwrights you would take your hat off to?
AW: I'm sure there must be. But I don't like doing that because I'll leave somebody out. There are a lot of good playwrights out there. So, I don't want to say that Parks is the only one I'd tip my hat to, but then I don't want to name four or five because what you'd come up with is the list of the "usual suspects." I will say that I haven't seen anyone just blaze across the scene, but I imagine they are out there.

DW: Have you worked with Javon Johnson, who is often billed as "August Wilson's protégé?"

AW: I haven't worked with him, but I know Javon. And I support his work. What happened was *USA Today* had different artists, and they wanted the artists to sit down with a younger person in their field and to have a conversation with them. And they approached me about this. And I knew Javon, so I said I'd sit down with Javon and have this dialogue. So they published it side by side, and that's how the "Wilson protégé" thing came to be, which I think is unfortunate for Javon. If I were him, I wouldn't want to be tagged with being anyone's protégé. I say, "Let me do my own thing." And it's unfortunate for me also because it locks me in a certain support of his work, some of which I know and some of which I don't. But I think he's a very talented writer, which is why I chose him to sit down with.

SS: Why is it that the urban circuit theater, not theater about "big" things as you say, has large audiences now more than ever?

AW: I'm not sure that some folks know that there is any other kind of theater. That's what theater is to them. Let me say this—there is nothing wrong with it. That may in fact be the future of black theater. That aesthetic we're talking about may in fact come right out of there. But in order for that to happen, there has to be critical attention brought to bear on that. Some of that stuff, they shouldn't be able to get away with. And the audience has to demand more. Until they demand more, you aren't going to get more. And that audience doesn't know that there is more to be gotten from a play. And I think critical attention will drive that and lift the audience. And you'll have a whole new way of doing theater—black folks' way of doing theater that has its own conventions. Folks will say, "Well, where did they get them from?" And they'll say, "We made them up."

SS: What kinds of subjects are worthy of theater, worth putting on stage?

AW: Love, honor, duty, betrayal, the human condition . . . those things. How we respond to the world. . .

SS: So the urban circuit plays would fit the bill?

AW: Well, my understanding of them, and I could be wrong, is that they are driven by the church. The Christian church has been the one institution that has enabled us and contributed tremendously to our survival. It's the most stable organization in the black community and has been for years. "My grandmother prayed for me." Well, my grandmother prayed for me too. Now that becomes a play. But to me, that's still pathology driven. It's driven by the lowest common denominator that connects everybody, and it's influenced by television. So, they make it a sitcom. The only problem I see with that though is that is the black pathology. It's like writing about all the horrible things that happened. Well, what about your grandfather who didn't do all that? The guy who wasn't on drugs . . . let's deal with that stuff. And in the process of doing that, other stuff will emerge as part of who we are.

SS: But it seems like those plays have hit a moneymaking formula.
AW: Because people are starved to see themselves. So, the church organizes a trip, and you have three thousand people in the audience. And they get something out of these plays. It's almost like a church experience, which is where black people have traditionally gotten their theater from. They've consolidated the experience. Church functions for black folks the way theater functions for European Americans, who don't have that church-as-theater experience. For them, church is very quiet. So, they developed a theater to get that experience. But we already had that. So we didn't need theater. All we had to do is walk into a church. And the emotions Aristotle talks about are played out every Sunday . . . pity, fear, anger. . . . It's right there. Of course, that's not what they call it in the church, but theater's what they're doing.

DW: Does black theater, then, have to have a different function from white theater?
AW: I think the function is the same—to create art that responds to or illu-minates the human condition. In other words, I don't think they are any different. And I don't want to force a writer or an actor into "this is what you should be doing." I don't want to say that what you're doing should fit this set of rules. Art should be liberating; it should be functional. This is from the sixties—art has to be functional, collective, and committing. Well, maybe it does. Let's assume it does. But you can't force that on anyone. If it doesn't emerge from the people, you can't lay that on them. You can't tell people "you guys are doing that, but you should be dealing with black liberation or that which presents positive role models to our kids." Maybe that's not the way the artist sees it. And I don't want to tell anybody what to do, and I don't think you can force it on the people. The people decide, and if that's what the

people want, that's what the people get. And you can't let down the people. All you can do is expose them to other things so that when they are making their decisions about what black theater is supposed to be they can see what black theater is capable of first before figuring out where they should be going.

SS: What would you tell a class of aspiring playwrights about being a part of black theater?

AW: I'd tell them to walk on the other side of the street. And that's simply saying you have to get out of the usual mode of viewing the world. If you walk on the other side of the street, you'd be surprised at what you see over there. So, that's the first thing—walk on the other side of the street, and know that there are other things in the world than what you think is in the world. The difficulty is in getting to the thing that is inside you or finding something worth writing about. Everything is not worth writing about. I personally do not want to see any more novels written by a young black person talking about their dating experiences in New York. No more. I've had it up to here. There's got to be more stuff to write about than that. It's sad when people have talent and don't put that talent to any use. So, I'm assuming that all the writers have talent. Now, let's find a way to put the talent to some use other than just saying you wrote a play. So, I would say to them that they are all potentially talented writers. But unless they claim it, claim being an artist, they're just a writer, which means you'll write anything for anybody. But if you're an artist, then you're not for sale. You have to have a belief in yourself that's larger than anybody's disbelief, and find something to say.

SS: What's the critic's role in what you find to say?

AW: I don't allow criticism to influence my art. Sometimes critics will give you a different way of thinking about a play. They'll describe a character a certain way. And I'll say, "Well, I never thought of him that way. I haven't thought of him as a subversive vagabond." But I've always placed my own value on my art. Now, do I read the critics? Yes, and I think that any playwright who tells you they don't is being at least intellectually dishonest. It might be true, but I don't believe it. Do I pay attention to what the critics are saying? Yes.

SS: I remember in "The Ground" speech, you challenge critics to evolve just as the aesthetic evolves.

AW: Absolutely. Let's say I'm reading this critic who is responding to a play, and it's a white play, but he's still responding to a play as having a neoclassical German influence. You recognize that. And that's good. So if you can do that, when you come to a black play, you should be able to say, "Oh, that's the blues" or whatever the influence is. And if you aren't able to do that, accept it on those terms, then you have the wrong analytical tools when you come because you're not going to find the neoclassical German influence. You have to be aware of what's going on. You have to know something about black culture and be able to say, "Oh that's a jazz influence." And I think you should be able to do that. But generally critics develop a single set of analytical tools, and they apply them to everyone. And all the references are mostly to Europeans—white critics, black critics, myself included. Generally, your first reference is to a Western piece of literature. So the critic has to develop a single set of analytical tools, and I think that's where you start. You have to have that in your tool bag. But if you're a music critic, and we have this thing called rap now, and you haven't paid any attention to it, you're out of step. So you're looking at rap and saying "that's new R&B or doo-wop" when it's this other thing that's going on. So the critic has to keep adding to his tools. But I think the responsibility of critics is to do two things—they drive the art, or they should drive the art. And they are the keeper of the gate, so to speak; they work at what [Robert] Brustein would call "preserving thought." So that if you're a critic and you're going to maintain a certain quality, then the critic has to demand that you [the playwright] come up to the bar. They have to maintain that quality. As a playwright, it's a privilege to stand here in this art form, and along with that privilege comes some responsibility and duty to the art form. And if the playwright assumes that then the playwright has to do the work. And the critics can't let them get away with anything else.

SS: And that's different from what race you are. I think the issue of the black director [for the film version of *Fences*] was another issue for you that was blown out of proportion. The individual ought to be sensitive to the culture, right?

AW: It's not just that. No matter how sensitive you are, no matter how well meaning you are, you're an outsider. I'm sensitive to all the issues of Italians, but I'm not qualified to direct *The Godfather*. You have to go and get an Italian. You cannot learn the Italian experience. No matter how well meaning I am or how long I study, I cannot learn it. And everybody in the world knows I'm right, and it's been proven. Steven Spielberg did not direct *The Godfather*. And when they decided to make the movie about the Holocaust, they didn't go get Spike Lee. They got Steven Spielberg. When you have a situation where a film is about the culture of the people like *The Godfather* or *Schindler's List*, then you go get someone who has lived the culture, except when it's black. And I just said, "Wait a minute. That ain't right." Why can't I get a black director? There are occasions when a movie is about a car chase, and you can get anybody to direct that because it's not about the culture. The problem you run into is times when people are trying to prove that race doesn't matter. I was in L.A. a few months after I first made the comment, and a guy came up to me and said, "I'm a director. And I've been out here telling these folks for fifteen years that it doesn't matter that I'm black. And here you come along telling them that it does. So, I direct your movie. Then what?" If he were to accept the fact that he could only direct black movies, then he'd only work every five years or whenever they decided to put out a black movie. He told me not to do him any favors. And I responded that I wasn't trying to do him any favors. I was just trying to get my movie made in the best possible way I can. I wasn't out there carrying a banner saying "hire black directors," and I'm still not. But I am saying, as a black playwright, if you want to make a movie of my work, I want it to be done in the best possible way, with a black director. And that's the way I want it done.

DW: But you've had white directors for your plays. What's the difference between that and having a white director for the film?
AW: I've had white directors work on my plays. In fact, the guy who directed my one-man show is white—Todd [Kreidler]. But I think there is a difference. The difference is that the film is forever. There was a production of *Ma Rainey's Black Bottom* in London that I saw. They didn't do too bad. There were a few things that they didn't understand, but I corrected them. But that's over and done with. A film will be here 150 years from now. I would want that permanent record to be best reflected by a person of my culture.

DW: The film version of *Fences* is also likely to be used as a reflection of the culture, much more so than someone going to theater. Someone going to the theater is not likely going to the theater specifically to look at the play's representation of the culture. But in teaching moments, especially, people are looking at a film expressly to identify the culture and the social context out of which the text emerges.

AW: Here again, it is a permanent record. It can be used for anything. So it has to be a good reflection of the culture.

SS: Do you consider *Fences* your signature play?
AW: I want to say here for the record [laughter], of the plays that I have written, it is my least favorite play. It's not my signature play.

DW: Oddly, in spite of your point about why you want a black director for the movie version (because it's so specifically about the culture), *Fences* is also considered the most universal of your plays. What do you say to an all-white production of *Fences* that misses the cultural underpinnings of the play?
AW: An all-white production *would* miss the cultural underpinnings, but there is nothing I can do about that. My signature play would be *Joe Turner's Come and Gone.* Most of the ideas of the other plays are contained in that one play. So, if I had to pick one play as my signature play, that would be it, but certainly not *Fences. Fences* is the only one that's not an ensemble play. The rest of them are ensembles. *Fences* has Troy Maxson in every scene, and all the other characters revolve around him. But with *Joe Turner*, there are like ten people, and they are all involved in the scenes.

SS: But *Fences* has been done more widely. I know of the all-Chinese production, for instance. And the audience got it from what I understand.
AW: It was also done in Ghana. And even though they were Africans, it was different because they were British. For instance, one of the things that they did was Gabriel was a chorus. He would talk to the audience. He would say the same things that were in the play—they didn't add lines, but he would talk directly to the audience. And I thought that was interesting. And I would have said that black culture is black culture until I went over to London and they were doing *Ma Rainey's Black Bottom.* And I found out that the black folks over there are very influenced by British culture. So, the kinds of mistakes that a white director might make because he isn't familiar with the culture, I found the black cast making the same mistakes because they are British. Toledo [from *Ma Rainey*] was sitting around reading a newspaper, and Levee is saying something. And then Levee jumps up on the table and kicks the newspaper out of Toledo's hands. And I said, "No, you can't do that."

DW: That's a fight waiting to happen [laughter].

AW: Yes, that's an assault that would call for a different response in the text. So, he can't do that. And I thought that a black cast should have known that. The guy playing Toledo should have known that. So, they took it out. Other than that it was fine.

DW: What are some diasporic aesthetic ideas that do cross geographical boundaries?

AW: Music, for instance. My assumption would be that music is cross-cultural. One of the driving things of any black aesthetic is improvisation or the idea of improvising. It's the thing that enabled us to survive—the ability to think on our feet. We're essentially the same people. For instance, I was watching these Japanese guys in a hotel, and there was a jukebox in the restaurant. And they didn't play the jukebox. It never occurred to them to play the jukebox. But if six black guys walk in there, the first thing one of them is going to do is go over to the jukebox. And it's the aesthetic. Music is more important to them maybe. I don't know what it is exactly. I just know the black guys would have played the jukebox.

SS: If you had to do the speech again would there be any changes made?

AW: I think so. I think I would leave the colorblind casting alone.

SS: But that wasn't really the big picture.

AW: That's why I would leave it alone, because that became the lightning rod that everyone focused on as if that was the only thing I was saying. I think it muddled the speech. So leaving that aside would force people to focus on what I was really saying because that was not it. That was an addendum to it and part of it all, but I think I would say some things differently. I would still have said it, but I would have talked about that the next week.

SS: Well, thank you very much for the interview.

DW: Yes, thank you for the interview and for the inspiration for *August Wilson and Black Aesthetics.*

AW: You're welcome.

A 10-Play Odyssey Continues with *Gem of the Ocean*

Maureen Dezell / 2004

From *Boston Sunday Globe*, September 5, 2004, N1, N7. Reprinted with permission of the *Boston Globe*.

"We've spent four hundred years trying to civilize white people," says playwright August Wilson, lighting a cigarette at a table outside Pizzeria Uno near the Huntington Theatre on a steamy Saturday morning.

The eatery has been a regular perch in recent weeks for the celebrated author of *The Piano Lesson, Fences,* and *Ma Rainey's Black Bottom.* Wilson and an all-star cast led by Phylicia Rashad and Delroy Lindo are rehearsing Wilson's new play, *Gem of the Ocean,* which opens Sept. 24 in previews at the Huntington. (Due to sudden illness, director Marion McClinton has had to withdraw from the production, and the play will not open Friday as originally scheduled. Kenny Leon, who most recently helmed the Broadway production of *A Raisin in the Sun,* will direct.) After its local run, *Gem* moves immediately to New York for a Broadway premiere.

Sipping what he says will be one of a dozen cups of coffee he will drink this day, Wilson is talking about what he calls the black American odyssey, an epic journey that began in 1619 with the capture, bondage, and transport of the first of more than ten million Africans to the Americas, where they were sold into slavery. The topic is central to *Gem,* the ninth entry in Wilson's ten-play saga that traces the twentieth-century African American experience. Set in 1904, *Gem* chronicles a time when slavery and the Civil War were living memories for many black Americans.

"If you look at even a bit of history, you see that in most of the experiences of black America—most of black America's confrontations with white America—it is white America that has acted uncivilized," Wilson says, puffing on a Marlboro Light. "Taking people away from their freedom is not civilized behavior. Hanging them from trees is not civilized behavior. Refusing citizens' rights to legal protection, the right to vote, is not civilized."

The prolific fifty-nine-year-old playwright, who had his Broadway break-through twenty years ago this fall with *Ma Rainey's Black Bottom*, won a Tony Award and his first Pulitzer in 1987 for *Fences*, a play set in the 1950s, and another Pulitzer in 1990 for *The Piano Lesson*, a 1930s family drama.

Each play is set during a different decade and explores the underpinnings of the African American experience as Wilson perceives it: a culture whose concepts of freedom, citizenship, and spirituality were shaped by bondage and an ongoing fight for freedom.

The plays were not written in sequence. *Gem of the Ocean* is the opening story of the saga, which will conclude with *Radio Golf*, a play Wilson is writing now that takes place in middle-class black Pittsburgh in the 1990s. Its protagonists are the children and grandchildren of characters in *Gem*, a fictionalized rendering of Pittsburgh's Hill District at the turn of the last century.

"In this play, you have a generation that has just claimed its citizenship," he says. "Anyone who was forty-something or older in 1904 was born into slavery. These are people who are trying to find out what freedom means—and so far, it doesn't mean very much.

"As Solly [Two Kings, a former slave in the play] puts it, 'All it means is you've got a long way to hoe with no plow, no mule,'" Wilson continues. "The question he asks is whether it's freedom if you can't do nothing with it. You're still restricted."

During the Reconstruction period after the Civil War, Jim Crow laws were enacted that systematically circumscribed civil liberties for blacks. The laws—and lack of freedom—drew tens of thousands of rural African Americans to northern urban areas during what is known as the Great Migration of the early twentieth century.

"That generation really defined [freedom] for my generation," says the playwright. "We owe a tremendous debt to them 'cause they're the ones who figured out how to live in the world, exactly what it meant to be free after hundreds of years of bondage. Some people didn't have any idea."

Wilson, whose plays are notoriously dense with plot, history, and multiple meanings, says that *Gem of the Ocean* is really a very simple story.

"It's a play about a man [a mill worker named Garret Brown] who's accused of stealing a bucket of nails and refuses to accept that," Wilson says. "He'd rather die than be accused of something that's a lie, and he does."

Gem opens in the kitchen of Aunt Ester (Rashad), a formidable offstage figure in other Wilson dramas who has never before appeared in the flesh. *Gem* takes place in her home, which is both a working-class domicile and a spiritual sanctuary. Those who come, go, and gather here are members of a community in tumult over Brown's death. He jumped into a freezing river rather than confess to a crime he didn't commit. Meanwhile, Citizen Barlow, a recent migrant from Alabama who did steal the nails, comes to see Aunt Ester (Rashad) seeking a way to cleanse his soul.

"Aunt Ester resembles any black woman in her early seventies—someone you wouldn't look at twice if she stepped outside," says Wilson. Yet she is "the embodiment of African wisdom and tradition—the person who has been alive since 1619 [when the first slaves were brought to Virginia] and has remained with us."

Ester would be a strikingly improbable character in plays other than those of Wilson, whose works portray a culture that combines traditional African spirituality, Christianity, and a sense of community.

"At the center of this play is the incredible spirituality of African people who honor their ancestors," Wilson says. "They have concepts of God—trees that have spirits. All of these things have been part of their belief system, which is different than the European belief system, just as our reality, our music, our humor is different.

"Of course no one is going to live to be 285 years old," continues the writer. "She represents any old person in the community that keeps its traditions alive. She's not mystical or magical. She can't help you find your way to redemption. You have to find it."

What Aunt Ester has that no Wilson character has possessed before is a map to the City of Bones, Wilson's mythic spiritual center of African American life. She leads Citizen on a journey to the city, where he discovers his spirit. Citizen, says Wilson, enters the play as an individual and leaves it as a member of a community.

Wilson has evoked the City of Bones in other plays, calling it the largest unmarked graveyard in the world.

"What we're doing in the play is we're marking it," he says. "There are hundreds of millions of bones of slaves in chains, entangled in ships. The city is part of all of our history, our experience."

In *Gem*, the city has grown larger and stronger, embracing the experiences of the descendants of those who perished in the Atlantic. "It is our experience in America—it's what made America a rich country. It jump-started the Industrial Revolution," says Wilson. "It isn't just blues or the black aesthetic. This is our experience—an American experience.

"People look at black American history and they say, 'Oh, you poor people, what you were subjected to, that's such a horrendous thing. I'm sure you want to forget that.' And I say no, no, I don't want to forget that, because it's a triumph. Black America is a tremendous triumph."

Index